7-08

THE LOST TRAPPERS

THE
LOST TRAPPERS

By DAVID H. COYNER

Edited and with an Introduction and a new Afterword

By DAVID J. WEBER

UNIVERSITY OF OKLAHOMA PRESS
NORMAN AND LONDON

This book contains the complete text of the original edition, published in 1847 under the same title.

Library of Congress Cataloging-in-Publication Data

Coyner, David H.
      The lost trappers / by David H. Coyner ; edited and with an introduction and a new afterword by David J. Weber.
          p.   cm.
      Includes index.
      ISBN 0–8061–2725–2
      1. West (U.S.)—Description and travel.   2. Overland journeys to the Pacific.   3. Williams, Ezekiel, ca. 1780–1844.   4. Trappers—West (U.S.)—Biography.   5. Fur trade—West (U.S.)   6. West (U.S.)—History—To 1848.
I. Weber, David J.   II. Title.
F592.C88   1994
978'.02'092—dc20

                                                                            94-36584
                                                                            CIP

The paper in this book meets the guidelines for permanence and durability of the Committee on Production Guidelines for Book Longevity of the Council on Library Resources, Inc. ∞

1   2   3   4   5   6   7   8   9   10

Editor's Introduction

SINCE ITS PUBLICATION in 1847, *The Lost Trappers* has both intrigued and bedeviled students of the early Trans-Mississippi West for, despite its author's protestations of fidelity to fact, the book contains a generous amount of fiction. The heart of David H. Coyner's narrative concerns the adventures of Ezekiel Williams, who allegedly led twenty trappers up the Missouri River in 1807, the year after the return of the Lewis and Clark Expedition. Williams' party reputedly made their way to the Yellowstone and trapped the Rockies, working their way south. By the time Williams reached the Arkansas River, only two of his twenty companions were alive. The others had been killed by Indians in a series of battles and mishaps. At the Arkansas, the three survivors separated: James Workman and Samuel Spencer started for Santa Fe, but became lost; they crossed the Rockies by a circuitous route and luckily met a Spanish caravan bound for California. And Ezekiel Williams placed a canoe in the Arkansas and set out alone for home, reaching the Missouri in 1809—or so the story of "the lost trappers" goes.

Although historians have since raised serious questions about the veracity of David Coyner's *The Lost Trappers*, most nineteenth century readers found the book convincing and would have agreed with the California bookdealer and historian, Hubert Howe Bancroft, who wrote in 1886 that Coyner told his story in a "homely but truthful and direct way which commands the reader's respect and confidence." In both his *History of the Northwest Coast* and his *History of Arizona and New Mexico* (published, respectively, in 1886 and 1889), Bancroft accepted Coyner's version of Ezekiel Williams' expedition in its entirety. In the latter work, however, Bancroft expressed doubt that Workman and Spencer had journeyed to California in 1809 since caravans did not operate between Santa Fe and Los Angeles that early. Bancroft suggested that this was "evidently a serious error in dates."[1]

Another nineteenth-century writer, Colonel Henry Inman, was less critical than Bancroft. He told his readers that *The Lost Trappers* contained the journal of Ezekiel Williams (which it does not) ; and in two books, *The Old Santa Fe Trail* and *The Great Salt Lake Trail*, he recounted Williams' expedition as fact and even added an occasional embellishment of his own. Inman averred, for example, that Williams and his men "were splendid shots with the rifle, and could hit the eye of a squirrel whether the animal stood still or was running up the trunk of a tree."[2] Even Coyner, for all of his exaggerating, would have been hard pressed to top that.

The fact that early writers viewed *The Lost Trappers* as authoritative is, in part, testimony to Coyner's ability as a writer for he had never seen the Far West. Born and raised in Virginia, Coyner had not traveled west of Missouri in gathering material for his book. Up to now, however, Coyner's own story has been completely unknown to students of the American West.

David Holmes Coyner was one of numerous grandchildren of Michael Keinadt, a German, who according to family legend had made several trading voyages to Philadelphia in the 1740s before settling permanently in Pennsylvania. By 1749 Michael Keinadt had married Margaret Diller at New Holland, Lancaster County, Pennsylvania. David Coyner's father, Martin Luther Coyner, born in 1771, was the ninth of thirteen children produced by this marriage. In 1789, when the family moved to Augusta County, Virginia, Martin went along with his father who was then sixty-nine. Three years later, in 1792, Martin Coyner married Elizabeth Rhea, of Raleigh, North Carolina. Elizabeth was a Scotch Presbyterian, which might explain why Martin Luther Coyner forsook the Lutheranism of his father to become and remain Presbyterian. In 1792, the Martin Coyners bought a farm they called

"Long Glade," about twelve miles north of Staunton in Augusta County, Virginia. It was at "Long Glade" that David Holmes Coyner was born on April 13, 1807, the eighth of nine children.[3]

Young Coyner's formal education began in a classical school run by the family pastor, Reverend John Hendren, in Augusta County. Early training in the classics may explain Coyner's occasional lapses into Latin in *The Lost Trappers*. Coyner attended Washington College, now Washington and Lee University, at Lexington, Virginia, where there is record of his matriculation in the summer of 1827, although he later remembered graduating on April 15, 1827. Coyner spent the year 1827-28 at the Princeton Theological Seminary in Princeton, New Jersey. Poor health, he later said, forced him to leave the Seminary in the fall of 1829, a year before his class was scheduled to graduate. Still, he continued to study theology under his first teacher, Reverend John Hendren, and in October 1831, was licensed to practice as a minister by the Lexington Presbytery of Virginia.[4]

Soon after being licensed, Coyner crossed the Blue Ridge Mountains and settled near the south branch of the Potomac in what is today Hardy County in northeast West Virginia. There he married Catherine McNeill on August 13, 1833. Sometime after the birth of their first child, Coyner's wife died. On March 26, 1839, he married another Hardy County girl, Catherine Eliza Snodgrass, by whom he had eight boys and two girls. Coyner remained in western Virginia "not less than ten years," by his own recollection, and preached in Hardy and neighboring Hampshire counties. When the Presbyterian Church was split by a schism in 1837, Coyner remained with the "old school" or predominantly Southern half of the church.[5] He considered his years in western Virginia as a time of great achievement during which he "built up strong Presbyterian churches."[6]

Coyner's reason for leaving Virginia, presumably about 1841, and his activities in the years that immediately followed, remain a mystery. We know from his statement in *The Lost Trappers* that he lived "in the upper part of the State of Missouri" between 1845 and 1847 and that he was not "formally" engaged in the ministry. In fact, his license to practice as a Presbyterian minister was withdrawn at Lexington, Virginia, on October 25, 1842.[7] Since Coyner had no children born between 1842 and 1848 (and children were born regularly before and after those years), it might be surmised that Coyner had left his family behind when he traveled to the Missouri frontier.

Coyner's explanation of his activities during those years was that he "went as Indian Agent west in the country between Missouri and New Mexico." While an Indian agent, Coyner claimed to have "organized [the] first Sabbath school in the upper Osage country."[8] If he was an Indian Agent, however, it is doubtful that he served in an official capacity for the United States government. His name does not appear in the known historical records of the period,[9] and it seems likely that if Coyner had been working among Indians some hint of this would have appeared in *The Lost Trappers*. Yet there is no reason to disbelieve Coyner unless he was undergoing a personal crisis that he later wished to cover up.

Coyner seems to have spent part of his time in Missouri in Howard and Cooper counties, which he mentions in *The Lost Trappers*. Perhaps it was in these adjacent counties—the historic Boon's Lick country, watered by the Missouri and cut by the roads to Santa Fe and Oregon—that Coyner found inspiration and information to write of the Far West. Information, according to Coyner, came from various persons he met in Missouri who "had spent years in the Rocky Mountains, and had traveled through Oregon and California." From them he learned many "interesting facts," but his chief source of information was "an old musty, mutilated journal, kept by Captain Williams."

At first, readers of *The Lost Trappers* had no reason to doubt that Coyner had access to Williams' journal, but as historians learned more about the early Trans-Mississippi West and about Ezekiel Williams in particular, Coyner's work fell into disrepute.

The name of Ezekiel Williams, the hero of *The Lost Trappers*, is cited so frequently in studies of early Anglo activity in the Far West that Edwin L. Sabin in his *Kit Carson Days* was moved to write of "the famed Ezekiel Williams."[10] Yet, despite the appearance of Frederic Voelker's article-length biography,[11] Williams remains an enigma. He left few written records, and there is no contemporary description of him or his personality except Coyner's questionable statements or vague assertion that Williams "was a man for whom nature had done a good part, both in mind and in body."[12]

Williams was probably born in Kentucky about 1780, but nothing is definitely known of his early life until he showed up in St. Louis in 1809 to join a group of trappers headed up the Missouri. Coyner states that Williams ascended the Missouri in 1807 at the head of an expedition that took Big White (or Shahaka), a Mandan chief, back to his village in present-day North Dakota. Big White had been brought to St. Louis in the fall of 1806 by Lewis and Clark and was taken to Washington, D.C., to see the "Great Father." The next year an expedition did try to escort Big White safely home. It was not, however, led by Ezekiel Williams, nor was he part of it. Rather, fourteen soldiers under Nathaniel Pryor made the journey, but they were attacked by Arikaras and failed to reach their destination.[13]

The next attempt to deliver Big White to his people succeeded. In 1809, the newly founded Missouri Fur Company contracted with the federal government to take the chief home and sent a large expedition of perhaps 350 men up the Missouri that summer. Led by the experienced, wily Manuel Lisa, the group reached the Mandan villages by September 24.[14]

If Coyner was correct that Ezekiel Williams was with the group escorting Big White to his village, then he clearly traveled with this party. Williams' own spare account of his activities during these years points to 1809 as the year that he ascended the Missouri. Furthermore, Williams later referred to himself as an employee of the Missouri Fur Company, and his name appears in the company records in 1814.[15] Coyner's version of the expedition that returned Big White is, however, fictitious. Williams did not lead the group, nor did it travel by land as Coyner says. Rather, Lisa took his men upriver in the customary manner—by barge and pirogue.

Most of the men who ascended the river in 1809 continued beyond the Mandan villages to the junction of the Yellowstone and the Big Horn, where Manuel Lisa had built Fort Raymond in 1807. From there, Lisa dispatched the men in small parties to trap and trade. Williams was probably among them, although his own statement is not revealing as to his precise whereabouts: "I went with the Fur Company up the Missouri, near the head of the river, where I hunted two years."[16]

Sometime in 1810 or 1811, Lisa sent Jean Baptiste Champlain as head of twenty-three trappers (perhaps including Williams) toward the Platte River. There Champlain met Arapahoes who told him that Spaniards from New Mexico sent trading parties to them annually. Champlain took this news to Lisa at Fort Mandan in the summer of 1811. Excited at the prospect of opening trade with New Mexico, Lisa sent another group of twenty-some trappers to the Arapahoes with merchandise that might entice the New Mexicans to trade with him. This group, which left Fort Mandan in August 1811, was led by Champlain and Jean Baptiste Lafargue; and Ezekiel Williams, according to his own testimony, was one of them.[17]

In spite of Champlain's experience and knowledge of the country, the trappers encountered serious trouble. After a year had passed with nothing heard from them, Lisa, in September 1812, dispatched Charles Sanguinet, Charles Latour, and Cadet Chevalier to search for Champlain. Always the businessman, Lisa also sent a letter to New Mexico officials with Sanguinet, inviting Spaniards to trade with him. The letter got through, but Sanguinet never found Champlain.[18] In December 1812, he sent Lisa a gloomy report. Arapahoes had told Sanguinet that Blackfeet had killed three of Champlain's party, and it was supposed that Champlain was among the murdered. Lafargue and five others, Sanguinet also reported, "had run off to the————Spaniards," and eight had gone to join Reuben Lewis, who was with the Crows on the Big Horn. Three or four others were missing, Ezekiel Williams apparently among them.[19]

A year later, in December 1813, Williams reached St. Louis alone and there gave Manuel Lisa more details of the disastrous expedition.[20] Champlain's men, Williams said, had trapped on the Arkansas through the winter of 1811-12, but Indians harassed them in the spring and forced them north to the Platte where the group divided. Williams said that "eight or ten crossed the Rocky Mountains," doubtless referring to those men whom Sanguinet reported had gone to the Big Horn. The remainder of the group, including Champlain and Williams, headed south again, apparently traveling to the east of the Front

Range of the Rockies to the Arkansas. There, Williams said, "four of our company determined to find the Spanish settlement."

These four must have been led by Lafargue, whom Sanguinet told Lisa had "run off" to the Spaniards; they were probably the same four Frenchmen who met José Antonio Casados of Taos, New Mexico, on the "Llano" or "Llara" River in March 1812. The four had asked Casados for directions to New Mexico. By July 30, 1812, they had found their way to Santa Fe where Spanish officials interrogated them and sent them farther south to Chihuahua.[21] They were held captive in Mexico at least until 1815 when an American who had been in Santa Fe learned that four of Lisa's men, "Lafargue, Vesina, Grenie, and Roi," were among some prisoners recently released in Chihuahua. Lafargue is said to have returned to St. Louis in 1817 with a group of American traders who had visited Santa Fe that year.[22] The fanciful adventures of James Workman and Samuel Spencer in Santa Fe and California, as told in *The Lost Trappers*, probably represent Coyner's imaginative retelling of the stories that he heard about Lafargue, Vesina, Grenie, and Roi nearly thirty years later.

Meanwhile, according to Williams, Lafargue's departure for New Mexico left only six of Lisa's men trapping in the mountains. By November 1812, Indians had reduced the group to three: Williams, Champlain, and Porteau. These three spent the winter among Arapahoes who, they suspected, had murdered their companions. In the spring the trappers separated, just as Coyner said. Champlain and Porteau, according to Williams, wanted "to stay with the Indians until some white person came there. . . ." Williams, however, was determined to leave and set out down the Arkansas alone in a canoe, trapping as he went.

Williams' journey down the Arkansas and his subsequent capture by Kansas Indians, both of which are described in *The Lost Trappers*, are substantiated by a letter that Williams wrote while captive and that somehow reached the *Missouri Gazette* at St. Louis. On October 9, 1813, that paper reported:

A few days ago, a letter was received from Mr. Williams, a principal hunter belonging to the Missouri Fur Company; dated Cansas [*sic*] village. Williams says that twenty men belonging to the Missouri Fur Company, were sent some time ago to hunt and trade with the Indians in that part of the country where the Arkansas River, Rio del Nord [Norte], Yellow Stone, Big Horn and Columbia take their source. Unsuspicious of danger, and while in the peaceful pursuit of their business, they were attacked by a party of Spaniards, who killed thirteen and sent the remaining seven, prisoners to the Mines.

Mr. W. also says that whilst trapping Beaver on the head waters of the Arkansas, he met with a Spaniard, who informed him that ten Americans were taken by the Spanish troops at an Indian village in the neighborhood of Sta. Fe and sent prisoners to the mines. . . .

As the article went on to point out, Williams had learned of the capture of a trading party that Robert McKnight, James Baird, and Samuel Chambers had led out of St. Louis. New Mexico officials had incarcerated these traders in June 1812 (about the same time that Lafargue reached Santa Fe) and kept them in confinement until 1820.[23] Williams' reported reference to Spaniards attacking his party is not substantiated by other contemporary documents, and Williams himself later charged Indians with the destruction. Perhaps the editor of the *Gazette*, angered at the New Mexicans' treatment of the McKnight party, added this information to Williams' letter gratuitously.

Coyner relates that after the Kansas Indians released Williams he traveled to Cooper's Fort and then to Arrow Rock on the Missouri where, "at the beginning of winter," an Indian agent named "Cibley" helped him to retrieve furs that the Kansas had kept. The year, however, was 1813—not 1809 as Coyner suggests—and Williams had been gone for over four years instead of eighteen months, nor was the amount of furs as large as Coyner indicates. But, in its main outline, Coyner's story is here correct. On November 30, 1813, Indian Agent George C. Sibley, at Arrow Rock, wrote the following letter to Governor William Clark:

Ezekiel Williams, hunter of the Missouri Fur Company, was on his way from the Rocky Mountains with a considerable quantity of fine fur.

He struck the Arkansas River below the mountains and descended that river within about 150 miles of the Verdigrise when a band of the Kansas found him on the 23d of June last, who robbed him of all he had with him, and very much abused him, as he says, and kept him prisoner to about the 15 Augt. when they released him and restored the greater part of his property. The balance (except a few articles they deny having taken) I have this day caused the Kansas to refund and pay for. . . .[24]

From Arrow Rock, Williams journeyed to St. Louis, which he reached at least by December 15. He stayed long enough to see Governor William Clark and Manuel Lisa, and to sell $591 worth of furs to the Missouri Fur Company. Then he returned to Cooper's Fort near Arrow Rock, where he married on January 16, 1814.[25]

If either Lisa or Clark had talked to Ezekiel Williams for long, these experienced frontiersmen would have learned about the unique geographical knowledge of the Rockies that Williams had acquired. As William Goetzmann summed up Williams' trek:

. . . although the best maps of the day indicated that Santa Fe was not far from the headwaters of the Yellowstone, at least one member of Lisa's company survived to say nay. Ezekiel Williams had seen the mountain country, explored the Platte, spanned the immense mountain distance from north to south, and long before anyone else in his profession, floated down the Arkansas to civilization. In effect, he had discovered Colorado [for Anglo-Americans].[26]

According to Coyner, Williams remained a year in the settlements before he managed to find two brave young men, Joseph and William Cooper, who would return to the Arkansas with him and help him bring in some furs he had cached near the Rockies. Actually, Williams started out for the Arkansas with Braxton Cooper and Morris May as his companions in May 1814 after only a few months' rest. These three traveled with a large group of French trappers under Joseph Philibert, a fact that, had Coyner known or cared to tell it, would have taken some of the drama out of his story. Williams did raise his cache and start back down the Arkansas, but low water made transportation impossible and forced him to cache the furs again after taking them some 500 miles downstream. In the winter of 1814-15, Williams did hire Joseph and William Cooper and successfully brought his furs in from the Arkansas. Some of the incidents Coyner relates may have occurred on this second journey to the Arkansas. Coyner seems to have been unaware, however, that Williams made two trips to retrieve his furs.

Further details of Williams' attempts to bring his furs down the Arkansas are told in his own words in an 1816 letter which is reprinted at the end of this volume. This terse document is Williams' only known account of his expedition to the Rockies and is of considerable value in illuminating Coyner's narrative. It is fortunate that the letter survived, for Williams did not write it for posterity but rather to clear himself of a curious accusation.

Nearly three years after Williams returned from the upper Arkansas, he was accused of murdering Jean Baptiste Champlain. The charge appeared in an unsigned article in the *Western Intelligencer* which told of the discovery of a grave some twenty-five miles west of Boon's Lick. The article reported that the grave had been discovered by "a gentleman of respectability" who, apparently unable to contain his curiosity, had opened the grave and found

> . . . the skeleton of a man dressed in uniform, he had a nice pair of epaulettes; the buttons on his coat marked U.S. He was buried sitting up with his sword cane between his legs, which had, as is supposed the initials of his name on it.[27]

The story went on to suggest that this was Champlain's grave and that Williams had murdered his trapping companion "for the sake of lucre!" which happened, in this case, to be furs.

This accusation contains many of the earmarks of fiction. Surely Champlain would not have been so attired, nor would a murderer take such care in burying his victim. Furthermore, Williams had a number of witnesses who had heard an Arapaho chief tell, in 1814, of Champlain's being alive after Williams left him on the Arkansas. The evidence seems to be on Williams' side, although the motive of his anonymous accuser remains unclear.[28]

Charges were never pressed against Ezekiel Williams for the death of Champlain, and he settled in Missouri to become a respected citizen and something of an authority on the West. In 1824, for example, the *Missouri Intelligencer* of Franklin spoke of Ezekiel Williams "who spent several years on the head waters of the Missouri, Arkansas and Columbia," and told of how Williams had accurately predicted that Major Andrew Henry would be attacked by Blackfeet Indians when he tried to ascend the Missouri River in 1822.[29]

In 1820, when the "Father of the Santa Fe Trade," William Becknell, advertised for men to accompany him on a hunting expedition destined to open trade with New Mexico, Becknell designated Ezekiel Williams' farm as the place of departure. In 1827, Williams himself made the trip to Santa Fe as the elected captain of the large annual caravan that year—a position which reflected the trust and esteem with which other merchants must have regarded him. His biographer, Frederic Voelker, suspects that Williams made subsequent trips to Santa Fe in 1828 and 1829, but evidence of this has not come to light. Williams almost certainly invested in merchandise that went to Santa Fe, for many of his acquaintances, including Abraham Barnes who became his son-in-law, were Santa Fe traders.[30]

Although "Old Zeke," as Ezekiel Williams came to be called, lived comfortably in Missouri, he was not one to stay in one place very long. In 1817, following his adventures on the Arkansas, Williams bought a farm on the rich bottomland along the Missouri a few miles north of Franklin in Howard County. In 1822, he crossed the Missouri and bought land along the river to the west of Boonville in Cooper County, where he resumed farming. By 1831, Williams had moved some seventy miles south and west of Boonville to present-day Benton County in what was then a nearly uninhabited corner of Cooper County. Williams settled on a creek that now bears his name, near today's Cole Camp, and there lived out his days while civilization gradually overtook him again before his death on December 24, 1844.[31]

As details of Ezekiel Williams' life came to light around the turn of the century, it became clear to historians that much of what David Coyner had presented as fact in *The Lost Trappers* was actually based on his imagination. At first, reaction against the book was severe.

Elliott Coues, in the introduction to his 1898 edition of *The Journal of Jacob Fowler*, wrote that *The Lost Trappers* was "an apocryphal book, never materializing out of fable-land into historical environment."

Hiram Martin Chittenden, in his classic *History of the American Fur Trade of the Far West*, published in 1902, devoted several pages to Coyner's book. He called it "one of the completest fabrications that was ever published under the guise of history." Terming the book an "ingenious creation" was as close to praise as Chittenden ever came. Otherwise, he suggested that "the author, Coyner, was chiefly a coiner of lies," and he stated flatly that "in the first part of the narrative there is not a semblance of truth, and the details of the story are themselves physically impossible."[32]

Much of Chittenden's annoyance centered on Coyner's faulty chronology, for Chittenden recognized that the book was not completely fictitious. He knew that Williams was a real person, but that he could not have ascended the Missouri in 1807. Chittenden also had evidence that Williams returned to civilization several years later than Coyner said, for he had a copy of Williams' 1816 letter. Thus, Chittenden wrote a realistic alternative to Coyner's confused account, and Judge Walter B. Douglas helped historians to understand Chittenden's position by publishing Williams' letter in the *Missouri Historical Society Collections* in 1913.[33]

Some historians, however, remained unconvinced that Coyner had seriously erred. One was Louis Houck, whose three-volume *History of Missouri* was published in 1908. Houck took the position that "many of the details of Coyner's little volume no doubt are fictitious, but perhaps in its main features this narrative is true." Houck retold the story to his readers and suggested that the "Narrative" of one John B. Shaw, who recorded meeting three trappers along the Front Range of the Rockies in 1809, confirmed Coyner's chronology. Houck, however, should have been more critical of Shaw, who dictated his reminiscences in 1855 at age seventy-two.[34] If Shaw met Williams near the Rockies, it is clear from what is now known that the date was not 1809.

The Lost Trappers remained convincing enough, then, that Houck was unwilling to question it seriously, and as late as 1929 Clarence A. Vandiveer, in his *Fur Trade and Early Western Exploration*, wrote a sketch of Ezekiel Williams which accepted Coyner's account almost entirely, warning his readers only that Coyner's dates might be too early.[35] Today, however, most historians would agree with the judgment of Paul Crisler Phillips who wrote that *The Lost Trappers* "is discredited as history, but there is reason to believe that many of the adventures described therein really happened."[36] The question remains: Which adventures really happened? How credible is anything in *The Lost Trappers*? To answer this, Coyner's sources of information should be looked at carefully, for they are more revealing and more easily identifiable than has been supposed.

Perhaps because Coyner's account of Ezekiel Williams' adventures is based, roughly, on actual events, some historians have taken Coyner's word that he truly had access to Williams' "journal." In fact, Frederic Voelker went a step further by suggesting that Coyner traveled to Benton County, Missouri, to meet Williams.[37] Since Williams died in 1844 and Coyner says he arrived in Missouri in 1845, such a meeting seems unlikely unless Coyner, writing in 1847, had reason to misrepresent the year he had come to Missouri. Furthermore, Coyner took such pains to convince his readers of the authenticity of his work that if he had actually met Old Zeke, he certainly would have described him or told of their meeting.

Not only does it seem unlikely that Coyner and Williams ever met, but there is little reason to believe that Coyner actually had Williams' "journal." Even had it been, as Coyner says, a "very succinct and imperfect and much mutilated journal," it scarcely seems possible that it would have permitted Coyner to confuse all dates, almost all names, and to report that a journey by boat was made by land or to ascribe the terrible hardships of winter to a journey that occurred in the summer. A "journal," or day-by-day account of Williams' activities, surely would not have permitted such errors. If Coyner had any of Old Zeke's writing, it might have been a short reminiscence written long after his memory had grown dim.

Voelker argues that Coyner had adequate sources before him—Williams' weak journal, as well as "oral material"—and lays most of the blame for errors in *The Lost Trappers* on Coyner's "superficial and careless method." Voelker also suggests, "Had Coyner checked his information against other available sources he could have produced a work of great importance. . . ."[38]

It seems to me, however, that the situation was just the opposite. Coyner appears to have taken the most fragmentary evidence and blown it up into a book through the checking and adaptation of readily available sources. As my annotations to this new edition of *The Lost Trappers* reveal, Coyner depended heavily upon published accounts to fill in background for his story. He leaned particularly on Washington Irving's *Astoria, or Anecdotes of an Enterprise Beyond the Rocky Mountains* (first published in 1836) and on Irving's *Adventures of Captain Bonneville, U.S.A. in the Rocky Mountains and the Far West*, which appeared in 1837. Coyner also drew information from Lansford W. Hastings' *The Emigrants' Guide to Oregon and California*, John C. Frémont's narratives, Zebulon Montgomery Pike's journals, and Nicholas Biddle's account of the Lewis and Clark Expedition.[39]

Coyner often paraphrases and plagiarizes these publications without acknowledging them (a technique with which Washington Irving and other contemporary writers were familiar), and occasionally makes it appear that he is instead paraphrasing Williams or another informant. This explains why *The Lost Trappers* has such an air of authenticity about it, even though Coyner never saw the Far West. It also means that Coyner's descriptions of Indian groups, geographical phenomena, animals, and hunting are reliable—or at least as reliable as the sources from which he took the descriptions.

Of course, not all of Coyner's story was derived from published materials. Coyner had some source which provided him with a sketchy outline of Williams' life. If this did not come from Williams' own hand, it might have come from any number of Missourians who knew Old Zeke, for he was apparently given to reminiscing about his exploits and may have "stretched" the truth on occasion himself.

Felix Renick, a young traveler, who visited Williams' farm in 1819, recalled that the tales he heard were "truly astonishing. We could hardly have given credit to his story, had it not been corroborated by colonel Cooper." Renick made an attempt in 1843 to have Williams write down his stories, but apparently he failed. Perhaps this was, as Voelker suggested, "the germ of the idea that resulted in David H. Coyner's *The Lost Trappers*."[40]

The clearest link between Coyner and Ezekiel Williams, however, seems to have been through the Cooper family. Prominent pioneers in the Boon's Lick country, the three Cooper brothers and their children knew Williams well. In 1814, Williams served at Cooper's Fort under Captain Sarshall Cooper (for whom Cooper County is named). In May, after Sarshall's death, his brother, Braxton Cooper, went up the Arkansas with Williams. Later that year, Sarshall's son Joseph, along with his cousin William, the son of Colonel Benjamin Cooper, accompanied Williams up the Arkansas. When Williams lived near Franklin in 1819, Benjamin Cooper was one of his neighbors.[41] In *The Lost Trappers* the names of Joseph and William Cooper are among the very few that Coyner records. Coyner also acknowledges that he used "papers furnished by Workman and Col. Cooper, of Howard county, Missouri." Which "Colonel" Cooper this was is not clear, for Benjamin, the veteran Santa Fe trader who was known as "Colonel," died in 1842. Perhaps one of his sons carried on the "title."

If Coyner also received "papers" from someone named Workman, it was probably David Workman, an Englishman who lived in Missouri at least as early as 1821, operating a saddlery at Franklin, New Franklin, and at Boonville after 1840. He, too, would have had ample opportunity to talk to Old Zeke. David Workman's brother, William, had trapped in the Southwest and lived in New Mexico and California and might have told his brother much Western lore. David Workman himself traveled on the Santa Fe Trail in 1827 (probably with Williams) and in 1846, and was knowledgeable about the West. The

"James Workman" whom Coyner tells of is almost certainly a fictional name, and his experiences clearly are. The Workman brothers had no close relative by that name in America.[42]

Coyner probably had other sources of information in the Boon's Lick country, such as Williams' son-in-law, Abraham Barnes, who probably told Coyner about his experiences on the Santa Fe Trail. It would be impossible, though, to identify all of those informants whom Coyner says "had spent years in the Rocky Mountains, and had traveled through Oregon and California." Through conversations with such men, Coyner picked up facts that seem to be available in no other published source. Thus, he has been cited by reputable scholars (and should continue to be) on such varied matters as the cooking of beaver tails, the toughness of wild horse meat, and the way to smuggle goods into Santa Fe.[43] Coyner's technique of combining firsthand information with gleanings from published accounts resulted in a volume that seemed authentic to contemporaries and that provided later and more critical readers with insights into the fur trade and the Santa Fe Trade.

Beyond the question of historical facts and details that Coyner may or may not have portrayed accurately, *The Lost Trappers* is of value to historians in that it reflects many notions about the West that prevailed in Coyner's day. His knowledge of Indians, for example, is shallow, and he over-generalizes about "Western Tribes." He usually views Indians as not-too-noble savages, a "lazy race," "taciturn and grave," who hopefully through tribal wars will kill one another off to make room for westward expansion. At times, though, Coyner reveals a characteristic American ambivalence toward the "rude and unpolished children of the forest."

Coyner's view of mountain men seems to have been borrowed chiefly from Washington Irving. Like Irving, Coyner admires the trapper as a man who despises civilization and thrives in the freedom of the wilderness.[44] Thus, *The Lost Trappers* may be of as much value in revealing what Coyner *believed* had happened in the West as for telling what actually had happened in the West. Then, too, *The Lost Trappers* not only mirrored American opinion, but also might have influenced it, for the book went through several editions and seems to have been available to the reading public for half a century after publication.

Although family tradition has it that David H. Coyner was "a successful author and historian,"[45] his success was such that neither fame nor fortune ever threatened him. Certainly, the West was much in the public eye when Coyner put the finishing touches to his manuscript in the fall of 1846. The long-disputed Oregon Territory had fallen to the United States that June and, even as Coyner wrote, news arrived in Missouri of how United States forces had wrested New Mexico and California from Mexican control. But, if there was great interest in the Far West in 1847, there were also enough writers to satiate public demand. When Coyner's book appeared, it had to compete with such newly published, firsthand accounts of western travel as those of George Frederick Ruxton, George Simpson, and Pierre-Jean De Smet. In 1847, Coyner's own publisher, the Cincinnati house of J. A. and U. P. James, brought out Joel Palmer's *Journal of Travels Over the Rocky Mountains* and John Taylor Hughes' *Doniphan's Expedition*— and so it went. Perhaps a desire to meet this competition led Coyner to add sections on the Santa Fe Trail, Oregon, and California to his story of Ezekiel Williams. If so, the tactic was only slightly successful.

When *The Lost Trappers* was published in late July or early August of 1847,[46] it made no great or immediate impact on the literary community. National magazines, such as *The Spirit of the Times* and *The North American Review*, carried no notice of it. Even bookdealers at St. Louis, the "gateway to the West," published no advertisement of the book. Rather, such timely if less enduring volumes as *Taylor and His Generals* and an *Illustrated Life of General Scott* were featured along with perennial volumes of Shakespeare and the Scriptures and on health and gardening.[47]

The Lost Trappers apparently did not sell well enough to remain on the list of the prestigious publishing house of J. A. and U. P. James, known to some contemporaries as the "Harper's of the West." The plates for *The Lost Trappers* were transferred to a Cincinnati bookseller and occasional publisher, E. E. Truman, who reprinted the book in 1850. In 1855, bookseller and publisher H. M. Rulison of Cincinnati brought out a new printing, which, in 1858, was followed by Anderson,

Gates & Wright, a Cincinnati company that went out of business two years later. Printings of *The Lost Trappers* dated 1853, 1856, and 1859 are also reported to exist, perhaps made by the publishers named.[48] Although Coyner's book caused no initial sensation, it did generate sufficient interest for small publishers to keep it in print. Toward the end of the century, perhaps in 1892, Hurst & Company of New York reissued *The Lost Trappers* on inexpensive paper, charging twenty-five cents a copy in hard cover. That was a bargain, since the first printing in 1847 had cost a dollar.

Today all printings of *The Lost Trappers* are scarce and expensive. In 1969, the first edition in good condition would have brought about $65.[49] All of the early printings are rare. Bibliophile and historian Hubert Howe Bancroft thought the book to have been first published in 1859, as did historian Hiram M. Chittenden. But, regardless of the edition, all were identical, having been printed from the same plates. The present volume, then, is not a facsimile but represents the first truly new edition of *The Lost Trappers* ever to appear.

Following publication of *The Lost Trappers*, Coyner continued to live in obscurity. In 1847, he settled north of Columbus in Delaware County, Ohio, where he was in charge of a classical school for several years. He was ordained in the new school of the Presbyterian Church in the Franklin Presbytery, Synod of Ohio, in August 1848. In Ohio, Coyner seems to have preached in a number of churches, traveling as far as Indiana in 1853.[50] From 1853 to 1857, he preached quite regularly at the Genoa Church at Galena in Delaware County, Ohio.[51] From 1857-60, he lived at Lexington in Richland County just south of Mansfield, Ohio.[52] In 1863, if not earlier, he moved to northern Ohio and preached at Monroeville, then at Clyde in the following year. At this time he was licensed in the Western Reserve Presbytery, associated with the old school of the church[53] with which he remained affiliated until he retired from preaching.

The Civil War was a time of great sadness for Coyner. Four of his sons served in the Union Army and only two returned home. On April 20, 1864, before the war ended, his wife died and Coyner took his family back to Virginia. There his northern sympathies made him unwelcome and his stay was short.[54] Perhaps he stayed long enough, however, to marry Harriet Frances Snodgrass, the sister of his deceased wife. Clearly this marriage took place before 1866.[55] After his visit to Virginia, Coyner returned to Ohio where he enlisted as Chaplain of the Eighty-Eighth Ohio Volunteer Infantry, garrisoned at Camp Chase just west of Columbus.

After the war, Coyner settled at Eden, which is today Kilbourne, Ohio. Coyner preached for two years at Brown Church and at nearby Kingston Church, then retired from the ministry.[56] In April 1867, he asked to be transferred from the Marion Presbytery to the Presbytery of the Missouri River. The request was granted, but he never moved and his name was restored to the Marion rolls the next year. In 1869, the Marion Presbytery denied Coyner's request to continue to preach, apparently because a scandal had arisen regarding his collection and use of church funds. A year later, following an investigation of Coyner's activities, the Marion Presbytery concluded that "certain rumors" concerning Coyner's "ministerial and Christian character" were not justified.[57] By that time, however, Coyner had moved to West Virginia.

Coyner seems to have made no attempt to preach on religious matters in West Virginia. Instead, he occupied himself with the more earthly concern of attracting immigrants to West Virginia and addressed the state legislature on this subject in February 1870. This talk resulted in his writing a sixteen-page pamphlet, "Cheap, Healthy and Happy Homes in West Virginia for Northern and New England Emigrants," five thousand copies of which were printed at Wheeling in 1870 at the expense of the state.[58] Aside from a few sermons and *The Lost Trappers*, this pamphlet was Coyner's only other published work. In it, Coyner's description of the "undeveloped wealth in West Virginia" was as lavish as the praises that he had bestowed on California and Missouri in *The Lost Trappers*. In "Cheap, Healthy and Happy Homes," Coyner argued that "West Virginia has many of the advantages not to be had anywhere in the 'far west.'"

Just as David H. Coyner did not succumb to the rhetoric of *The Lost Trappers* and move to California or remain in Missouri, neither did he allow his own writing about West Virginia in 1870 to keep him there.

He soon returned to Eden, Ohio, where he spent his last years in bad health. He died, suffering with dropsy, on January 21, 1892, at age eighty-five.[59]

The author of *The Lost Trappers*, then, died before scholars began to vilify his book; and he did not live to read Chittenden's charge that he was "chiefly a coiner of lies." It is just as well. Coyner would hardly have understood Chittenden and other literal-minded historians. As was common for many "historians" of his day, Coyner had drawn from published and unpublished sources to create an impressionistic picture that was reasonably accurate, even if it erred in some details which he surely thought were minor. Or, as Mark Twain had Huckleberry Finn say, "There was things which he stretched, but mainly he told the truth."

All annotations in this new edition of *The Lost Trappers* are those of the editor. They are designed to clarify the narrative for the modern reader and to indicate published sources from which Coyner borrowed. Coyner was a literate man and can be forgiven for "Camanches" and "Lewis and Clark*e*," for such were the common usage of the time. And if Coyner uses "farther" when he ought to say "further," or renders "valleys" as "vallies," these too are understandable, for they remain common errors today. Thus, with the exception of an occasional printer's error that has been corrected, this edition of *The Lost Trappers* is faithful to the original. Because diverse sources were used in annotating this volume and receive a full bibliographical citation on first and often only use, a bibliography has not been added.

This volume owes much to the University of New Mexico Press which recognizes the value of an edited and indexed volume over the expedient and all-too-common facsimile reprint. Numerous other persons and institutions gave of their time to answer inquiries. Their help is acknowledged in the footnotes. My work was also facilitated by a grant from the San Diego State College Foundation, and by the efforts of my wife Carol, and my young children, Scott and Amy. The former worked closely with me and the latter kept judiciously far away.

La Mesa, California   *David J. Weber*

NOTES

1. *Northwest Coast*, vol. II, pp. 126-28, and *Arizona and New Mexico*, p. 300.

2. *Old Santa Fe Trail* (New York, 1897), pp. 30-37, and *Great Salt Lake Trail* (New York, 1898), pp. 32-62.

3. Absalom Koiner (comp.), *A Historical Sketch of Michael Keinadt and Margaret Diller, His Wife. The History and Genealogy of Their Numerous Posterity in the American States, Up to the Year 1893* (Staunton, Va., 1893), pp. 11, 15-17, 108-21. A personal copy of this volume was loaned to me by Helena Koiner of the University of Virginia Library.

4. Letter to me from Frank A. Parson, Assistant to the President, Washington and Lee University, August 15, 1969. Letter from the Office of the President, the Princeton Theological Seminary, August 18, 1969. David H. Coyner to Reverend William E. Schenck, Kilbourne, Ohio, March 14, 1878, in response to an Alumni Questionnaire from Princeton Theological Seminary. Coyner folder, Princeton Theological Seminary.

5. Willis J. Beecher (comp.), *Index of Presbyterian Ministers . . . 1706-1881* (Philadelphia, 1888), p. 125.

6. Coyner to Schenck, March 14, 1878. Koiner, *Historical Sketch*, pp. 120-21.

7. General Catalogue, Princeton Theological Seminary.

8. Coyner to Schenck, March 14, 1878.

9. Coyner's name as an Indian agent does not appear, for example, in the U.S. Department of Interior's eight-volume *Biographical and Historical Index of American Indians and Persons Involved in Indian Affairs* (Boston, 1966). Mrs. Alma Vaughan, State Historical Society of Missouri, August 28, 1969, finds no record of Coyner in Missouri or Kansas.

10. (New York, 1935), vol. I, p. 33.

11. "Ezekiel Williams of Boon's Lick," *Bulletin of the Missouri Historical Society*, vol. 8, no. 1 (October 1951), pp. 17-51.

12. Felix Renick to John S. Williams, editor, January 23, 1843, *American Pioneer*, vol. II, no. 7 (July 1843), p. 330. This letter is cited in Voelker, "Ezekiel Williams." Voelker quotes extensively from it.

13. Richard Edward Oglesby, *Manuel Lisa and the Opening of the Missouri Fur Trade* (Norman, Okla., 1963), pp. 50-51.   14. Ibid., pp. 68, 70, 75.

15. See Williams to Charless, August 7, 1816, in the Documents at the end of this volume. Douglas, "Williams," p. 196. [Walter B. Douglas], "Ezekiel Williams' Adventures in Colorado," *Missouri Historical Society Collections*, vol. IV, no. 2 (1913), p. 196.

16. Williams to Charless, August 7, 1816.

17. Ibid. Herbert E. Bolton, "New Light on Manuel Lisa and the Spanish Fur Trade," *Southwestern Historical Quarterly*, vol. XVII, no. 1 (July 1913), p. 63.

NOTES

18. Bolton, "Lisa," pp. 60-66. Oglesby, *Lisa*, pp. 115, 131-32.

19. John C. Luttig, *Journal of a Fur-Trading Expedition on the Upper Missouri, 1812-1813*. Edited by Stella M. Drumm with preface and notes by Abraham P. Nasatir (New York, 1964), pp. 102-03.

20. Williams to Charless, August 7, 1816. Oglesby, *Lisa*, p. 145.

21. José Antonio Casados to Ignacio Elías Gonzales, Santa Fe, April 11, 1813, document number 2484, Spanish Archives of New Mexico, State Records Center, Santa Fe, N.M. Bolton, "Lisa," p. 64.

22. Letter of Joseph Philibert in the St. Louis *Missouri Gazette*, July 29, 1815. Luttig, *Journal*, p. 103 n151.

23. Rex W. Strickland, "James Baird," in LeRoy R. Hafen (ed.), *The Mountain Men and the Fur Trade of the Far West* (Glendale, Calif., 1966), vol. III, pp. 27-37.

24. Quoted in Douglas, "Ezekiel Williams," p. 199.

25. Voelker, "Ezekiel Williams," pp. 24-26.

26. William H. Goetzmann, *Exploration and Empire: The Explorer and the Scientist in the Winning of the American West* (New York, 1967), p. 28.

27. This article, which appeared in the July 9, 1816, *Western Intelligencer* published at Kaskaskia, Illinois, is printed in entirety and further analyzed in Voelker, "Ezekiel Williams," pp. 29-33.

28. Williams to Charless, August 7, 1816. Adding to the mystery surrounding Champlain's death, Blackfeet Indians are said to have learned that Arapahoes killed Champlain and three others in the summer of 1812, according to the entry of October 18, 1812, in the journal of Robert Stuart in Philip A. Rollins (ed.), *The Discovery of the Oregon Trail: Robert Stuart's Narratives* (New York, 1935), pp. 161, 179. Since this story passed through several hands before it reached Stuart, since translation was involved, and since other evidence points to Champlain's death having occurred after 1812, it seems wise to dismiss this piece of information. Assuming that the Blackfeet had heard correctly that Arapahoes had killed some trappers, it seems unlikely that they would have known a trapper's name.

29. Quoted in Dale L. Morgan (ed.), *The West of William H. Ashley, 1822-1828* (Denver, 1964), p. 248 n205.

30. Voelker, "Ezekiel Williams," pp. 39, 43. David J. Weber, *The Extranjeros: Selected Documents from the Mexican Side of the Santa Fe Trail, 1825-1828* (Santa Fe, N.M., 1967), p. 41.

31. For a more detailed account of Williams' life in Missouri, see Voelker, "Ezekiel Williams."

32. (Stanford, Calif., 1954), vol. II, pp. 651-56.

33. "Ezekiel Williams' Adventures in Colorado," *Missouri Historical Society Collections*, vol. IV, no. 2 (1913), pp. 194-208.

34. Houck, *History of Missouri* (Chicago, 1908), vol. III, pp. 93-94. Shaw's "Narrative" is in *Wisconsin Historical Collections*, vol. II (1903 reprint), pp. 197-232.

35. (Cleveland, 1929), pp. 164-67.

36. *The Fur Trade* (Norman, Okla., 1961), vol. II, p. 267. See also such works as W. J. Ghent, *The Road to Oregon* (London, 1929), p. 12; and Dale L. Morgan (ed.), *The West of William H. Ashley* (Denver, 1964), p. xliii.

37. Voelker, "Ezekiel Williams," p. 50. 38. Ibid.

39. Subsequent references to these works are to Edgeley W. Todd's editions of *Bonneville* (Norman, Okla., 1961) and *Astoria* (Norman, Okla., 1964); to the facsimile of the 1845 Hastings' *Emigrants' Guide*, edited by Charles Henry Carey (Princeton, N.J., 1932); Allan Nevins' edition of the *Narratives of Exploration and Adventure* by John C. Frémont (New York, 1956); Donald Jackson's edition of Pike's *Journals* (2 vols., Norman, Okla., 1966); Elliott Coues' edition of the *History of the Expedition under the Command of Lewis and Clarke* (4 vols., New York, 1893).

40. Voelker, "Ezekiel Williams," pp. 37, 48.

41. Ibid., pp. 25-26. Houck, *History of Missouri*, vol. III, p. 121.

42. David J. Weber, "William Workman," in LeRoy R. Hafen (ed.), *The Mountain Men and the Fur Trade of the Far West* (Glendale, Calif., 1969), vol. VII, pp. 381-392. *History of Howard and Cooper Counties* (St. Louis, 1883), p. 172. Advertisement in the Boonville *Western Emigrant*, March 21, 1840, announcing David Workman's move to that city. LeRoy R. Hafen (ed.), *Ruxton of the Rockies* (Norman, Okla., 1950), p. 136.

43. Sabin, *Kit Carson Days*, vol. I, pp. 125, 156. Max L. Moorhead, *New Mexico's Royal Road* (Norman, Okla., 1954), p. 127.

44. See Henry Nash Smith, *Virgin Land: The American West As Symbol and Myth* (New York, 1950), who quotes Coyner on p. 90.

45. Koiner, *Historical Sketch*, p. 121.

46. Advertisements in the *Cincinnati Daily Enquirer* on July 26 and 27, 1847, and in the *Cincinnati Daily Gazette* on July 22, 1847, indicated that the book would be published "in a few days." Subsequent advertisements do not reveal when the book was actually published.

47. *The Lost Trappers* does not show up in *Poole's Index to Literature*, or the *Nineteenth Century Reader's Guide to Periodical Literature*. A check of the St. Louis *Daily Union* and the St. Louis *Missouri Republican* for fall and winter of 1847 revealed no advertisement of the book.

48. Walter Sutton, *The Western Book Trade: Cincinnati as a Book-Trade Center* (Columbus, 1961), pp. 88-95, 115-18, 312, 336, 340. *Library of Congress Catalogue* (Ann Arbor, Mich., 1943), vol. V, pp. 34, 293-94. Wright Howes (comp.), *U.S. Iana, 1650-1950* (rev. ed., New York, 1962), p. 138.

49. *United States Catalogue* [Books in Print], 1899, p. 149. Letter to me from Arthur H. Clark, Bookseller, Glendale, California, July 25, 1969.

50. Arthur M. Byers, Jr., Secretary, Princeton Theological Seminary, to Weber, August 21, 1969, citing the Minutes of the General Assembly of the Presbyterian Church.

51. Coyner to Schenck, March 14, 1878. *History of Delaware County* (Chicago, 1880), p. 610.

52. Miss Dorothy Kurtz to Weber, Presbyterian Historical Society, September 3, 1969, citing the Minutes of the General Assembly of the United Presbyterian Church. That this was the Lexington in Richland County is confirmed by the birth of George Coyner there in 1858.

53. Reverend C. Arthur Phillips to Weber, Office of the Stated Clerk, Presbytery of Wooster, Ohio, August 29, 1969.

54. James R. Lytle, *20th Century History of Delaware County, Ohio, and Representative Citizens* (Chicago, 1908), pp. 850-51, contains a sketch of Coyner's son, George.

55. On February 2, 1867, Coyner's third wife bore a son, Clarence. A genealogical chart containing information by the son of Clarence Coyner, Rolland G. Coyner, was provided by Mrs. Fay Bouic of the Delaware County Historical Society, Delaware, Ohio.

56. A. C. Crist, *The History of Marion Presbytery, Its Churches, Elders, Ministers, Missionary Societies, Etc.* (Delaware, Ohio, 1908), pp. 76, 116. Coyner to Schenck, March 14, 1878.

57. Minutes of the Presbytery of Marion, provided by Miss Dorothy Kurtz, Presbyterian Historical Society.

58. West Virginia *Senate Journal*, p. 96, and *Acts of the West Virginia Legislature, Joint Resolutions, 1870*, p. 146.

59. Obituaries in the *Delaware Gazette*, January 22, 1892, and the *Delaware Democratic Herald*, January 28, 1892. Letter of C. C. Coyner, Kilbourne, Ohio, February 9, 1894, in Coyner folder, Princeton Theological Seminary.

OVERLEAF: MAP OF PLACES MENTIONED IN THE LOST TRAPPERS

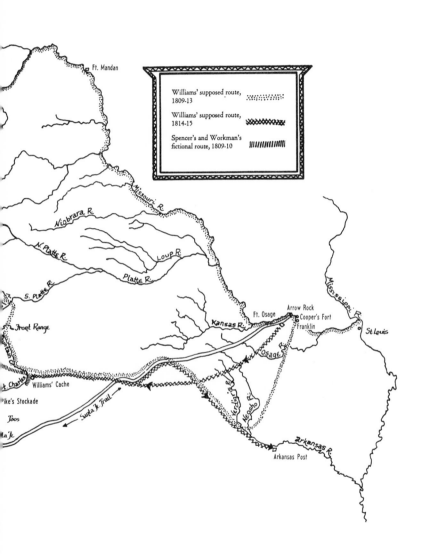

Williams' supposed route, 1809-13

Williams' supposed route, 1814-15

Spencer's and Workman's fictional route, 1809-10

Ft. Mandan

Missouri R.

Niobrara R.

N. Platte R.

Loup R.

Platte R.

S. Platte R.

Front Range

Williams' Cache

Pike's Stockade

Taos

Santa Fe

Santa Fe Trail

Kansas R.

Ft. Osage

Arrow Rock

Cooper's Fort

Franklin

Osage R.

Verdigris R.

Neosho R.

Mississippi R.

St. Louis

Arkansas R.

Arkansas Post

THE

LOST TRAPPERS;

A COLLECTION OF

INTERESTING SCENES AND EVENTS

IN THE

ROCKY MOUNTAINS;

TOGETHER WITH

A SHORT DESCRIPTION OF CALIFORNIA:

ALSO,

SOME ACCOUNT OF THE FUR TRADE,

ESPECIALLY AS CARRIED ON ABOUT THE SOURCES OF MISSOURI, YELLOW
STONE, AND ON THE WATERS OF THE COLUMBIA,
IN THE ROCKY MOUNTAINS.

BY DAVID H. COYNER.

CINCINNATI:
J. A. & U. P. JAMES, WALNUT STREET,
BETWEEN FOURTH AND FIFTH.
1847.

Facsimile of title page of the first edition, 1847.
(Courtesy Yale University Library)

Contents

CONTENTS

in a buffalo hunt by the Black-feet—Danger of the company—they leave that region—Crows—One of their men leaves them.

CONTENTS

CONTENTS

Author's Introduction

During a residence of three years, 1845-6-7, in the upper part of the State of Missouri, I was occasionally employed in redeeming a promise made to an editor of a newspaper in Virginia, the state from which I emigrated, to send him for his paper such materials of a frontier character, as I might be able to pick up, and as would form interesting communications for his columns. When I took up my residence in that State, I found myself among a people much moved and stimulated by western enterprise; a people not only familiar with frontier scenes and events, but deeply interested in things far beyond the limits of their own state. Many of them I observed were engaged in the Santa Fe trade, and were making their regular annual trips across the plains to New Mexico. I frequently sought the company of such gentlemen, whom I found not only intelligent, but kind, and ready to communicate any thing I desired. Some of them, indeed all that I met with, would entertain me for hours frequently, with interesting accounts of their difficulties in the various expeditions in which they had been engaged. I made it a rule to note down all the important oral information, that I was able to procure. Several gentlemen furnished me with a number of very interesting facts on paper, which were of great service to me in the work I now offer to the public. I soon found that the materials accumulated on my hands too fast, and in too great quantity to be published in a newspaper, at so great a distance. I also met with a number of men who had been to Oregon and California, and some who had spent several years in the Rocky Mountains. From such I drew a great many interesting facts, which are interwoven in this

1

work. The most interesting facts, however, that I was able to gather, I found in an old musty, mutilated journal, kept by Captain Williams, and other papers furnished by Workman and Col. Cooper, of Howard county, Missouri, giving an account of the expedition, the history of which, makes the greater part of this volume. It is due to myself to state, that these papers were so badly written, and so defective in many respects, that I aimed simply to get the facts, which I always clothed in my own words. Many of the most interesting facts that are interspersed through this work, I procured in conversation with gentlemen, who as I have said, had spent years in the Rocky Mountains, and had traveled through Oregon and California.

My reasons for offering an account of Captain Williams' expedition to the public, are, that I believe that just at this time, it would be interesting to the great majority of readers. Indeed any book detailing the trials and difficulties of those early adventurers, will be read with avidity. Any publication, throwing any light on that vast wilderness between the States and the Pacific, and calculated to open its secrets, will be read with interest. Events are now transpiring, that throw around the regions of the far west, an interest, which they never possessed before. The Oregon question is settled, and our citizens are going there every summer season by thousands. California is likely to become ours, and who will venture to limit the number of persons emigrating there, if it should be attached to our domain? A mail route from the States across the Rocky Mountains, is talked of in high places, and among the great ones of our government; and even the idea of a great rail-way across the Rocky Mountains has entered the minds of some. Our government will, doubtless, soon adopt measures to establish a cordon of military posts between the State of Missouri and the settlements on the waters of the Columbia. Each one of those posts will be a nucleus around which our adventurous citizens will be sure to collect and form colonies, that will expand and cover the whole land. It may be said that such enterprises will be beset with dangers and trials and hardships, and these things will deter men from such undertakings. But these are the very exciting causes that will prompt men to bold adventure. Those frontier men are fond of excitement, and they desire to be surrounded by exciting circumstances. They are even fond of trials and hardships and dangers, for they stimulate and sustain. Look at the trapper as he dashes into a wilderness full of danger, to pursue his favorite employment. He is conscious that his undertaking is very hazardous. He is aware that he is liable to be discovered by the savages every day, and to be cut off. As he paddles about in his little canoe on some nameless stream, he expects every moment to be surprised by the hideous yells of ruthless foes, from whom no mercy can be expected. As he passes along through some solitary and dark ravine of the mountains, he sees the bones and grinning skulls of his brethren, who were waylaid by the savages, and fell by their cruel hand. He is compelled to keep his arms in his hands, night as well as day; nor does he dare for one moment to relax in his vigilance. If he venture to close his eyes in sleep, it is only to snatch a morsel of rest, and then to start up, perhaps to witness some new danger in his vicinity. This is a trapper's life; a life of sleepless vigilance, of constant toil and danger: and yet he prefers it to any other kind of life. A strange infatuation possesses him, that makes him passionately fond of the excitement of the wilderness. He despises the dull uniformity and monotony of civilized life, when compared in his mind with the stirring scenes of wild western adventure. The security and protection of the laws have no attraction for him; for he wants no other means of defence than his rifle, which is his daily companion. He is impatient of the formalities and the galling restrictions of well organized society, and prefers the latitude and liberty of a life in the woods. Seated by his fire, in his camp, with a beaver tail spitted before him, or feasting upon his buffalo tongue, or buffalo beef, or buffalo marrow bones, with a piece of dry bark for a plate, he lives better and feels better, and enjoys his repast with a better zest than the citizen who is surrounded with all the comforts and luxuries of a metropolis.

As to the statements that I have made about California, I would mention that they were furnished by men whose veracity I had no right to question. I have not seen that country. But if I had, and my account had been made from personal observation, my statements would have been those of one man only. I furnish that kind of representation of California which speaks the larger aye of a majority of those who have been there. I collected quite a number of items in relation to the climate, fertility, and soil, and productions of that country, which I withhold in this book, not that I disbelieve them, but because I was apprehensive that I might be regarded as imposing too heavy a tax on the credulity of my readers. I know that many descriptions of the far west are too highly colored; that many have been misled by them, and are ready to deplore the hour they read them. But it seems to me that men ought to be able to distinguish those accounts that are extravagant and wild from those that are sober and wear the aspect of truth. Again, there are many persons who will receive any thing as truth, that may be said about the many and superior advantages in the regions of the west. It is no wonder, then, that they are misled, and do not find things as they expected, in those countries. I met with persons in Missouri, who had moved to Oregon and California; but whilst there they became dissatisfied, and returned over a long journey of two thousand miles. I have also been informed that many are moving from Oregon to California, and from California to Oregon. This only proves that as long as there is any country ahead, or to which emigrants can go there are some persons of unsettled and dissatisfied feelings, who will always be traveling. I never ask information from such persons about the countries they may have seen.

As to all the representations then, in this volume, I honestly believe that they may be assumed as *credenda*, in which every confidence may be reposed by those who may read them.

Chapter 1

Lewis and Clarke's expedition across the Rocky Mountains—their efforts to secure the friendship of the western tribes—their presents to the natives. They persuade a Mandan chief, Big White, to descend the Missouri with them to the States. Object of Captain Williams' expedition—number of men and their outfit—the route they took—annoyed by a band of wolves—one caught in a trap—difficulty in regaining the trap. Frontier mode of driving off wolves—dose of fish-hooks—some of the horses missing. The Mandan chief of great service to the party.

By THOSE WHO have read the expedition of Lewis and Clarke, across the Rocky mountains, it will be remembered that they endeavored, by all possible means, to assure the many Indian tribes in the far west, of the kind feelings and intentions entertained towards them by the government of the United States, and the desire of said government to create and establish upon a permanent basis, those friendly relations, between the different tribes themselves and the United States, that were preferable to those constant hostilities that then existed, and would prove a source of great and almost innumerable blessings and benefits to all parties. To effect this the more readily, that party took with them a considerable amount of merchandise, consisting of such articles as were most likely to please those rude and unpolished children of the forest. It was also the design of Lewis and Clarke to impress them as far as they could, with the num-

5

ber, strength and greatness of our people, that they might see the importance and advantage of always being at peace with such a people. To this end, on their return they were anxious to bring with them, to the States, as many of the chiefs of the different tribes as could be persuaded to accompany them. But in this they almost entirely failed, as the Indians, generally, were very suspicious, and expressed their fears that those, that might go, would never return to their tribes. Having wintered [in 1804-05], among the Mandans, whose villages are high up the Missouri river, on their way across the Rocky Mountains, the company, to some extent, had gained the confidence of that tribe, and on their way home prevailed on one of their chiefs, Big White,[1] to go with them, and to take with him his wife and son, to see our people and President. The Mandans, at that time, were at war with the Sioux, a numerous, war-like and formidable tribe, whose villages were below on the Missouri, and who would intercept, if they could, any of the Mandans going down the river, and cut them off. This fact was a matter of much dread and anxiety to the chief, Big White, and promised to be an insuperable barrier in the way; but Capt. Lewis placed himself under every obligation to protect him, and gave a pledge in behalf of his government, that a company of armed men should guard him on his return to his tribe. As this pledge was redeemed by the government of the United States, it is our purpose in this volume to give the history of the expedition, the object of which was, not only to guard the Mandan brave to his home in the far west, but to explore the country on the waters of the Missouri, to trap for beaver, and even to penetrate and cross the Rocky Mountains.

It was in the spring of 1807, that this expedition set out from St. Louis. The party consisted of twenty men, under the direction of Captain Ezekiel Williams, a man of great perseverance, patience, and much unflinching determination of character. His men, being citizens of Missouri, which was, at that early day, an almost unbroken wilderness, were all accustomed to the privations and hardships of a frontier life, and like most frontier men, fond of adventures and daring enter-

---

[1] Big White, or Shahaka, was head chief of the southernmost of two Mandan villages located on the west bank of the Missouri about four miles below the mouth of Knife River in present-day North Dakota.

6

prises; well skilled in the use of the rifle, and entertaining a strong partiality for those hazards and exploits that are peculiar to a frontier and savage life.

The outfit of each man was a rifle, together with as much powder and lead as it was supposed would last for two years. Each one took six traps, which were packed upon an extra horse with which each man was furnished. Pistols, awls, axes, knives, camp kettles, blankets, and various other essential little articles, also made a part of the equipage. Captain Williams provided himself with an assortment of light portable little notions, intended as presents for the Indians. To the expedition belonged also four dogs, (great favorites of their masters,) one of which was a very superior gray-hound, that was taken along by his owner to catch deer on the plains.[2]

On the 25th of April the party were on their way, exhibiting all the glee, and excitement, and laughter, of men enjoying the wild freedom of frontier life, and expecting to pass through scenes of adventure and danger that would fully test their patience and courage, and perhaps be marked by the effusion of blood. At that season of the year, there was a sufficiency of grass for their horses, and as for themselves, it was their purpose to depend on their rifles for provisions. As it was the purpose of Captain Williams to reach Fort Mandan[3] as early in the trapping season as practicable, the party abandoned the meanderings of the Missouri, and launched forth into those seas of prairie on the south side of said river, with no other guide than that very imperfect knowledge which was then had of the country. The expedition of Lewis and Clarke was confined to the Missouri, as they went up and came down. The party headed by Captain Williams was the first overland expedition ever undertaken to and across the Rocky Mountains, from the United States.[4] Some of the party had been up the Missouri river some distance, trading with the Indians for furs, but none of the com-

---

[2] Although not commonly used in the West, greyhounds were sometimes used as hunting dogs as they had been for centuries in England.

[3] Fort Mandan was built in the fall of 1804 by Lewis and Clark who spent the winter there among the Mandans.

[4] Even had Williams made such a trip, Lewis and Clark would still have been first to cross the Rockies within the continental United States. Coyner apparently defined the Rockies more narrowly than is done today.

pany had any knowledge of the country through which they had to pass, from personal observation. The difficulties, therefore, which they had to encounter, were very numerous and trying. But they found the Mandan chief, Big White, to be of great value to them, as an observance of his timely suggestions and counsel, very often prevented the party from being entirely cut off. He always urged upon Captain Williams the great importance of constant vigilance day and night, the strictest attention to the position of their encampments, and the situation of their horses. The captain learned from him, that the Indian, although generally inclined to surprise, assault, and kill, was not given to rash and careless adventure; and that he would never attack a party that were prepared and on the alert.

About twenty-five miles was the distance they traveled each day. When night approached, they selected a position to camp where wood, water, and grass were convenient. Large fires for the first eight or ten nights were kindled up, around which they gathered and roasted their fat venison, and ate, and laughed, and talked, and passed their rough jokes, until they sunk into the embraces of sleep. This unguarded and careless way of encamping, however, was abandoned when they entered the region of country infested with savage and hostile bands of Indians, against whose assaults they found it necessary to guard at all times. For the first two hundred miles, game was not very abundant, although they killed enough to supply them with provisions. About the twelfth day, the prairies seemed to enlarge and approach nearer the river. Timber was not so abundant. The face of the country improved and was much more interesting, and the soil was evidently richer as they traveled westward.

On the evening of the twelfth day, the party were encamped in the edge of a beautiful prairie about two hundred and forty miles from St. Louis having crossed the Gasconade, the Osage, and several affluents to the Missouri. Two very fine deer were killed by some of the company near the encampment, the blood and entrails of which attracted a band of hungry, saucy wolves near the company. There were not less than twenty, of different sizes and color; and some of the smaller kind, that were crowded out of the feast, kept up a very plaintive whine and howl. The dogs belonging to the company began to bark very fiercely, and rushed out after them and pursued them round a point of timber; but as soon as they were out of sight of the company, the wolves turned upon their pursuers and chased them back within a short distance of the camp. One of the dogs, the most resolute of the pack, in a bold attempt to stand his ground, was seized by as many as could get at him, and was torn to pieces almost instantly. That evening, one of the men set one of his traps, which he baited by a piece of venison, hung on a bush immediately above the trap. In the morning, not only the venison, but the trap was gone, much to the surprise and mortification of the inexperienced trapper, who, knowing but little about the business, had not observed the precaution of fastening the trap to something permanent.

Whilst breakfast was being prepared, and the horses were filling themselves with grass, the unlucky trapper went in quest of his trap. A wolf had been caught, and as he dragged the trap along he left a very distinct trace in the grass, by which he was easily followed. But he had crept into a very thick patch of brush, made almost impenetrable by a rank growth of hazel. And how was the trap to be recovered? The wolf was doubtless alive, and it would be very hazardous to attempt to enter his place of refuge. An effort was made to encourage the dogs to go in, but they recollected the rough fare they experienced the previous evening, and would not go beyond the edge of the thicket. In the midst of his perplexities, the young trapper was relieved by the arrival of two of the company, one of whom climbed a pin-oak tree, that stood in the edge of the brush, and from the top of which he had a fair view of the formidable occupant of the brush-patch, and shot him with his rifle. All danger being now removed, the dead wolf was dragged from his fastness, with one of his fore feet in the trap. He was of the largest kind, and almost black. As there were no wolves to be seen on the prairie in the morning, it was feared that all of them had been led off by the one in the trap: and that trap and wolf would not be seen again.

On the frontier, where wolves are very troublesome, the following expedient is sometimes resorted to, to drive them out of the country. Several fishhooks are tied together by their shanks, with a silk thread, and put in a piece of fresh meat, which is dropped where it is likely to be found by them. The hooks are buried completely in the meat and made very fast to prevent the wolf from shaking them off; for it is said by those acquainted with the habits of wolves, that they never eat a morsel of any thing without first picking it up very cautiously and giving it a shake. When the piece of meat is swallowed, the hooks generally stick fast in the throat, inflicting the most excruciating pain. The unlucky wolf immediately begins to scratch and tear his neck, and howl most piteously. In this condition he hurries away from the place of his great mishap, running, and raving, and scratching, and howling. Curiosity and fellow-feeling, or some other feeling, equally active, prompts every other wolf in sight and in hearing, to follow. Away the gang goes, increasing as it goes, until every wolf in the vicinity of their route is taken in, and taken away perhaps fifty miles from the place where the matter began.[5]

On the evening of the fourteenth day of the expedition, which was the ninth of May, another little mishap took place, which created some anxiety of mind and loss of time. Five of the horses were missing. The party, at first, were inclined to think they were taken by the Indians; but, as yet, they had not apprehended any thing of this kind, as they had not reached the country beset with danger. The horses, perhaps, had broken their fetters and straggled off. Big White told them that their horses were not stolen; that Indians could have stolen *all* of them as easily, if not more easily than five, and if they had taken five, they would have taken all. This very reasonable suggestion of one ac-quainted with the practices and customs of Indians, prompted the men to make an effort to find them. Their trail was soon found in the grass, and was made very plain by the dew. It led back, the way the party had come. The horses had, by some means, cleared themselves of their shackles, and were now striking for home; and it was not until evening that they were overtaken and brought back.

A day was lost, but the company, by the circumstance, were taught the importance of being more cautious, particularly at night. The Mandan chief also took occasion to allude to that which had been a matter of much anxious concern, to his mind. He told them, that thus far they had been on safe ground, and that no harm might result from

[5] I have been unable to locate any other account of this ingenious and plausible stratagem.

the absence of that vigilance and caution, that elsewhere would be indispensable for their safety. An Indian by birth and education, he knew the habits and practices of the different tribes in the far west, much better than any of the party. Their journey was long, very long, and led through a country occupied by tribes that would waylay them in every ravine, and watch their movements from the top of every eminence, for the purpose of surprising them and taking their equipage, horses, and perhaps scalps. The counsel of the venerable warrior, delivered with great earnestness and Indian gravity, had its effect. The company adopted the plan of journeying until about an hour before sunset, when they came to a halt, relieved their horses of their burdens, and turned them out to grass. In the mean time, a fire was struck, and repast for the men prepared. About dark the horses were brought in, and saddles and baggage placed upon them. The fires were renewed, and the company would then spring into their saddles and push on some eight or ten miles further: where they would come to a second stop, relieve their horses of their burdens, tether them, and station their guards. They divided the night into four watches, and each watch was kept by three men, whilst the others, wrapped up in their blankets, were reposing upon the ground. Fires were not raised, as the light could be seen at a great distance on those extensive prairies, and might betray them into the hands of some lurking foe.

In the morning, some moved the horses to fresh grass, that they might the more easily fill themselves; whilst others were expediting their morning repast, and attending to the other offices belonging to an encampment. By sunrise, generally they were going ahead.

Chapter 2

Kansas Indians and Kansas river—Signs of buffalo—Speed of the
Antelope—A hunting party of the Kansas—A man frightened in a
dream. Kansas braves visit Captain Williams' camp—The company
visit the Kansas village, and are received with great parade—Kind
feelings of the tribe for the party. A buffalo hunt on hand—Kansas
were experienced horsemen and hunters—Buffalo plenty, and a
great hunt—The grace and spirit of the Indians in the hunt.

IN THE JOURNAL before me, nothing is noted of much
importance, until they reached the Kansas river, an affluent to the
Missouri. This river rises in the plains west, and runs east into the
Missouri. It is about three hundred and thirty yards wide.[1] The party
were able to ford it. When they were about ten miles from this river,
they saw, as they thought, several Indians; but they soon lost sight of
them. As they approached the Kansas, they observed a great many
horse tracks, some of which were very fresh, and several places where
buffalo had been killed by the Indians. They were evidently in the
neighborhood of Indian villages. Big White said they were the Kansas
tribe, a fierce and warlike nation. They had lived higher up the Missouri, where they were involved in a number of unfortunate wars with
some of the neighboring tribes, which nearly resulted in their extinc-

[1] Coyner probably obtained this information from Lewis and Clark, who described the Kansas as "340¼ yards wide" at the mouth. Coues (ed.), *Lewis
and Clark*, vol. I, p. 33.

tion. They had been nearly broken down, and lost quite a number of their braves. They were driven down towards the Kansas, about one hundred miles. There was much sign of buffalo, and the men were anxious to engage in a buffalo hunt.[2] Two antelopes were seen on the prairies, wheeling and prancing about, and gazing upon the party with much curiosity. As the men had heard a great deal about the speed of this animal, a general desire was expressed to test the relative speed of the gray-hound and the antelope, as an opportunity now presented. Accordingly the dog was started, and the antelopes suffered him to get within fifty yards of them. They then wheeled, and put off, and the space between them and the dog widened[3] so fast, that the latter stopped suddenly, apparently abashed and disappointed, and returned to the company. All descriptions of this beautiful animal represent its speed as not only very great, but equal, if not superior, to that of any other animal in the world. Its motions are very graceful and easy, and made without any visible effort. It runs very level, and as it moves over the plains, it seems to fly rather than run.

The company encamped on the west side of the Kansas river, and about a mile and a half from it, on the border of a prairie. They had not been there long before they saw a small party of Kansas Indians, passing not very far from the company. Some of the men approached them, making signs of friendship, and induced them to come to the camp. They cast very inquisitive looks upon the white men, and at first seemed rather alarmed; but the kindness of the party towards them soon dispelled their fears. By the aid of the Mandan chief, who partially understood their language, and acted as a kind of interpreter, Captain Williams learned that they belonged to the Kansas nation, and had been out on a hunt to procure buffalo meat. They represented one of their villages as being about six miles down the Kansas river. With a view of securing their friendship, Captain Williams gave them several little presents, with which they were greatly pleased. In return, they gave Captain Williams some buffalo meat, upon which his men feasted very heartily that night. Big White, acting in behalf of the

[2] Lewis and Clark described the Kansas Indians in a similar manner and also saw buffalo "for the first time" at the Kansas River. Ibid., p. 34.
[3] Should such a race have occurred, the greyhound would, indeed, have lost.

company, sent word to the chiefs that the party would visit their village the next day. It was deemed advisable by the men to take every pains to secure the horses, and to be prepared for any emergency.

A very amusing circumstance occurred during the night. One of the men, who in all probability had overloaded his stomach with buffalo meat, and whose mind, perhaps, had been haunted, in day time, by frightful visions of Indians, suddenly started up, shouting "Indians, Indians, Indians; yonder they are—shoot, shoot;" at the same time running back and forth, and making the most violent gestures. In a moment all were wide awake, and in another moment, all were in possession of their arms. The guard rushed in to see what was wrong. The very dogs partook of the excitement and barked fiercely. The frantic vociferations of the frightened man continued—"Indians, Indians, Indians." "And where are they?" was asked every where. It was, however, soon discovered that the fellow was asleep and dreaming; and a camp-kettle full of water was thrown into his face, which brought him to his right mind. It was sometime before quietude and sleep resumed their reign in the camp. The next morning the frightened dreamer and his dream was quite a laughing stock and matter of much amusement. As he was compelled to tell his dream, he said that he thought, the company had come in contact with a band of hostile Indians, with whom they were about to have a difficulty, but his unpleasant dream was interrupted by the cold water, that was thrown into his face.

After breakfast, the principal chiefs and several of the warriors of the Kansas came to the camp on horseback. Captain Williams received them with very marked respect and kindness. The pipe of peace was passed round. The object of the expedition was explained, and several little articles were given to them by the captain. As they had heard of Big White going down with Lewis and Clarke, they very much admired the conduct of the whites in being thus true to their promise by taking the Mandan brave back to his people. This circumstance induced them to repose great confidence in the party, and to place the most implicit faith in all their statements. The party agreed to accompany the Kansas to their village, as the men were generally anxious to join them in a buffalo hunt. As they went to their village the Kansas asked Big White a thousand questions about the country he had recently visited,

14

and seemed greatly interested with his answers. They gathered around him and received the information they sought for with a great deal of avidity. Capt. Williams expressed a desire to salute the village with a round or two from their rifles. As the Kansas had a few fire arms, they expressed a wish to return the salutes, but they had nothing to make their arms *talk*, by this meaning they had no ammunition. Capt. Williams therefore gave them some powder, with which one of their warriors hurried off to the village to make the necessary arrangements. When the party came in view of the village, all the women and children were out of their wigwams and looked wild and much affrighted. Their men had advanced a little, out from the village, and from their few fire arms answered to the salute of Captain Williams' men. When this ceremony was over, by which the chiefs and warriors seemed to feel themselves much honored, the party, including Big White, his wife and son,[4] were conducted to lodges fitted up expressly for their reception. The pipe, according to a uniform practice among the tribes in the far west, was passed around. Captain Williams renewed his efforts to secure their good will by distributing among them a few of such articles as were most likely to please. The kind feelings of the Kansas were manifested by serving the company the best they had and in great profusion; such as the meat of buffalo, deer and the antelope, besides several kinds of roots. Big White made a speech, in which he alluded to the kindness with which he was received by his white *brothers*, and their great riches and number and strength. He advised them to cultivate the most friendly relations with his white brothers and their father the President of the United States, as they would furnish his poor red brothers with every thing they wanted; such as knives, guns, powder, lead, blankets, whisky. He advised them to go and see their white brothers. Nearly the whole of the night was spent by the Kansas in putting questions to the Mandans, particularly the Chief, about his trip to the land of the pale faces.

Captain Williams and his party resolved to spend two or three days with this tribe, to take a buffalo hunt, and arrangements were made with the Kansas to take the hunt the next day. The plains were said to

---

[4] One of Big White's conditions for going with Lewis and Clark was that he be allowed to take his wife and son along.

be darkened with thousands and thousands of buffalo, not more than twenty miles from their village. They had not been frightened, and were in all probability, in the same neighborhood yet. Accordingly early the next morning, ten Kansas hunters on horseback, with spears and bows and arrows, with the same number of Captain Williams' men, set out for the buffalo ground. The Indians were not only good hunters, but very superior horse men. Their horses too were familiarized to buffalo-hunts and buffalo baits, and well trained in all those dexterous movements to be practised in a buffalo battle.

Not so with Captain Williams' men. Most of them had never seen a buffalo, and their horses were as inexperienced as their riders; and horses are generally very much frightened the first time they are rode into a hunt of this kind. And then again, they had to use rifles, which are a kind of arms, too unwieldy and ponderous for such business. Inexperienced men, too, are very apt to become too much excited and run themselves into dangers from which it is difficult if not impossible to extricate themselves. Untried men, therefore, upon untried horses, with unhandy arms and greatly excited in the bargain, are very apt to fail in their first attempts to kill buffalo; if they do not share a worse fate than simply failure. For it often happens that horse and horseman are killed.

After sweeping over the prairie for twelve miles the hunting party came to a halt, to hold a conference about their future movements. They believed they were in the vicinity of the buffalo. Two of the Kansas hunters were sent ahead to reconnoitre the plains, and report by signs when they saw the buffalo. They set off at a brisk hand-gallop upon their ponies, whilst the company moved along more at their leisure. In less than an hour, the two Kansas were seen on an eminence, making signs that the buffalo were in view. The party rushed up and they saw the buffalo within a mile in thousands, all quiet and feeding on the plains. The men dismounted and girthed their saddles more securely, and adjusting their arms for the attack, sprung again into their saddles, and in a few minutes were in the outskirts of the multitudinous herd. Each man selected his object and dashed after it. The Indians picked out the males, as they were fatter than the cows, which, at that season, had their calves. In a moment the innumerable multitude were in motion, frightened by the horrible yelling of the Kansas Indians, and men and horses and buffalo were seen in every direction. The very plains seemed to tremble, and the rumbling sound created by the running of the buffalo resembled distant thunder, and could be heard for many miles. The Indians seemed to be perfectly at home when mounted on horseback and dashing among the buffalo, shooting their sharp-pointed arrows, and launching their spears. Their horses too seemed to understand the business. They would advance close up to the buffalo, and when they heard the twang of the bow, that sped the arrow, they would wheel and bound off. When they perceived that they had shot an arrow and launched a spear in a fatal place, the Kansas would abandon the bleeding victim to die, and dash off after another. In this way they continued for an hour, when men and horses were overcome by labor and fatigue. Some ten or twelve bulls lay bleeding on the plains, some dead and others badly wounded.[5] Captain Williams' men, not being able to manage their rifles and horses, failed to accomplish anything. Indeed, one of their horses took fright and ran away, a mile or two from the scene of action, before the rider was able to stop him. Another hurled his rider with violence from his saddle, upon the ground. A third one rushed upon an infuriated bull, that one of the Kansas had wounded, and had his entrails torn out by his horns, and was left dead on the ground, his chagrined and deeply mortified rider being left to foot it back to the camp. The chase being ended, the party went to work to dispatch those that were wounded, which, by the way, was accompanied with no little danger. Some of the bulls were very furious, and made desperate bounds at the horses, and even pursued them. Captain Williams observed, that the Indians exercised a great deal of coolness and judgment. They reserved their arrows, until they were able to make a sure and effective shot. They always aimed to launch their spears and arrows behind the ribs, so as to range forward and in this way penetrate the vitals. A single arrow, in several instances, would dispatch a large bull, and when the carcasses were opened by the Indians to get their arrows, they were found

[5] This description of a buffalo hunt is sound, although Indians fired with great rapidity and ordinarily would have killed many more than ten or twelve bulls in an hour.

to have passed from the flank, obliquely through the body, and lodged against some of the bones on the opposite side. It is very common, for an arrow to pass completely through the body, when it does not strike a bone.[6] The points of their arrows and spears are made of iron and steel, procured of the whites, and made very sharp. Their bows are sometimes made of wood, but their strongest and most efficient weapons of this kind are made of pieces of bone and horn spliced and glued together, and are strung with sinews of buffalo. Their spears are generally eight or ten feet long, including the handle, which is made of light elastic wood, and wrapped with the sinews of buffalo. Having taken as much of the choicest portions of the meat as they could carry, the party turned their faces toward the Kansas village. But as it was late in the afternoon before they set off, they raised a fire, around which they prepared their hunter's repast, the horses at the same time being permitted to refresh themselves upon the grass. They traveled about eight miles from their grand scamper, that evening, and then stopped, until the next morning, when very early they reached the Kansas village, richly ladened with fat buffalo meat, it was true, but *minus* a very fine horse.

---

[6] Other accounts substantiate Coyner. See, for example, Josiah Gregg, *Commerce of the Prairies*, edited by Max L. Moorhead (Norman, Okla., 1954), p. 370.

Chapter 3

A black bear is killed. A trade, a horse for a dog—A panorama—
The party overtaken by the dog traded to the chief—They meet a
small party of Kansas, by whom the renegade dog is returned to his
owner—Running of buffalo, and danger to be apprehended—The
plan to avoid it—Vast number of buffalo. A man is lost—His critical
situation—He is found the next day—His report of his night in
the prairie.

WHILST AMONG the Kansas, Captain Williams' men
were informed that a large black bear had been frequently seen on an
island in the river, about a mile from the village, and that several
efforts made by the Indians to take him had been unsuccessful. There
was a dense thicket of plum bushes and hazel, to which he always
betook himself when assailed, and into which his pursuers thought it
unsafe to follow him. As the dogs belonging to the expedition were
trained to hunt such game, they were taken across the river to the
island by some of the men. A number of the Kansas went with them to
witness the performance of the dogs, which they were disposed very
much to admire for their superior size. Within a very short time, the
bear was started from his hitherto safe retreat, and being pursued
closely, and now and then nipped by the dogs, took a tree. One of the
men shot him. He was uncommonly large and very fat, and furnished
a fine repast for the company that night. The Kansas were delighted
with the courage of the dogs, and the principal chief of the village ex-

19

pressed a desire to purchase one of them. He gave Captain Williams to understand that he would give him a fine young horse in exchange for a large mastiff, for which he took a particular fancy. As the party had began to consider the canine part of the expedition as not only useless, but calculated by their barking to betray them into the hands of lurking parties of Indians, a bargain was soon struck. The chief took his dog, and Captain Williams his horse, both alike well pleased with their trade. The village generally seemed delighted with the new acquisition of an animal so much superior, in every way, to the small, half-starved, half-wolf, roguish-looking breed, which they had in their village. Indian dogs seem to be wolves of the smaller kind domesticated, and are of no value except to those tribes who have no horses. By such poor wretches they are frequently used to convey baggage.

Having passed three days with this tribe, Captain Williams resumed his journey with his men, greeted with the best wishes of these unsophisticated children of nature, for their future good luck. He was advised by Big White to bear more to the west, to avoid the broken, hilly country near the Missouri, and to avoid the difficulty sometimes experienced in crossing its tributaries near their mouths. The hostile parties of Indians, too, with whom they might fall in, would not be very large, and of course less formidable, as their villages generally were near the Missouri. Captain Williams therefore, determined to cross the Platte, a short distance below the junction of the north and south forks, and pursued his course accordingly. The company traveled over a dry, elevated, rich prairie country. Buffalo were seen in great numbers. Elk, deer, and the antelope were frequently to be seen, scampering and curveting, and sometimes gazing with wild curiosity upon the company as they passed along. Frequent signs of Indians were seen through the day, but the fears of the party were not excited, as they were made, in all probability, by the hunting parties of the Kansas.

An hour before sunset the company came to a halt to refresh themselves and horses. This evening the dog that had been exchanged for a horse overtook them, and seemed much pleased with rejoining his old acquaintances. There was a piece of raw hide attached to his neck, by which he had been tied, and which he had cut, and in this way made his escape. How he passed, without being attacked by wolves and torn to pieces, was a matter of surprise to the party, who had observed that wolves were very numerous. At dark a light was observed across the prairie, which was most likely that of an Indian camp. The company put out their fires, mounted their horses, and traveled eight or ten miles further, and then unpacked and fettered their horses, and turned them out to graze, whilst they wrapped themselves up in their blankets and laid themselves down to sleep. The light of the ensuing morning revealed to the men the most extensive and beautiful prospect they had ever seen. They found themselves on the most elevated point in a grand prairie, that spread almost immeasurably in every direction. In every way they looked, a beautiful sea green surface spread onward and onward, until it united with the utmost verge of the sky, bearing a striking resemblance to the undulating surface of the ocean. The prairie was dotted, here and there, with bands of the different kinds of animals, which at that early day, were very numerous in the far west. Far away, in the distance, was to be seen a herd of buffalo, some quietly grazing, and others reposing upon the grass. Near at hand was a band of hungry and roguish-looking wolves, curiously eyeing the company, and patiently licking their lips in anticipation of the sweet morsels and bones they expected to pick up about the camp when the party were gone. In this beautiful exciting panorama of nature were the elk and the antelope, the one crowned with his stately, wide-spreading antlers; the other sweeping and curveting around with so much grace and ease, as scarcely to appear to make a singular muscular effort. And then, hard-by, was a little village of prairie dogs, the industrious inhabitants of which were up at the first break of day, yelping, and skipping about, darting into their holes, and as quickly coming out again, and in this way expressing the surprise and curiosity created by the presence of these intruders upon their territory. We promise the reader, in another part of this volume, a fuller account of this curious, antic little inhabitant of the prairie.[1] Although the company was delighted with the scene, they did not think it safe policy to occupy so conspicuous a place very long, as they might be espied many

---

[1] Coyner fails to keep his promise, for no description of prairie dogs is given.

miles in every direction, by any roving bands of Indians that might be in that region. Without, therefore enjoying their usual morning repast, they hurried off, and traveled until noon, when they came to timber, in which they passed several hours of repose both to themselves and their horses. In the afternoon of this day they met a small hunting party of Kansas, belonging to the village the party had visited, and held a short parley with them, in which they were informed of the trade made by Captain Williams and the chief of the Kansas village. They seemed to place confidence in the statements of Captain Williams, confirmed as they were by the testimony of the Mandans, and took possession of the renegado [sic] dog for the purpose of conveying him back to his legitimate owner.

In the latter part of this day, a rumbling, rolling noise was heard by the company, in the south, resembling distant thunder. Big White, who was an experienced buffalo hunter, said that it was made by the running of a very large herd of frightened buffalo, and, as the sound became more and more distinct, he stated that they, in all probability, were coming toward the company, a circumstance that would be attended with danger, if they were as numerous as the noise indicated.

For one hour the thundering continued, becoming more and more audible, until the dark rolling mass of living, moving animals was seen on the verge of the horizon, coming directly towards the company, and apparently covering the whole earth.[2] Under such circumstances there is no retreating, and a party of men in such a situation, are reduced to the desperate expedient of standing their ground and facing the danger. A part of the men secured the horses by tethering them, and at the same time rid them of their burdens; whilst the others rushed forward with their arms to meet the herd two or three hundred yards in advance of the horses. The thing to be effected, and the only thing that can be effected, to prevent being overrun and trampled to death, is to divide the crowd. This, the company was able to accomplish by

[2] Perhaps since he had never experienced this phenomenon, Coyner later expressed concern that his readers would think he had exaggerated. Yet others also described the approach of a galloping herd of buffalo in similar terms. See, for example, *Ruxton of the Rockies*, edited by LeRoy R. Hafen (Norman, Okla., 1950), p. 180.

firing their guns as fast as they could load, and shouting and waving their hats. As the vast throng came up, they divided to the right and the left, leaving a passage about forty or fifty yards wide, which was occupied by the men and horses. But the shouting, and shooting, and waving of hats had to be kept up whilst the denser part of the throng was passing by, which consumed at least one entire hour. Big White and his son, who understood the disposition of the buffalo better than any present, aided in the matter, and rendered most efficient help by their tremendous yells, which seemed to frighten the buffalo more than any thing else. The gray-hound dog belonging to the company became frightened and confused, and darted into the crowd, and was trampled to death.

To some, these statements about the vast number of buffalo may seem to invite incredulity, and may be classed among those extravagant stories that are frequently associated with the excitement belonging to frontier adventure. They may be thought to be true, only, in part; but it should be remembered that they are confirmed by the observation of all men who have traveled through a buffalo country, some of whom are certainly entitled to credit for what they say. The same statements are made about their vast number even at the present day; and if they be correct *now*, how much more true were they forty years ago. That the number of buffalo has been diminished very fast is certainly true, and in another part of this book there will be found some interesting data to this effect, which we gathered from the expeditions of Captain Fremont.[3]

When buffalo are seen frightened and running, it is regarded as evident that they are pursued by Indians. It was not the case, however, in the present instance. As the company expected the buffalo would be followed by Indians, they did not once think of securing a supply of meat, but suffered the opportunity to pass unimproved. Captain Williams thought it wisdom to be on the alert, as this was a season for hunting, and the prairies were doubtless infested by hunting parties, by whom he was liable to be surprised. They therefore traveled hard and late before they came to a halt. Three men left the main body of

[3] See Chapter XIV.

the company to kill some game, as provisions were somewhat scarce. They were to join the company at a point of timber, that was visible at that time, and seemed to be about six miles off; but the distance proved much greater. The men were strictly ordered by Captain Williams not to separate from each other, as they were now on very dangerous ground, and their safety required the strictest vigilance. The party reached the point of timber about sunset, and supped upon a very scanty supply of meat. About dark two of the hunters came in, bringing a fine deer. They reported that the other hunter had left them to get a shot at some elk that were about the half of a mile off, whilst they wound around and about to kill their deer. In this way they lost sight of him. They further stated that they had seen three men on horses, going in the direction the absent man had gone. This circumstance awakened the most painful apprehensions in the camp as to his safety. It was now too late to go in search of him, and, if alive, he was doomed to spend the night in the prairie, entirely unprotected. Captain Williams thought, at one time, of kindling up a large fire, hoping that the lost man might see the light and find his way to the camp; but then this plan might betray the whole company into the hands of hostile Indians, and on that account it was abandoned. The fires were extinguished, and the guard required to be very cautious. If the missing man had fallen into the hands of the Indians, these savages would most likely meditate an attack upon the main body. The night passed without anything to disturb their slumbers, except their concern for the lost hunter, and at the earliest dawn of day, ten men, including the two that had acted as hunters the evening before, set off to look up the one that was absent. They went to the place where Carson,[4] (for that was his name) was represented as being last seen; but no signs of his being there could be found. The surface of the ground was such that if he had been there, he would have left some impression that would still be perceptible. No tracks made by his horse could be found. It could not be the place where he had been last seen, for he could not

[4] This Carson, described later as an "impetuous youth," is clearly not Kit, for he loses his life in Coyner's tale. Perhaps Coyner chose this name to capitalize on the growing interest in Kit Carson. Or, since Coyner frequently took material from Washington Irving, perhaps this name was suggested to Coyner through Irving's *Astoria*, p. 170, in which Alexander Carson is mentioned.

have been there at all. The men frequently fired their guns, and rode about and shouted at the top of their voices, and waved their hats, but no answer was received, and nothing like a man could be seen any where on the wide expanse of prairie that spread around. As they swept around, however, they saw a horse standing in a patch of brush. When they approached him, he recognized the company and neighed. This brought the men to a halt, to ascertain what it meant. They called and shouted, but no one answered. This tended to confirm their un-favorable apprehension as to the fate of Carson. He was, in all prob-ability, killed, and his horse and equipage were in the possession of savages, at that time concealed in the thicket just before them. But they were determined to know for themselves, and approached the horse very cautiously, with their fingers upon the triggers of their guns, ready to fire, and expecting, every moment, to be fired upon. When they were sufficiently near, they discovered the horse was carefully tied, and a short distance off lay Carson under a tree, with his head upon his saddle. The men thought he was dead, but they soon found out that he was in a sound sleep, and indeed enjoying a very pleasant dream, at the same time. When they aroused him, he at first seemed bewildered and wild. He gave a doleful account of himself, as he passed the night lost and alone. In his eagerness to shoot an elk, he lost his course, and wandered about long after dark, perhaps till mid-night, hoping that he might see the light of the encampment. Failing in this, fatigued and hungry, he laid himself down to sleep if he could, but his mind was so much impressed with the dangers by which he was beset, that he lay wide awake until about the break of day, which was the cause of his being asleep when they found him. He saw the Indians seen by the other men. They passed within an hundred yards from him, but did not see him, as he was hid, as he thought, in the same thicket in which he spent the night. As his horse was very impatient to join the company again, and frequently neighed, Carson was very much afraid that he would betray him into the hands of those three Indians that passed so near. To prevent this he blindfolded him by binding his handkerchief over his eyes, an expedient that had the effect of entirely subduing his restiveness and ill-timed impatience. He thought the Indians were traveling in a southern direction, and their horses seemed very much fatigued. They were well armed with bows and arrows, and long spears, and Carson thought each one had several scalps dangling to their bridle bits. They were evidently returning home, perhaps from some adventurous tramp, in which they may have sought revenge on some rival party.

From the description of these Indians, Big White thought they were of the Kite Indians,[5] who were savage in the extreme, and would have shown no mercy whatever to Carson, if they had seen him. He spoke of them as being very much reduced in number, by their constant wars with other tribes, and yet perfectly indomitable. They were great horsemen, and very swift. Captain Williams embraced the opportunity, which this occur[r]ence furnished, to urge upon his men the most scrupulous observance of the regulations belonging to the company, as very necessary for their safety.

[5] Lewis and Clark so named a group of Crow Indians who, they reported, were living on the headwaters of the Cheyenne River. Coues (ed.), *Lewis and Clark*, vol. I, p. 58.

Chapter 4

Indian scouts—Vigilance of the party—They reach the Platte—One of the party becomes sick—The way to kill antelope—Pawnees come to the camp—They feel very much for the sick man—The vapor bath cure for every thing—The sick man dies—Indian honors bestowed upon their dead—A band of wolves on the grave of Hamilton, digging up his body—This is a common thing.

THE LOST MAN being found, the party resumed their journey, exercising renewed caution, as they saw abundant signs of Indians. The tracks of their horses and their vacated camps were frequently observed; whilst the game along the route seemed alarmed and easily frightened. About noon some Indian scouts were seen by the aid of a glass on an eminence, a long way off, evidently reconnoitering the movements of the company. Toward the latter part of the day, the same scouts were again following along at a distance, on their trail. They were supposed to be spies belonging to some hostile tribe, perhaps large, in that neighborhood, who intended, that night, if an opportunity offered, to steal their horses, and perhaps attack the company. Late in the afternoon, they came to a small stream of very pure water, where they determined to take a little refreshment, and to permit their horses to fill themselves with grass. The Mandan Chief told Captain Williams that the party that were dogging them, and no doubt entertained bad designs towards his company, would not attempt to execute those designs until a late hour in the night, perhaps a short time before day, when they would be asleep; and that it was good policy on his part, to act as though he suspected nothing of the kind, and to be perfectly at his ease. At dark, they renewed their fires to deceive the lurking foe, and then quietly and silently put off. Turning their course rather to the north, they traveled about ten miles, and then stretched their weary limbs on the green grass, until the light of another morning.

Immediately after day-break the company were on their way, exulting in their present security and in having out-witted as well as out-traveled the enemy; nor did they in the least relax their speedy gait until noon, at which time they reached a ravine, where wood and water were abundant. There they remained for two hours. A scout or out sentinel was stationed on an eminence in the prairie to scan the country around, and report, by signs, any and every thing, that looked in any degree suspicious.

We pass on to that part of the journal which details the events of the expedition, when they arrived on the Platte. They reached the waters of this river about the first of June. One of the men, whose name was William Hamilton,[1] had taken sick the day before, and not being able to travel, the party were compelled to encamp. He had a very high fever, and was frequently wild and flighty. Captain Williams made several efforts to bleed him, but without success. He also exhibited a dose of calomel, which, likewise, was not accompanied with any salutary effect. Poor fellow! in his lucid moments, he frequently expressed an earnest wish to see once more his native home and his friends: but he had bid them adieu for the last time, and it was his fate to end his days in a land of Arabs.[2]

As they would, in all probability, be compelled, by the situation of Hamilton, to remain there, perhaps for several days, the men on the first day were engaged in constructing a sort of breast-work for the greater safety of the party. Five men, the next morning swept around a mile or two from the camp, and returned with part of the meat of a fine young buffalo, and the carcass of an antelope, which was the first that had been killed by any of the party. Its meat was thought to be

[1] This common name is probably one of Coyner's inventions.
[2] A common term for nomadic Indians of the West in Coyner's day.

very fine, and much like venison. Indeed the antelope exactly resembles the common deer, in every respect, except as to its horns, which differ from those of the deer, being straight, slender, erect and without any branches. The man who killed it, said that it would not permit him to approach within the range of his rifle; he threw himself upon the ground and elevated his handkerchief on the end of his gun-stick, and as it waved in the wind the curiosity of the animal seemed to gain the ascendancy over its caution and shyness; and it wheeled about and returned, running round and round, drawing still nearer every circuit it made, until it actually came within thirty steps of him. He then shot it, as he lay in a horizontal position.[3]

During this day, a party of Indians, on horseback, and bearing a warlike aspect, made their appearance near the camp, and gazed with much curiosity upon the company. Captain Williams, accompanied by Big White, advanced towards them, making signs of friendship. With some little difficulty they were brought to a parley, in which he learned that they were a war-party of Pawnees, who had been out in pursuit of some Osages who had stolen some of their horses. They had overtaken and killed the most of them. They were in possession of a number of scalps, as so many trophies, and had regained the stolen horses. There were thirty Pawnees, well armed with bows and arrows, and shields, and spears. They seemed very friendly, especially when they learned that the object of the expedition was to take the Mandan chief home to his tribe. They had received presents from Lewis and Clark the year before,[4] which laid the foundation of partiality for the whites; a feeling which Captain Williams strengthened very much, by giving them tobacco, and several other trifling articles. Having been conducted to the camp, they received every kindness that the party could bestow upon them. They seemed to feel very much for Hamilton, who continued very ill, and were greatly surprised to witness Captain Williams' effort to extract blood; nor was it possible to make them understand how it could benefit the sufferer. They brought in a number

[3] Coyner probably took this story from Washington Irving who tells it in almost identical fashion in *Astoria*, p. 192. Variants of this method of attracting antelope were frequently used.

[4] In 1804, Lewis and Clark sent two men up the Platte to a Pawnee village with a present of tobacco. Coues (ed.), *Lewis and Clark*, vol. I, pp. 54-55.

29

of roots and weeds, which they eloquently affirmed, by signs, would be an infallible remedy. They also urged sweating and bathing, to which the Indians east and west of the mountains always resort, as a remedy not only for fever, but almost every kind of disease. As the reader may not understand their *modus operandi* in the use of this remedy, it may not be improper to describe it. A vapor bath, or sweating house, is "a hollow square, of six or eight feet deep, formed against the river bank, by damming up, with mud, the other three sides, and covering the top completely, except an aperture about two feet wide. The bather descends by this hole, taking with him a number of heated stones and jugs of water; and after seating himself, throws the water on the stones, till the steam becomes of a temperature sufficiently high for his purpose. The baths of the Indians in the Rocky Mountains are of different sizes, the most common being made of mud and sticks like an oven; but the mode of raising the steam is exactly the same. Among those nations, when a man bathes for pleasure, he is generally accompanied by one, and sometimes by several of his acquaintances. Indeed it is so essentially a social amusement, that to decline going in the bath when invited by a friend, is one of the highest indignities which can be offered. The Indians on the frontier generally use a bath that will accommodate only one person, and which is formed of wicker-work of willows, about four feet high, arched at the top and covered with skins. In this the bather sits till, by means of the steam from the heated stones, he has perspired sufficiently. These baths are almost universally in the neighborhood of running water, into which the bather plunges immediately on coming out; and sometimes he returns again and subjects himself to a second perspiration. The bath is employed for pleasure, as well as health, and is used indiscriminately for all kinds of diseases."[5] It is also used for another purpose. When an Indian trapper is unsuccessful in trapping for beaver, he enters the sweating house, where he remains for some time, sweating most profusely. In this condition, he immediately plunges into the cold stream, fancying that, by this means, he rids himself of some peculiar odor, or impurity of body, that kept the keen-scented beaver from his traps.

[5] Coyner is quoting (and occasionally paraphrasing) the description given by Lewis and Clark. Ibid., vol. II, pp. 626-27.

Having passed through this purification and cleansing, he returns to his work with renewed confidence and hopes of success.

Two of the men went with the Pawnee warriors to their village, which was about fifteen miles north-east. They took with them some presents for their chiefs, as they had learned that the various tribes were very great beggars, and always expect the white men to confirm their professions of friendship, by things that are visible as well as tangible. The latter part of this day the sick man died; a melancholy event that was not expected so soon. His body was immediately wrapped in a blanket and deposited in a grave. In the bark of a tree standing at the head of his grave, his name was cut by one of the men with his pocket knife. His death cast a deep gloom over the camp, as he was greatly beloved by the company, and esteemed and admired for his great fortitude and prudence. The Mandan chief, who sympathized very much with the party in their great loss and affliction, expected that the burial of a white brave would have been accompanied with more parade and ceremony, and was particularly surprised, that he was not furnished with horses and arms to use when he should reach those happy hunting grounds, to which the braves are conducted after death. It is the custom of the various tribes to furnish their heroes with horses, that are slain on their graves, and with moccasins and arms of every description, to be used in that Elysium to which they pass in death. On the grave of a very distinguished brave, fifteen or twenty horses are sometimes sacrificed, together with a corresponding outfit for hunting in the other world.[6]

Early the next morning after the death of Hamilton mingled feelings of sadness and indignation were created in the camp, by seeing a band of wolves on his grave, most industriously digging out the loose earth to get at his body. The men suddenly and simultaneously grasped their rifles to revenge the indignity offered to the dead, by a general fire upon the pack; but Captain Williams checked them, by suggesting that the report of their arms might be heard by marauders, and bring them into a difficulty. They therefore quietly drove them away, and covered

[6] It was not uncommon for Shoshonean tribes, especially, to sacrifice the horse or horses of a warrior. But fifteen horses would have been an extraordinary occurrence.

the grave with long heavy pieces of timber which the wolves would not be able to remove.

Captain Williams learned from Big White that the wolves would always dig up the dead, if not buried so as to prevent it, and that they always most greedily devour the slain on the field of battle, if left on the surface of the ground. Their scent is so very acute, they can smell a dead body three or four feet under ground, and having dug it up, feed upon it with the greedy rapacity of the hyena. The two men sent to the Pawnee village returned about noon, stating that there were none but women, and children, and very old men at the village; the chiefs and the young men having gone to hold a council with the Ottoes and the Missouries.[7] This afternoon the party were again under way, traveling due west, as the most direct route to the Mandan country.

[7] Spelled "Otos" and "Missouris" today, these were Siouan-speaking peoples.

Chapter 5

IT MAY BE REMARKED, as the general character of the country between the State of Missouri and the Rocky Mountains, that the greater part of it is undulating prairie, almost as vast and trackless as the ocean, and, at the time we treat, a *terra incognita* to the white man. Some geologists suppose them to have formed the ancient floor of the Ocean, countless ages since, when its primeval waves beat against the granite bases of the Rocky Mountains. But the opinion, most generally entertained by those persons who reside in the great prairies of the West, is, that they are formed by the fires by which they are overrun every autumn. In favor of this opinion, quite a number of facts can be brought up. Where the fires still prevail, they encroach upon the timber that exists, and diminish its quantity every year; and it is not difficult to see that, in the process of time, these regular autumnal fires would destroy all the timber on the surface of the earth, where it may be unprotected. Again, it is to be remarked that in all low places, such as ravines, hollows and river bottoms and small vallies, where the dampness of the soil and vegetation is such as to check the progress of these great fires, there and there only is timber

33

to be found. It may be further stated, that where the fire has been kept out for twenty five or thirty years, the face of the country becomes covered again with a growth of young timber, thirty and forty feet high. The trunks of trees are sometimes found in those prairies, in a state of petrifaction, which is evidence that those vast plains were once clothed with timber.[1] Although in many parts of the prairie country timber is scarce, yet the supply is sufficient for present purposes, and as its growth is very rapid in consequence of the great fertility of the soil, the increase of timber it is believed will be amply sufficient for all future demands.

These great fires are sometimes very beautiful and even grand when seen in a dark night. As the light of the sun is withdrawn, and night-fall comes on, the light of those fires becomes more and more distinct and bright, until a beautiful long, and luminous line is to be seen stretching afar to the right and the left, across the plains. The flames generally rise to the height of five or six feet; but when the consuming element reaches those places where the growth of vegetation is luxuriant, it blazes up thirty or forty feet high; and such is the reflection of the light in the distant horizon, that it may be seen for fifty miles, and looks like the approach of the great luminary of day.

It sometimes happens, that a solitary tree, from some peculiar locality, remains unscathed and is permitted to grow and attain considerable dimensions; whilst not a shrub or twig of any description is to be seen, in any direction, for many miles. Alone and isolated, it stands a beacon to the traveler over a sea of prairie, and constitutes a pleasant and permanent object, on which he may rest his eyes, that are wearied with the monotony around him.

June 5th. This afternoon something in motion was discovered on the prairie ahead of the company, but so far off, they were not able to determine what it was. As they approached it, Captain Williams, by the aid of a glass, ascertained that it was a band of wolves in full chase after a buffalo coming directly towards the party. As all were anxious to see the race, and how it would terminate, they placed themselves in a position not to be noticed very readily by the wolves, and, in a few

[1] Coyner's theory, while interesting, is of course incorrect.

minutes, they had a fair view of the whole affair. The buffalo proved to be a well grown young bull, in fine condition. There were about twelve wolves of the largest kind, and must have had a long and a tight race, as they seemed (both wolves and buffalo) very much fatigued. As they ran the wolves were close around the buffalo, snapping and snatching all the time; but they were observed not to seize and hold on like a dog. Their mode of taking the buffalo is to run them down; and when they are completely out of breath, by a constant worrying and snatching kept up by all hands, they drag their victim to the ground, and then fill themselves with his flesh, sometimes before he is entirely dead.

Indeed in this case they seemed to feed upon their victim as they ran, for every thrust they made at him they took away a mouthful of his flesh, which they gulped as they ran, and by the time they had brought him to the ground, the flesh of his hind quarters was taken away to the bone. So eager were they in the chase, and so fierce was the contest, that they did not observe the company until they rode up within ten steps from them, and even then they did not appear to be much frightened, but scampered off a short distance and sat down and licked their lips, and waited with much impatience to be permitted to return to their hard-earned feast. The buffalo had suffered violence in every part. The tendons of his hind legs were cut asunder; the tuft of hair at the end of the tail was taken away, with part of the tail; pieces of hide and flesh, as large as a man's hand, were jerked out of his sides in several places; his ears were much torn, and in the battle he lost one of his eyes. Just before they succeeded in bringing him to the ground, one of the pack, a very large gray wolf, was seen to spring upon his back, tear out a mouthful of his hump, and then bound off. Having gratified their curiosity, the men withdrew, and the hungry pack in a moment set in, with fresh rapacity, tearing away and gulping the bloody flesh of their victim, that still faintly struggled for life.

Captain Williams represents the wolves as being very numerous, and always to be seen hanging about the outskirts of a buffalo herd. They kill a great many calves, and any that are unable, from any untoward circumstances, to resist successfully their attacks, are sure to fall victims to their rapacity.

35

This evening, when the company had gone into camp, and when they were enjoying their usual repast, two young Indians, a young man and a squaw, rode up and alighted in the midst of the men, apparently much fatigued and way-worn. Their presence filled the company with amazement, and the safety of the party required of them a very prompt explanation. They might belong to some marauders in that vicinity, who might give some trouble. The young Indian, under the pretext of friendship, might be the spy of a hostile band, who were meditating an attack upon them. But what means this pretty young girl, who is with him? War parties are never encumbered with women. The jaded condition of their horses, too, to some extent allayed their fears, as it was evidence that they were on a long and a severe journey.

The Mandan chief interrogated him as to his object and destination, and learned that he was a Pawnee, who had been taken captive about a year before by the Sioux, and was conveyed by them up the Missouri to one of their villages, in which he remained until an opportunity to make his escape to his own tribe presented itself. The young girl with him was a Sioux, for whom he conceived a fondness whilst among that tribe. The attachment was not only mutual, but that they might consummate their bliss, they found it necessary to elope. They were now flying to his native village, to which another night's ride, he thought, would bring them. As they seemed very much fatigued, and were without any provisions, the party very promptly tendered them the best they had, which was consumed with all good relish by the two lovers. After they had enjoyed a little repose Captain Williams, through Big White, drew from the young Pawnee the following details, that shall furnish matter for a short chapter.

Chapter 6

Story of the Renegade Lovers, Doranto and Niargua.

Doranto belonged to the Pawnee Loups, who dwelt, (if an Indian can be said to dwell any where) on the Wolf fork of the Platte.[1] In company with several of his young brethren, he had sauntered some distance from their village, and were bathing and swimming about in a small stream of water, when some marauders belonging to the Tetons of the Burnt Woods, a tribe of Sioux, suddenly came upon them, and made a prisoner of him, whilst the others were able to effect their escape. He was instantly snatched up, tied on a horse, and hurried away. The horse that he rode was led by one of the Sioux, and goaded on by another that followed immediately behind. They traveled night and day, and traveled hard, until they had reached a point entirely out of the reach of danger. The Tetons of the Burnt Woods have their main village in the Grand Detour or Great Bend of the Missouri river, the circuit of which is thirty miles whilst the distance across is a little over a mile.[2]

When they reached their village, as Doranto proved to be a son of a grand chief of the Pawnee Loups, he was greatly prized as a captive,

[1] Coyner has taken the name of this tribe and its location from Lewis and Clark. He does the same with the Tetons of the Burnt Woods. Coues (ed.), *Lewis and Clark*, vol. I, pp. 56, 98.
[2] The Great Bend is located between the White and Bad rivers. Lewis and Clark found the distance across the bend to be 2,000 yards and the circuit thirty miles. Ibid., p. 125. Clearly, Coyner used their figure.

and, on that account, was placed in the family of a principal chief of the Tetons. There was something very interesting in the person of the young captive, which no doubt secured to him more consideration, and a kinder and more respectful treatment than captives generally experience in the hands of their captors. Although, according to his own statement, he had seen but sixteen winters, he was about five feet and nine or ten inches high, and, in the view of Captain Williams, one of the handsomest and best proportioned men he had ever seen. The expression of his countenance, which was very fine, was very different from that which human nature usually bears in its elementary state. He certainly possessed, to a remarkable degree, that daring intrepidity of character, so much admired by Indians, and which, of itself, and unassociated with other excellencies, in their view, constitute the great man and the brave.

It is frequently the lot of captives and prisoners to some extent, to occupy the relation of servants, and have assigned those menial and domestic offices which are never performed by men, but constitute the employment of women. To be compelled to occupy this position in society, was very mortifying to the Indian pride of Doranto; but he was somewhat reconciled to it, as it threw him in the company of a beautiful daughter of the chief, whose name was Niargua.[3] He was not permitted to go to war, or to hunt the buffalo, the elk, and the antelope, a mode of life too tame and inactive, it was true, for his restless and mettlesome spirit, but then it gave him frequent opportunities of walking, and talking, and laughing with the Teton damsel over whose heart it was his good fortune to gain a complete victory. But it would not do for the daughter of a distinguished chief to be the wife of a captive slave, belonging to a tribe, too, against which the chief entertained a deep-seated hostility, for past insults and injuries. This would be a flagrant violation of every notion of Indian aristocracy. By the way, the mother of the young princess, who had noticed the growing familiarity of the two lovers, reported the matter to the chief, whose duties

[3] Henry Inman, who took this story from Coyner and retold it in his *Great Salt Lake Trail* (New York, 1898), p. 49, "improved" upon Coyner's version by rendering the Indian's names Ni-ar-gua and Do-ran-to, thereby giving them a more "Indian" flavor.

had kept him generally from home. As the intelligence was very unexpected, and by no means agreeable to his feelings, his daughter was not only very roughly reproved, but a severe flagellation must be inflicted to appease his wrath. He likewise threatened to shoot an arrow through Doranto for his bold pretensions. The result of this effort "to break the match," in this, as in similar cases in civilized life, was not only unsuccessful, but served to increase the flame it was intended to extinguish, and to strengthen, instead of dissolving, the attachment between the parties. If their partiality for each other was not so visible and open, they were not the less determined to carry out their designs. When Doranto perceived that difficulties were in the way, that would ever be insuperable whilst he remained among the Tetons, he immediately conceived the bold design of eloping to his own people, and embraced the first opportunity to apprise his betrothed of his thoughts. The proposition met with a prompt and a hearty response on her part. She was ready to go with him wherever he went, and to die where he died.

But there was a young warrior among the Tetons who also desired the hand of the Sioux belle, and greatly envied the position Doranto occupied in the eyes of Niargua. Indeed he entertained the most deadly hate toward the Pawnee captive, and suffered no opportunity to show it, to pass unimproved. Doranto was by no means ignorant of the young warrior's feelings of jealousy and hate, but he sensibly felt his disabilities as an alien in the tribe, and pursued a course of forbearance as most, likely to ensure the accomplishment of his designs. Still there were bounds beyond which his code of honor would not suffer his enemy to pass. On one occasion, the young brave offered Doranto the greatest and the most intolerable insult, which, in the estimation of the western tribes one man can give to another. "*You stink*," were the offensive words of the Teton warrior, embracing the great indignity.

The person upon whom this indignity is cast, by a law among those tribes, may take away the life of the offender, if he can; but it is customary, and thought more honorable, to settle the difficulty by single combat, in which the parties may use the kind of weapons on which they may mutually agree. Public sentiment will admit of no compromise. If no resistance is offered to the insult, the person insulted is thenceforth a disgraced wretch, a dog, and universally despised. Doranto forthwith demanded satisfaction of the young Sioux, who, by the way, was "cut and dry" to give it, being full of game and mettle, as well as sanguine as to the victory he would gain over the young Pawnee. They agreed to settle their difficulty by single combat, and the weapons to be used were war-clubs and short knives. A suitable place was selected. The whole village of the Tetons emptied itself to witness the combat. Men, women and children swarmed about the arena. The two youthful combatants made their appearance, stark naked, and took their positions about thirty yards apart. Just when the signal was given, Doranto caught the eye of Niargua in the crowd. Then said he "my heart was big and my arm strong; no fear, then, in Doranto." As the champions advanced towards each other, the Sioux was too precipitate, and by the impulse of his charge, was carried rather beyond Doranto, who, being more cool and deliberate, gave him a blow with his war club as he passed, on the back of his neck, that perfectly stunned him, and brought him to the ground. Doranto then sprung upon him and dispatched him by a single thrust of his blade. The relatives of the unfortunate Sioux raised a loud lament, and with that piteous kind of howling peculiar to Indians, bore him away. Doranto was now regarded as a young brave, and was greatly advanced in the general esteem of the village. He must now be an adopted son, and no longer a woman, but go to war, and hunt the buffalo, the elk, and the antelope.

The father of Niargua, however, in this matter, must be excepted. In the general excitement in behalf of the lucky captive, he lagged behind, and was reserved and sullen. Having conceived a dislike for him, he was not inclined to confer upon him the honors he had so fairly won. And then it would not do to appear delighted with the valor of the young Pawnee. Niargua was his favorite child, and she must be the wife of some distinguished personage. But the chief was doomed, as many a father is, to be out-witted by his daughter, in matters of this kind. At a time when he was absent, holding a council with a neighboring tribe of the Sioux, upon great national affairs, Doranto picked out two of the chief's best horses, on which to escape with his girl to his own tribe. Niargua was ready. When the village was sunk in a profound sleep, she met him in a sequestered place, bringing a supply of provisions for the trip. In a moment they were in their saddles and away. They were not less than three long sleeps from his own people, and would be followed by some of the Tetons as long as there was any hope of overtaking them. By morning, however, there would be such a wide space between them and their pursuers, as to make their escape entirely practicable if no mishap should befall them on the way. "They had good horses," said Doranto,[4] "good hearts, good moon, good weather, good country to travel over and above all a good cause, and why not good luck." They traveled day and night, never stopping any longer than was absolutely necessary to rest their horses. Captain Williams represented the Teton damsel as very pretty, but very young for an undertaking requiring so much self-denial, patience, and fortitude, and in which she was exposed to great fatigue and very severe toil. Her resolution was, however, quite commensurate to her difficulties and trials.

The company tried to prevail upon the young Pawnee to stay with them until morning, and enjoy that rest and refreshment which he and his girl so much needed; but he replied that they had not slept any since they set out on their flight, nor did they even dare to think of closing their eyes before they should reach the village of the Pawnees. He knew that he would be pursued, as long as there was the faintest hope of overtaking him; and he also knew what his doom would be, if he again fell into the hands of the Sioux. Having remained, therefore, in the camp scarcely an hour, the two fugitive lovers were again on the wing, flying over the green prairie, guided by the light of a full and beautiful moon, and animated and sustained by the purity of their motives, and the hope of soon reaching a place of safety and protection. The party could not but admire the courage of the Teton beauty, and the cheerfulness, and even hilarity, that she manifested while in their camp. When about to set off, she leaped from the ground, unassisted,

---

[4] Clearly, Doranto should have said, "*We* had good horses. . . ."

into her Indian saddle, reined up her horse, and was instantly beside *him* with whom she was now ready to share any trial and to brave any danger.

What an exhibition is this of female fortitude, that kind of heroism, peculiar to the sex, which elevates woman to a summit perfectly inaccessible to sublunary difficulties, and enables her to view, with undisturbed complacency of soul, all that occurs beneath her feet. What an auxiliary to man is woman ! in bearing his quota of life's trials and difficulties, and how does she light up his dark hours of adversity with her sunny smiles of cheerfulness, and prompt him to make *another effort,* when and where, unassisted and unencouraged, he would have yielded to despair.

Chapter 7

Sioux and Sioux country—Land Pirates—Strength of the Sioux—
Doubtful character of the statements about the numbers of the western tribes—Sioux's intention to intercept the return of Big White—
Carson lost again—His horse killed in a buffalo chase—Buffalo
hunting—Its dangers—Strength, activity and size of the buffalo—
Purity and dryness of the atmosphere—Indian encampment—Arrival at Fort Mandan.

HAVING REACHED the Platte country, Captain Williams
was aware of the fact, that increasing dangers beset their route, and
that he was now in a region full of hazard, and in which the utmost
caution was necessary to prevent his company from being cut off. The
greater part of the country, at that day, between the river Platte and the
Mandan nation, was infested with a variety of tribes of Sioux, whose
predatory habits had justly secured to them the title of "land pirates,"
who were a terror to all other tribes, on account of their superior numbers and their savage and ferocious disposition. Lewis and Clarke
represent them as being subdivided into ten tribes; the Yanktons,
Tetons, Minnake-nozzo, Tetons Saone, Yanktons of the Plains, or Big
Devils, Wapatone, Mindawarcarton, Wahpatoota, or Leaf Beds, and
the Sistasoona:[1] and by means of different interpreters, whilst in the

[1] Coyner names only nine tribes, omitting the "Tetons Okandandas" of Lewis
and Clark (the Oglala). Elliott Coues discusses the Sioux extensively in *Lewis
and Clark*, vol. I, pp. 97-101. I have been unable to determine the source of the
population figures.

Sioux country, they learned that their men of war numbered about two thousand five hundred. In 1836 the Sioux were represented as numbering about 27,000 men, women and children. A subsequent account speaks of these bands as probably numbering from 40,000 to 60,000. We are disposed to receive these accounts, as we receive all statements about the numerical strength of the tribes of the far west, as very uncertain. Correctness no doubt has been aimed at, but correctness in a great majority of cases can not be attained. One thing is certain, the Sioux have been diminishing very fast. Many of the tribes have been broken down, and lost their names; and the nation, *now* is not such a formidable body of freebooters as they were in the days of which we are treating.

The ten tribes, whose names we have furnished, were scattered up and down the Missouri river, and were constantly on the prowl, scouring the country from the waters of the Platte to the Black Hills and the Mandan region. They were very hostile to the Mandans, who dwelt above them on the Missouri, and as they had seen Big White on his way to the states, in company with Lewis and Clarke, they expected his return, and were on the alert to prevent his going back to his nation. They entertained the idea that the whites would furnish the Mandans with arms, and make them more formidable than they were, at that time. For this reason the Sioux aimed to intercept all communication between our people and the tribes above them. And for a number of years subsequent to 1807 they resisted all efforts made by various expeditions to push their way to those upper tribes.[2] Captain Williams was fully impressed with the fact, that the difficulties that were before him were much greater than those his party had already encountered, and that their vigilance must be increased and every expedient adopted to elude the observation of those "land pirates," through whose country they were now passing. It was some consolation to the party, that the Sioux expected them to ascend the Missouri river, and in all prob-

[2] Once beyond the Platte, the Sioux were indeed worrisome to traders, but they were not as hostile as the Arikaras, a Caddoan people who lived higher up the Missouri. It was Arikaras who attacked Manuel Lisa in the summer of 1807 and who drove Big White's escort party back to St. Louis in the fall of 1807.

ability, the greater part of their warriors would be collected on that river to drive them back.

For this reason, and another, stated in another place, Captain Williams left the Missouri not less than one hundred miles on his right, and thereby avoided all the large Indian towns on that river. If he should fall in with any of the Sioux on the route he was pursuing, they would be dispersed hunting parties, with whom he would be able to cope, if it should be his misfortune to be involved in a difficulty. Game, too, would be more abundant in that region, and the more easily and safely procured; which was an important consideration, as the safety of the party required that they should push their way through this dangerous country with all possible speed.

On the day after leaving the main Platte, a band of buffalo were observed feeding very quietly about the fourth of a mile from the party, offering an opportunity for those who desired it to show their horsemanship and skill in a buffalo hunt. Although they had a supply of meat, and it was the purpose of Captain Williams that there should be no more shooting than was necessary, the impetuous youth, Carson, begged permission to try his hand.

The captain granted his request, as it was near sun-set, and the company came to a halt to take their usual repast, as well as to witness the exploits of the young Nimrod.[3] The more experienced men of the company urged Carson not to venture too near the object of his pursuit, nor too far from the company, as both steps would be accompanied with much danger. The young man felt it to be the safer plan to undertake the matter on horseback, and as the rifle is not easily handled when horse and buffalo are at full speed, he armed himself with two braces of pistols. The buffalo very soon observed his approach, looked frightened, and put off at quite a fast gait. This made it necessary that he should increase the speed of his horse, and immediately hunter, horse and buffalo were out of sight.

Having refreshed themselves and horses, the party would have resumed their journey, but Carson had not returned. Night-fall came on,

---

[3] The Nimrod of *Genesis* 10:8 whose name has come to mean "hunter."

and still he did not make his appearance. Many unhappy fears now pervaded the camp as to his safety, and the suspicious circumstances of his absence prevented the men generally from sleeping that night. Early the next morning some of the men went to hunt Carson, and without much difficulty found him. He was sitting on a rock near a small stream, perfectly lost. Some of the men, when looking for him, had seen him when about a mile off, and supposed that he was an Indian, as he had no horse, and were very near leaving him to his fate; but the thought that they might be mistaken prompted them to approach him, and they recognized him. He had a doleful history to give of his buffalo hunt. According to his account, he pursued the buffalo four or five miles before he could overtake them. At first, and for some time, he could not get his horse near enough to use his pistols with any effect. After repeated unsuccessful efforts to ride up by the side of a very large bull, he fell immediately behind him, firing as he ran. His repeated shots threw the animal into the greatest rage, and as bull, horse and rider were in full drive down the side of a declivity, the infuriated buffalo stopped suddenly and wheeled about for battle. Carson's horse, not trained to such dangerous exercises, following immediately behind, and at the moment perfectly unmanageable, rushed upon the horns of his antagonist, and was thrown headlong to the ground, with his rider. When he had recovered from the confusion of the moment, and gained his feet again, Carson was glad to see his buffalo moving off as fast as his legs could carry him; but his horse was so badly wounded that he could be of no service to him. When he called to his recollection his party, and would have returned to them, he knew not the way to go. In the great excitement of the chase, he paid no attention to the direction he was going. And what was worse, he was now on foot, and several miles from the company. To be lost in a prairie country is worse than being lost in woods. His horse was so badly injured, that he abandoned him and wandered about, when he crept into a hazel patch, where he slept until morning without anything to disturb his rest except several bruises, he received in the fall from his horse. At the earliest dawn of day, he crawled out of his hiding place, and very cautiously examined the sea of prairie around him to ascertain whether any Indians were to be seen. Observing nothing that indicated danger, he set out in search for his party, and tramped about and around, until hunger and fatigue compelled him to sit down where he had been found. As they returned to the camp, they passed his unfortunate horse. He was dead, and a band of hungry wolves had already found his carcass and were greedily snatching and gulping his flesh. In fact, the men thought the wounded horse had been killed by the wolves, as they were very numerous and fierce, and would attack a horse as soon as any thing else, especially if they were incited by the smell of blood. They had even committed violence upon Carson's saddle, which he had removed from his horse, and left on the prairie, for want of a tree in which to secure it. They frequently get together in considerable gangs, and when emboldened by numbers, and especially when infuriated by hunger, dreadful is the fate of anything that crosses their path. The unlucky and now crestfallen hunter had a hundred questions to answer when he returned to camp; nor did he feel like being taunted in this way, as he had fasted for the last twelve or fifteen hours, had undergone great fatigue, and received several severe bruises in the bargain. The horse was a favorite animal; but he had learned a lesson (though dearly) that was worth a number of horses to him and the company. A party of raw and inexperienced men, in these expeditions, generally buy their wit, at this dear rate. And in a majority of cases they cannot be prevailed upon to practice the necessary caution, until by the want of it they are betrayed into a few and sometimes very serious difficulties. It is very rash and extremely hazardous for a single man to engage in a buffalo chase in a country infested with prowling bands of Indians, whose constant aim is to surprise and kill. It was viewed as a mere accident that Carson was not killed by the buffalo he had wounded, or that he had not fallen into the hands of hostile Indians. When he set off on the chase, Big White shook his head by way of disapprobation, and as prognostic of some mishap that was likely to befall him; and the party always found, that the suggestions of the old Mandan chief could not be neglected with safety, as he was a veteran warrior, habituated to all that kind of unremitting watchfulness, that an Indian begins to practice from his infancy.

We have said that it was very dangerous for an inexperienced hand to engage in a buffalo hunt on a horse that has not been trained to the business. A well trained horse will always bound off to one side or the other out of the way of the buffalo, when he stops to fight, and it frequently happens, if the rider is not "up to" the quick and sudden movements of his horse, he is thrown into the midst of danger. The buffalo stops to make battle only when he is wounded or finds escape impossible. He then wields his great strength and activity in self defence. We have read a number of incidents said to have occurred in buffalo hunts, the correctness of which we are disposed to doubt, as we think they are unauthorized, from what we have been able to gather from men who have spent the half of their lives in the buffalo country. We have alluded to their great strength and remarkable activity and quickness of motion. The horse that overtakes them must be very fast, and then they run for many miles over the plains, without seeming to fail.[4] When broke to work (a thing very easily done) one buffalo will break down three or four of our cattle. This has been fairly and frequently tried on the frontier. A gentleman living in Missouri informed me that he had a buffalo bull that could work all day on an inclined plane, whilst he was obliged to change his tame cattle every three hours. Another gentleman in the same region of country had a buffalo bull that would leap over an enclosure eight and ten rails high, without touching it.[5] This bull, in a contest with one of our domestic animals, would always prove himself victor in a very few moments. The males frequently attain an enormous size, and it is no uncommon thing to see on the plains those that will weigh three thousand pounds, gross.

As they were favored with moon light and very fine weather, the

---

[4] According to Walter Prescott Webb, the buffalo, or more properly the American bison, was "described by all observers . . . as a stupid animal, the easiest victim to the hunter . . . slow of gait, clumsy in movement." *The Great Plains* (New York, 1931), p. 44. Yet many observers agreed that running buffalo could attain considerable speed and could turn suddenly to surprise a pursuer. See Washington Irving's firsthand experience in *A Tour on the Prairies* (Norman, Okla., 1956), p. 173, and Irving's *Bonneville*, p. 351, which Coyner had read.

[5] Experiments at domesticating bison have never been successful, but whoever told Coyner about the high-jumping buffalo may not have been exaggerating too much. Charles Goodnight, who began raising buffalo in 1866, told of a bull that jumped a six-foot fence and claimed that his men had difficulty keeping the bull corralled. J. Evetts Haley, *Charles Goodnight: Cowman and Plainsman* (Norman, Okla., 1949), p. 441.

company thought it the safer plan to travel during the night, when circumstances were favorable, and to remain the greater part of the day in a state of inactivity, at least when it would be accompanied with much danger to move. They procured their meat, of course, during the day, and enjoyed their repast at the same time, as they never kindled fires after dark, for light in a prairie country is seen a great distance, and, more than any thing else, would lead to their discovery. During their passage through this region of danger, their usual way was to travel all night, until about eight o'clock the next morning, when they would seek some sequestered place to refresh themselves and horses. They always occupied an attitude of defence, and every one lay with his arms beside him, whilst they never failed to plant their scout around to look out for Indians. They slept by turns, and never more than half of the men slept at a time. In this way they traveled for twenty days, performing a greater part of their journeyings after night. Game was very abundant, but they killed no more than was necessary to furnish themselves with meat.

Their nocturnal movements were not, however, without interest, nor were they barren in interesting events. In those regions the atmosphere is very pure and elastic, and the sky has a delightful blue, in which cannot be seen for weeks and even months, any thing like vapour or clouds. When the moon shone, it was with an effulgence almost equal to that of a vertical sun. And when the moon did not favor them with her light, the starry firmament appeared with a brilliancy and a glory which they had never witnessed in any other country. This dryness, purity, and elasticity of atmosphere, this delicious transparent blue, said to belong also to Italian skies, increase as the traveler approaches the Rocky Mountains. The usual dry season that prevails in that country had already commenced; the water courses were very low, and threw but few obstructions in their way. Vast prairies generally spread around them, covered with a luxuriant growth of grass and wild flowers. But the face of the country was frequently cut up by deep, dry, ravines or gullies, which, being impassable, made the route sometimes very circuitous.

Along the rich bottoms of the rivers and ravines were groves of trees, with thick entangled undergrowth, in which our little party

49

generally sought to hide themselves from the observation of the prowling, free-booting Sioux. From one of those fastnesses, in the latter part of the day they would secretly and silently emerge and travel all night, when the next day they would turn aside into another of these hiding places. They dispensed with fire as often as they could, as the smoke ascending very high is very apt to attract the notice of Indians. They frequently saw bands of Indians, that invariably hovered about their route, but by making sham encampments and deceptive fires, and then traveling all night, they succeeded in escaping the clutches of the Arabs of the west.

One night about an hour after dark, they saw before them a light that indicated, as they thought an Indian encampment. As they approached it they found that they were not mistaken. Captain Williams thought it the safer plan for his party not to pass very near their camp, and when within a mile of it, he directed his men to come to a halt, and to remain where they were until he, in company with the Mandan chief, would approach the camp near enough to make some observations. Accordingly, accompanied by Big White, he crept up within a few hundred yards and reconnoitered their camp for a half-hour. They had twelve or fifteen fires, and there must have been not less than one hundred Indians. Some were lying down, and some were passing to and fro, whilst others were standing around the fires. A portion of them were squaws, who seemed to be very busy, for Captain Williams discovered they were a hunting party, who were procuring meat in that region, and the squaws were drying it for winter. He observed their long poles, on which they exposed their meat to the sun. A great number of horses were grazing around the camp.

Having gratified their curiosity, the captain and the chief quietly made their way back to their company, fully convinced of the expediency of getting out of that region as fast as their horses could carry them. They were apprehensive that these savages might observe their trail, and endeavor to overtake them. They therefore pushed ahead all that night, and the greater part of the next day, before they went into camp.

Without troubling the reader with all the incidents of this part of the expedition, we will state that on the first day of July Captain Williams, with his party, arrived safely at Fort Mandan, in the Mandan nation.[6]

[6] If, as I have conjectured in the Introduction, Ezekiel Williams accompanied the group that took Big White home, he reached the Mandan villages on September 24, 1809. Thomas James, *Three Years Among the Mexicans and Indians* (St. Louis, 1916), p. 30.

Chapter 8

Joy of the Mandans on the arrival of their chief—Indian gravity and silence—Their mutual attachment—Their grief for the dead—Repose of the party—They resume their journey—Unknown danger before them—Black-feet Indians—Their hostility to the whites—Yellow Stone—Hunter's Elysium—Indian caught in a trap—Five men killed in a buffalo hunt by the Black-feet—Danger of the company—they leave that region—Crows—One of their men leaves them.

Nothing could exceed, says Captain Williams, the enthusiastic joy of the Mandans upon the arrival of their old and much loved chief. It was something they had not expected, as they had heard, (a thing very likely to occur) that he had been killed by the Sioux, together with the party, that were conducting him home, on the Missouri river. As they had believed the report, knowing as they did the hostile character of the Sioux, they had mourned for their lost chief, and had gone through the usual forms intended to express their sorrow and regard for the dead. Their surprise was equalled only by their joy, when they had the unexpected pleasure of again looking upon the face of their venerated and long-absent hero. They received him as directly from the spirit land, and as one from the grave. For several days, the excitement produced by his arrival, was kept up, and kept everything in motion. There was feasting, and there was dancing, throughout the village. They sang their wild chants, and whilst they extolled the faith of the whites, in bringing back their chief and his family, they made their thanksgiving sacrifices to the Great Spirit, for that protection that had overshadowed their old warrior. Runners were sent to other villages in several directions to spread the news, and for several days hundreds of curious visitors consisting of men, women and children, came to see the party of white men, and especially Big White, who now in their eyes was something superhuman. The reader may be ready to suppose that the old acquaintances of Big White would tease him almost to death with innumerable questions about the country of the white man, from which he had just returned; but it may be stated, as something peculiar to Indians generally, that they always repress a curiosity of this kind, and conduct themselves with great dignity, gravity and silence, when one of their company may be detailing important information. This seems to be a part of their education, and a rule into the violation of which they are seldom betrayed by any kind of excitement.[1] Indians, generally, are prone to be taciturn and grave yet their natural sensibilities are very deep and strong. A mutual and ardent attachment pervades the whole tribe, however numerous, and binds them all together as closely as brothers; and although a tribe may number several hundred, if any one dies or is killed by a foe, all alike give themselves up to the most wild and extravagant grief: nor does the greatest victory over their enemies in battle atone for the loss of a single warrior. The lamentations and howlings about an Indian village after a battle are to be heard in every direction, although they generally aim to retire to some sequestered spot to empty the heart of its abounding grief.

Irving, in his Astoria, alludes to this practice among the western tribes in the following beautiful language: "But sounds of another kind were heard on the surrounding hills; piteous wailings of the women, who had retired thither to mourn in darkness and solitude for those who had fallen in battle. There the poor mother of the youthful warrior, who had returned home in triumph but to die, gave full vent to the anguish of a mother's heart. How much does this custom of the Indian women, of repairing to the hill tops in the night, and pouring

---

[1] Here Coyner did not read Irving carefully enough. In *Astoria*, p. 208, Irving talks of the "boisterous revelry" of an Indian village, which "proved the fallacy of the old fable of Indian apathy and stoicism."

53

forth their wailings for the dead, call to mind the beautiful and affecting passage of scripture, 'In Rama was there a voice heard, lamentation, and weeping, and great mourning; Rachel weeping for her children, and would not be comforted, because they are not.' "[2]

Big White made a long speech to his people, in which he spoke in eloquent terms of the kindness with which he was received by the whites. He also alluded to the riches, number, and great strength of our people, and urged upon them not only the necessity of maintaining a constant peace with us, but the advantages that they would experience from the existence of very friendly relations between them and the whites. "Brothers," said he, "do you see yon prairie (pointing at the same time to a prairie several miles wide) ; the white man has a gun that will kill Indians across that prairie." He had reference to the cannon that he had seen when in the states.[3]

An important point in the expedition being attained, and a long and perilous journey having brought our little party to the Mandan country, they once more felt themselves in a land of comparative safety, and among friends, not the less friendly because they were savages. They were now at liberty to relax themselves from that intense vigilance necessary to be practiced in a country full of danger, and to give to themselves and their way-worn horses that repose which they so much needed. A week, however, had not passed away, before Captain Williams' men manifested a restless spirit, and were anxious again to launch into the boundless wilderness, the great *terra incognita* that was before them. A recollection of their past good fortune greatly animated them, whilst they were stimulated by the prospects that were before them. They fancied that all danger was behind them, in the land of the piratical Sioux, through which they had passed without difficulty. But it was only fancy; delusive fancy. Little did they know of the

[2] Ibid., pp. 208-09.

[3] Shahaka did not impress his people as much as Coyner supposed. Henry M. Brackenridge, who visited the Mandans in 1811, recorded that Shahaka and his wife had "fallen into disrepute from the extravagant tales which they related as to what they had witnessed; for the Mandans treat with great ridicule the idea of their [sic] being a greater or more numerous people than themselves." Furthermore, Shahaka was "a little talkative, which is regarded amongst the Indians as a great defect." Reuben G. Thwaites (ed.), "Brackenridge's 'Journal,' " in *Early Western Travels* (Cleveland, 1904), vol. VI, p. 137.

dangers before them, and the unexpected and formidable foes that infested the country they were approaching. Little did they dream of the unhappy fate that awaited the greater part of their party. When they left the Mandan country, a few day's travel brought them to the country over which roves and prowls the ferocious Black-feet Indians, then as well as now one of the most cruel and relentless tribes of the far west. For the Black-feet Indian is an embodiment of every quality that is offensive to the feelings of civilized man. Lewis and Clarke, in passing through their country, killed one of their tribe, which act created an implacable hatred for the whites from that day till this.[4] Of the hostility of this tribe to the whites, on this account, Captain Williams' men were not apprized, and were not expecting to meet with a foe writhing under the recollection of past injuries, and who had sworn destruction to every white man that should venture to put his foot upon their territory.

We would state that it was the object of captain Williams and his party, to spend the approaching fall and winter on those upper rivers, trapping for beaver, until spring, when they intended to push their way into the Rocky Mountains, and carry on their trapping operations, on the head waters of the Columbia. It was also a very praiseworthy object of the expedition to find a more practicable pass through the Rocky Mountains, than the route of Lewis and Clarke. Such a pass, it was believed, could be found, south of the sources of the Missouri. When, therefore, they reached the mouth of the Yellow Stone, they turned in a southwest direction, following the meanderings of the river last named. Up the Yellow Stone they journeyed for several days, looking for a region where beaver were very abundant. Such a region they soon found, and the traps of the company were all as soon scattered up and down every little mountain brook and branch for several miles around. In the meantime, whilst some were constructing a temporary camp and fortress, others were beating up and down the adjacent hills and hollows in the pursuit of game. They were now in a perfect Elysium. Buffalo, elk, antelope, white and black-tail deer, *ah-sah-ta*, or big horn, could be seen every day; and the innumerable

[4] An idea that Coyner took from either Irving, *Astoria*, p. 177, or Coues (ed.), *Lewis and Clark*, vol. III, p. 1103.

little rills around abounded with fish of the finest flavor. In the way of trapping, the men had a great run of good luck, for every morning, nearly every trap in the neighborhood, was found holding in its iron jaws a fine beaver. These were the employments and enjoyments which the party had long craved, and they now had them in the greatest exuberance. From day to day, the men were variously engaged in trapping, and skinning beaver, fishing and hunting, eating, laughing and jesting. Their horses also were recovering very fast from the effects of the long journey they had performed, and were fattening. Their feet and backs were getting well and sound again, and they were soon in fine plight. The party had seen no signs of Indians to excite any apprehensions of danger, until, one morning, one of the men discovered that an Indian had been caught in a trap, from which however, he had succeeded in extricating himself, as it was found near the place where it had been set. It would seem that the savage was not disposed to carry it off, but was satisfied to be rid of a thing that, for a short time, at least, had held him in painful custody. He no doubt, was of the Black-feet tribe, and had been sent as a scout to pry into the condition of Captain Williams' camp, and report the same to his people, as another and very melancholy event which we will record, will prove. A day or two after this Indian was taken in a trap, some of the men, about ten, left the camp on a buffalo hunt. At the commencement of the chase, the buffalo were not more than a mile from the camp, but they were pursued for three or four miles, which led the men into danger. A company of Black-feet, numbering at least one hundred, suddenly appeared on horses from behind a covert of trees and undergrowth, and dashed toward the men as they were scattered over a plain pursuing and shooting the buffalo. Five of the men being on fast horses, and flying at the top of their speed, were able to effect their escape, but the others were intercepted by the savages, and their escape to the camp cut off. They fell an easy prey into their hands, and were in all probability the first whites that were killed by that tribe, and killed, too, to appease the vengeance awakened against the whites by the act of Lewis and Clarke. The five men who made their escape, were pursued within the half of a mile from the camp by several of the Black-feet. One of these savages manifested a disposition to follow the men into the very camp of our little party, after the others had wheeled their horses and were returning to the main body of their party. But he paid dearly for his rashness. One of the men, whose gun happened to be loaded, stopped his horse, and sent a ball whizzing through his body which caused him to tumble from his horse, dead.

The loss of five men, sustained by a party numbering only twenty at first; the killing of one of their band, which would rouse the vengeful feelings of those savages to a still greater pitch, and the fact that so large a party of those ruthless marauders was in their immediate vicinity, made the situation of Captain Williams and his now reduced party very critical and hazardous indeed. A consultation was immediately held, and they determined to leave that night, as it would be very unsafe to remain there. Indeed they expected every moment to see the whole body of the Black-feet coming upon them, especially if they had any knowledge of the size of their little party; but if they did not know the strength of Captain Williams' party they would be more cautious, as Indians rarely run dangerous risks. They were, however, *now* certain of one thing, and that was, they had been watched by the scouts of the Black-feet for several days, as they had observed something several times on the summit of an adjacent mountain, among the rocks, peering the country below, which they had supposed was wolves, but which was most probably Indians, examining their location, and endeavoring to ascertain their strength.

The melancholy event that we have just detailed took place in the latter part of the day, so that it was not long before the little party of Captain Williams was under the covert of night. All the horses were brought in when the alarm was first given. When night came on, all hands were busy collecting their traps and making ready for their departure that night as soon as possible. Large and numerous fires were made to deceive the enemy, from which the men withdrew at least a mile where they remained until they were ready to set off. About midnight they leaped into their saddles and set out south. They traveled as fast as they could for twenty-four hours, without giving repose to themselves or horses. Their journal states that they soon reached the country of the Crow Indians, who were very friendly to the whites at that time. At one of the villages of these Indians they remained about

a week, during which time they took a buffalo hunt; but as they desired
to reach a country where beaver were more abundant than in that of
the Crows, they continued to travel south, under the east side of the
Rocky Mountains, until they came to the sources of the Platte. This
route the Crows informed them, was greatly to be preferred if they
wished to penetrate the Rocky Mountains, and beaver were very abundant.[5]

We will conclude this chapter by stating that one of Captain Williams' men, whose name was Rose, expressed his intention to abandon
his party and remain among the Crows. It appears that whilst the men
were in the Crow village, Rose was not able to resist the charms of a
certain Crow beauty, whom he afterwards selected as his wife and
with whom he lived for several years. We will give some account of this
man Rose in the next chapter, as he was an egregious character in the
history of those times.[6]

[5] Since the sources of the Platte are in the Rockies, Coyner must have meant to
say that the men traveled along the east side of the Rockies until they reached
the Platte, then followed it west into the beaver-rich intermontane parks to its
sources.

[6] Edward Rose, a mulatto, came up the Missouri with Lisa in 1807 and was
sent from Fort Raymond to trade with the Crows. Rose, who did live among the
Crows from time to time, became one of the most notorious mountain men. Coyner describes him in Chapter IX.

Chapter 9

Rose, the scape-goat refugee—The Crow Indians, and a Crow's description of their country.

 THE CHARACTER of Rose was not known to Captain Williams when he joined his party. "This fellow, it appears, was one of those desperadoes of the frontiers, outlawed by their crimes, who combine the vices of civilized and savage life, and are ten times as bad as the Indians, with whom they consort. Rose had formerly belonged to one of the gangs of pirates who infested the islands of the Mississippi, plundering boats as they went up and down the river, and who sometimes shifted the scene of their robberies to the shore, waylaying travelers as they returned by land from New Orleans, with the proceeds of their downward voyage; plundering them of their money and effects, and often perpetrating the most atrocious murders."[1]

These hordes of villains being broken up and dispersed, Rose betook himself to the upper wilderness, and when Captain Williams was forming his company at St. Louis, this fellow came forward and offered his services. Captain Williams observed that he had a sinister look, and suspected that his character was not too fair, but it was difficult to get men to join an expedition so daring and full of danger. He was dropped among the Crows (or Upsarokas, as they are sometimes called,) a race of savages whose habitudes of life were much more

[1] Coyner has taken the description of Rose from Irving, *Astoria*, p. 225.

congenial to the feelings of such a man as Rose than the restraints of civilized life. He took several of their women as wives, by whom he had children, and became a great man among them. As he lived among the Crows several years, he could speak their language very fluently, and had a very general knowledge of the extensive country ranged by these Indians. In the year 1810 or 11 he was picked up somewhere on the Missouri, by Mr. [Wilson Price] Hunt, who was at that time on an expedition across the Rocky Mountains. From his knowledge of the Crow country and the Crow language, and from the fact of his affiliation with that tribe, Mr. Hunt thought he might be of great service to him whilst passing through their country, and in any intercourse he might have with them. Rose was therefore engaged as guide and interpreter when Hunt's party should reach the country of the Crows. He had been attached to this party but a few days before he began to exhibit his dark and perfidious spirit, by tampering with the fidelity of certain of the men, and suggesting to them a design he had been concocting in his own mind, in which he wished them to co-operate with him. The plan of this treacherous scoundrel was, that several of the men should join with him, when in the Crow country, in deserting to those Indians, taking with them as many horses and goods as they could. He assured the men of the kindest reception among the Crows, with whose principal chief he was well acquainted, and tempted them by artful stories of the honors and privileges they would enjoy. They could have the handsomest women and the daughters of the chiefs for wives, and as many as they pleased. This plan, too, would set them up for life. When the treachery of this vagabond became generally known, it created much anxiety in the breasts of Mr. Hunt and his friends, as they were sensible that he might do them much mischief, as he could succeed in carrying out his nefarious designs if he could seduce some of the men to co-operate with him. An affair of this kind might be ruinous to the expedition. To divert the mind of Rose from his wicked thoughts, and to tempt him to give up his perfidious purposes, Mr. Hunt treated him with great attention and kindness. He told him that in parting with him in the Crow country, he ["]would pay him half a year's wages in consideration of his past services, and would give him a horse, three beaver traps, and sundry other articles calculated to set him up in the world.["]²

This liberal proposition had the desired effect, and from that time the whole deportment of Rose underwent a change. He was no longer that surly, sullen, silent, designing fellow. Ever after he was cheerful, and seemed honestly to desire the success of the expedition. Still it was the fixed purpose of some of Hunt's party, that if Rose showed the least inclination to carry out his knavish designs, to shoot the desperado on the spot. Whilst among the Crows, however Rose exhibited no bad feelings towards the party, and when they took their leave of those savages, Mr. Hunt consigned him to their cherishing friendship and fraternal adoption as their worthy and old confederate.

"Rose was powerful in frame and fearless in spirit, and very soon by his daring deeds, took his rank among the first braves of the tribe."³ Nothing but daring deeds and desperate exploits in the estimation of an Indian, will make a brave. In repeated actions of the Crows with the Black-feet, Rose won many laurels. On one occasion, it is said, "a band of those savages had fortified themselves within a breastwork and could not be harmed. Rose proposed to storm the work. 'Who will take the lead,' was the demand. 'I,' cried he, and putting himself at their head rushed forward. The first Black-foot that opposed him, he shot down with his rifle, and snatching up the war-club of his victim, killed four others within the fort. This victory was complete, and Rose returned to the Crow village covered with glory, and bearing five Black-foot scalps, to be erected as a trophy before his lodge. From this time he was known among the Crows, by the name of Che-ku-kaats, or 'the man who killed five.'" The Crows and Black-feet have always been the most implacable and deadly foes; this daring deed of Rose, therefore, would naturally make him a popular idol of the village. But

² Occasionally, as here, Coyner's paraphrasing lapses into plagiarism. These lines are from *Astoria*, p. 229.

³ This quotation and the remainder of Coyner's description of Rose are close paraphrases of Irving, *The Adventures of Captain Bonneville, U.S.A.*, edited by Edgeley W. Todd (Norman, Okla., 1961), pp. 166-68. For a modern account of Rose's career, see Charles L. Camp, *James Clyman, Frontiersman* (Portland, Ore., 1960), pp. 31-34.

Indians, like white people, are invidious beings. The popularity of Rose awakened the envy of the native braves. He was a white man, and interloper. Two rival parties sprung up, between whom there were feuds and civil wars that lasted for two or three years, until Rose having contrived to set his adopted brethren by the ears, left them and went down the Missouri, in 1823. He afterwards enlisted as guide and interpreter, for Fitzpatrick and Sublette, who conducted a trapping expedition, sent by General Ashly across the mountains.[4] When they got among the Crows, he was able to some extent to revive his popularity, by being very liberal and kind among his old acquaintances, at the expense, however, of the expedition. This company was robbed of their horses, when in the Green river valley, and it was believed that this man Rose had a hand in the matter. When General [Henry] Atkinson went up the Missouri in 1825, he met with Rose among the Crows, who as usual, was a personage of much consequence among them. He is represented as suppressing a chance-medley fight, that was on the point of taking place between the military of General Atkinson and those savages. It appears the Crows contrived to stop the touch-holes of the field pieces of the expedition with dirt, and then became very insolent. A tumult arose, and blows began to be dealt out. As the Crows were evidently in the fault, Rose grasped his fusee and broke the stock of it over the head of a brave, and laid so vigorously about with the barrel that he soon put the whole throng to flight. Here the affair ended. Of the subsequent history of this voluntary exile from civilized life, but little is certainly known. Some reports say that he died of a disease brought on by his licentious life; and others state that he was killed by some of his adopted brethren, the Crows. He is said to have taught the Crows the policy of cultivating the friendship of the white men. A policy, which they still observe to some extent, since the death of Rose. "If we keep friends with the white men,["] said one of their chiefs, ["]we have nothing to fear from the Blackfeet, and can rule

[4] Thomas Fitzpatrick, William L. Sublette, and William H. Ashley are well-known figures in the fur trade. Each has been the subject of a book-length study by, respectively, LeRoy R. Hafen and W. J. Ghent, John E. Sunder, and Dale L. Morgan. Rose did aid a small party, led by Jedediah Smith, to winter among the Crows in 1823-24.

the mountains."[5] So much about Rose, the heroic vagabond and renegado.

Whilst we are with Captain Williams, among the Crows, we will state a few things about those savages, and the country over which they range. The Crows are to be found on the west of the Missouri, and on and along the east side of the Rocky Mountains, although they often cross the Mountains on their predatory excursions, which they are constantly making. They perhaps excel all tribes of the west in their roving, wandering habits, and horse-stealing propensities. They not only scour the country east of the Rocky Mountains for several hundred miles, but they are often on the wing along the head waters of the Columbia, carrying on their plundering and horse-stealing operations. The horse is the idol of the Crow Indians, and their skill and audacity in stealing this animal is said to be astonishing. It is the business of their lives, and their glory and delight. An accomplished horse-stealer fills up their idea of a hero. They are called Crows, because they are always on the scamper and the foray, and like the bird of the same name, winging their roguish flight from one region to another.[6] A Rocky Mountain trapper, with whom I met on the frontier of Missouri, and who had spent several years as a free trapper in the Black Hills and Rocky Mountains, told me that he once accompanied a party of Crows across the mountains, whose object was to steal horses. It was at a time of the year when trapping is suspended (June, July and August.) He had nothing to do, and therefore accompanied this party merely for the purpose of seeing the country and witnessing their mode of operating in their favorite employment. They were gone about eight weeks, and returned with eighty horses. My informant thought they were generally taken from the lower Nez Perces, and also the white settlers on the waters of the Columbia. They performed this trip, stole this number of horses, and returned, and such was their adroitness and skill, that they did not meet with a single difficulty. The Crows were

[5] Statement attributed to Arapooish in Irving, *Bonneville*, p. 168. Arikaras apparently killed Rose on the Yellowstone in late 1832. Dale L. Morgan (ed.), *The West of William H. Ashley* (Denver, 1964), p. 263 n52.
[6] To this point, Coyner's description of the Crows follows Irving, *Astoria*, pp. 224-25.

once a numerous and powerful tribe of Indians, but their constant wars with the Black-feet, and their roving and predatory habits, are wearing them away very fast. They seem doomed to that tendency to extinction which is to be seen among all the western tribes.

I will take the privilege of giving a very interesting account of the Crow country, which is to be found in Captain Bonneville's notes, prepared for publication by Irving.[7] It is a description of the Crow country, given by a Crow chief, Arapooish, to Mr. Robert Campbell,[8] of the Rocky Mountain Fur Company: "The Crow country," said he, "is a good country. The Great Spirit has put it exactly in the right place; while you are in it, you fare well; whenever you go out of it, which ever way you travel, you will fare worse.

"If you go to the south, there you have to wander over great barren plains; the water is warm and bad, and you meet the fever and ague.

"To the north it is cold; the winters are long and bitter, with no grass; you cannot keep horses there, but must travel with dogs. What is a country without horses!

"On the Columbia they are poor and dirty, paddle about in canoes, and eat fish. Their teeth are worn out; they are always taking fishbones out of their mouths. Fish is poor food.

"To the east they dwell in villages; they live well; but they drink the muddy water of the Missouri—that is bad. A Crow's dog would not drink such water.

"About the forks of the Missouri is a fine country; good water, good grass, plenty of buffalo. In summer it is almost as good as the Crow country; but in winter it is cold, the grass is gone, and there is no salt weed for the horses.

"The Crow country is exactly in the right place. It has snowy mountains and sunny plains; all kinds of climate, and good things for every season. When the summer heats scorch the prairies, you can draw up

[7] This quotation should extend through the last sentence of this chapter, for it is taken from Irving, *Bonneville*, pp. 164-65.

[8] A prominent figure in the Rockies, Irish-born Robert Campbell has not yet been the subject of a biography. He is best known as an associate and partner of William Sublette. See John E. Sunder, *Bill Sublette: Mountain Man* (Norman, Okla., 1959).

under the mountains, where the air is sweet and cool, the grass fresh, and the bright streams come tumbling out of the snow banks.

"There you can hunt the elk, the deer, and the antelope, when their skins are fit for dressing; there you will find plenty of white bears and mountain sheep.

"In the autumn, when your horses are fat and strong from the mountain pastures, you can go down into the plains and hunt the buffalo, or trap beaver on the streams. And when winter comes on, you can take shelter in the woody bottoms, along the rivers; there you will find buffalo meat for yourselves, and cotton-wood bark for your horses; or you may winter in the Wind river valley, where there is salt weed in abundance.

"The Crow country is exactly in the right place. Every thing good is to be found there. There is no country like the Crow country."

Such is the eulogium on his country by Arapooish.

Chapter 10

Another disaster befalls the party—All the horses are stolen—A fight with the Indians—Five more of the party killed, and nineteen savages killed and mortally wounded—The party *cache* their furs, etc., and leave the country—They reach the Arkansas—Their trapping operations there—All killed but Captain Williams and two others.

W<small>HILST JOURNEYING</small> on the head waters of the Platte, Captain Williams' party met with another disaster. One morning seven of the men, including Captain Williams, went to bring in the horses, which had been turned out to graze the previous evening. As they were still in the country of the Crows, whom they regarded as their friends, they had not exercised the usual precaution of bringing in their horses and carefully securing them for the night. They simply fastened two of their feet together, to prevent them from wandering too far, and then turned them out, whilst they retired a short distance, into the edge of some timber, and stretched themselves out upon their buffalo skins for the night. The next morning the horses were missing; but their trace in the deep, dewy grass was soon discovered, very fresh, and leading across a low ridge in the prairie. The men in pursuit of the horses soon found some of the cords by which they had been tied. They were not broken by the horses, but had evidently been taken off, a circumstance that filled their minds with painful anxiety. But they continued to follow the trace to the top of the ridge, from which they were suddenly struck with the sight of about sixty Indians at the base of the hill, in possession of their horses. They seemed very busy, preparing, no doubt, to make an attack upon the party; for when they observed the men at the top of the hill, they sprang upon their horses and dashed up the hill toward them, at the same time making every thing ring with their terrific and hideous yells. Captain Williams urged his men to escape to the timber, but before they could reach it, five of them were overtaken and killed. Captain Williams and another of the seven succeeded, though very closely pursued, in gaining the timber. The other men that had remained in the camp, seeing the savages coming, had snatched up their rifles, and, each one taking a tree, they opened a fire upon them that caused them to wheel and withdraw a short distance, leaving several of their men upon the ground dead and wounded. In a few minutes the savages dashed up again, shouting, and yelling, and launching their arrows in the timber. There was a dense undergrowth, that not only prevented them from riding into the timber, but also prevented them from seeing Captain Williams' men. This was a lucky circumstance, and but for it they would all have been cut off. Captain Williams told his men to take good aim, and not to fire until they were certain of making an effectual shot. By observing this plan, and reserving their shots until the savages would come to the very edge of the timber, the sharp report of each rifle was always followed by the tumbling of an Indian from his horse. For four successive times did these savages dash up to the timber, launch their arrows and then wheel and withdraw out of the reach of the rifles of Captain Williams' men. Being unable to dislodge our little band, and having sustained a great loss of men, the Indians abandoned the field of battle, and rode off.

As a scalp is a great and favorite trophy with an Indian, these savages did not neglect to carry off with them the scalps of the five men they had killed. They also took with them two or three (it was thought) of their wounded, but left nineteen on the ground. The party remained behind their fortress of trees and thick undergrowth, whilst one of the men went out to reconnoitre the motions of the savages. He returned, reporting that he had seen them at least three miles off, going at a brisk gait.

Captain Williams saw his party now reduced to ten,[1] without a single horse to carry their accoutrements, and what could they do in a country full of savages, on foot? It was probable that these same savages, knowing the almost helpless condition of the little party, and infuriated by the slaughter of so many of their men, would hurry off to the main body of their tribe, and return with increased forces to do a work of total destruction. There was therefore no time to be lost. The company gathered up their furs and as many traps as the ten could carry, and traveled about ten miles, keeping close to the timber. They avoided as well as they could making any trace by which they might be pursued. When night came on, they crept into a very dense thicket, where they spent the greater part of the night, in erecting a scaffold, upon which they *cached* their furs and traps and such things as they found inconvenient to carry.[2]

Captain Williams did not know to what tribe of Indians the band belonged that attacked his party. They were, in all probability, Crows, and perhaps from the very village in which our little party had spent several days; although they professed great friendship for the whites. This conjecture is the more plausible, when we remember, that the friendship of those savages is about as uncertain as their locality, and the consciences of these notorious horse-thieves would not let them rest very easy, if they should suffer such a cavalcade to pass through their country without, at least, an effort on their part to steal their horses. The party, however, did not suspect the Crows, as they supposed they were out of the Crow country, and on the Arkansas river; a supposition, however, that proved to be erroneous, as they were still in the country of those treacherous, crafty, roving free booters, and on the upper waters of the Platte.

As the prospects of the company were now gloomy in the extreme, the spirits of the men drooped, and their hearts became sad. They were many hundred miles from the adobes of civilized life, in the heart of a

---

[1] Coyner's lack of attention to detail is here revealed. In Chapter 8 he reported the death of five men and in this chapter he "killed off" five more. Since William Hamilton had died of illness and Edward Rose had stayed with the Crows, only eight of the original twenty should have been left at this point.

[2] Placing a "cache" in a tree was a highly unusual, but plausible, expedient.

wilderness almost boundless, where they found themselves beset on every side with lurking savages, ready, at a suitable opportunity, to pounce upon them and make them their easy prey. They were now without horses, and their number was so reduced they could scarcely indulge a hope of escaping the cruel hands of the natives. It is hardly necessary to state that they were compelled to abandon their intentions of crossing the Rocky Mountains, and trapping on the waters of the Columbia. But Captain Williams who is represented by one who knew him well, "as brave and cautious, and the best and most feeling companion in the world," in all his difficulties, wore a serene and cheerful countenance, and encouraged his men not to give up the hope of yet succeeding in their trapping enterprise. Should they succeed, they would not only be independent, but rich for life. They left this region of danger, and the following spring found them on the sources of the Arkansas,[3] where they encamped, as beaver were very abundant, and there was a prospect of their gathering in a large harvest of rich peltries.

The very succinct and imperfect and much mutilated journal before me states that the party scattered about on the various little streams that put into the Arkansas, and that one after another was cut off by a fierce tribe of Indians called the Camanches, until but three of the party remained, Captain Williams and two others, whose names were James Workman and Samuel Spencer.[4] These three were all that were left of those early adventurers in the fur trade, a melancholy fate indeed, that verifies the assertion "that of the hardy bands of trappers that first entered those regions, three-fifths have fallen by the hands of savage foes."[5]

Williams, Workman and Spencer now determined to return, if they could, to St. Louis. But what route should they take to reach there, and *where* were they? were the perplexing questions that sprung up in the anxious minds of the lost trappers. Captain Williams thought, from

[3] As becomes clearer in Chapter XI, Coyner envisioned the trappers crossing over the Front Range of the Rockies to the headwaters of the Arkansas. Ezekiel Williams, however, seems to have stayed east of the Front Range.

[4] James Workman and Samuel Spencer are almost certainly fictitious names. Champlain and Porteau were Williams' final companions.

[5] Almost a quotation from Irving, *Bonneville*, p. 6.

the distance they had traveled, they were on the Red river, and proposed descending it in canoes. Workman and Spencer thought they were not far from Santa Fe, in New Mexico, and proposed going there, as the only way they could adopt to avoid being killed by the savages. Strange as it may appear, and dangerous as their situation was, the three lost trappers separated; Workman and Spencer striking out towards the Spanish country, and Captain Williams descending, as he supposed, the Red river. Before they separated, however, they *cached* all their peltries, and such traps as they could not take with them.

As it is our object to give a faithful and full account of these three wandering trappers, subsequent to the time when they parted in a region of great danger, we will furnish the reader with that of Captain Williams first.

Chapter 11

The forlorn situation of the three trappers—Their separation—
Ignorance on the part of Indians at this day of the efficiency of our
rifles—Great sacrifice of life—Policy to be observed in fighting
Indians—*Cache* their furs—Williams holds on to his purpose—His
perplexities—His mistake—A bull bait—Travel day and night—
Vast number of buffalo—A bull fight—Gangs of wild horses—Contest with a bear—Beaver tail great delicacy—Description of the
beaver, and mode of taking him in traps—Beaver resembles a dog;
his food—Williams' firmness—Three Kansas; their treacherous designs—Williams runs into danger; is made a prisoner—Set at liberty
again, but loses all his furs.

W<small>E HAVE ALREADY</small> alluded, with great surprise, to the
fact, that these three lost trappers should have separated, when all hope
of regaining their homes depended upon their remaining together.
When their party was now reduced to three, by the ferocity of the
Arabs of the West, how could *they* expect to escape the clutches of
these savages? How could two men expect to escape! How could one?
Yet startling as the fact may be, they separated, and separated in a
region where several of their party had been killed, a region full of
danger and lurking foes. We would state, that at that early day, our
men were not as well acquainted as they are now, with the modes of
warfare practised by the western tribes; nor were those tribes as well
apprised as they are now, of the efficiency of our rifles. The melancholy

consequence has been, as already stated, the loss of three-fifths at least of those early adventurers into those regions, and the killing of a great many savages. Since, however, our men have gained a knowledge of the way in which the Indians practice their hostilities, and especially since the various tribes have ascertained the distance and accuracy with which our rifles shoot, those savages are much more cautious, and the consequence is, the loss of life on either side has not been so great for a number of years. Our men, too, have found it to be good policy to take with them into that country, guns that carry very heavy balls. These are better for killing buffalo, and they keep off hostile Indians, at a greater distance. In a prairie country, men engaged in shooting at any thing, are apt to mistake the distance, always supposing the object nearer, than it really is. Hence, the advantage in having guns that will carry up for several hundred yards. Indians will never rush upon a party of white men, unless they know their guns are empty, or when they may have some other advantage. "They know," said a free trapper of great intrepidity, "that the crack of a rifle is always followed by the loss of one of their men." They therefore regard the rifles of our men as very dangerous things. A handful of men behind a fortification of some kind, may keep off a hundred Indians. Their guns, (all of them) should not be empty at the same time. It is the custom of experienced men to reserve several shots, or in other words, to always keep some of their rifles charged. The same free trapper informed the author, "that in several difficulties with the Black-feet, two other trappers and himself, snugly entrenched behind some logs had compelled a large body of those savages to leave the field of battle, howling and whining most mournfully for their losses. They will not rush upon a loaded rifle." It was the misfortune of Captain Williams' men, that they did not understand the most successful and the safest way of fighting those savages, and the results were the melancholy events we have detailed.

Before Williams, Workman and Spencer separated, they *cached* the skins they had procured, expecting, if they should be fortunate enough to reach the abodes of civilization, to form another company and return for the purpose of conveying their peltries to St. Louis. They also *cached* all their traps, except as many as they could conveniently carry. Workman and Spencer could take none, as they intended to strike across the water courses for the Spanish country. Captain Williams was able to take six or eight traps, as he constructed a canoe in which he conveyed them. We have said that we would follow Captain Williams throughout his subsequent history, and then return to that of Workman and Spencer, whom we now leave on the head waters of a strange river, entangled in a labyrinth of wild and unexplored region, scarcely knowing which way to go. Captain Williams, although a great woodsman, very cool and brave, and holding on with great tenacity to his original purpose of making himself rich by the traffic in the rich peltries of those nameless and unknown rivers, was no less perplexed in his own mind about his locality.

As the country was an unexplored region, he might be on a river that flowed into the Pacific, or he might be drifting down a stream that was an affluent to the Gulf of Mexico. He was, however, inclined to believe that he was on the sources of the Red river. He therefore resolved to launch his canoe, and go wherever the stream might convey him, trapping on his descent, when beaver might be plenty. The first canoe that he used he made of buffalo skins. As these kind of water conveyances soon begin to leak and rot,[1] he made another of cotton-wood, as soon as he came to timber sufficiently large, in which he embarked for a port, he knew not where. The most of his journeyings Captain Williams performed during the hours of night, except when he felt it perfectly safe to travel in daylight. His usual plan was to glide along down the stream, until he came to a place where beaver signs were abundant. There he would push his little bark to the shore, into some eddy among the willows, where he remained concealed, except when he was setting his traps or visiting them in the morning. He always set his traps between sun-set and dark, and visited them at the earliest break of day. When he had taken all the beaver in one neighborhood, he would untie his little conveyance and glide onward and downward to try his luck in another place.

Thus, for hundreds of miles did this solitary trapper float down this

---

[1] Buffalo-skin boats needed to be removed frequently from the water and dried, or else covered with pitch or tar. See R. G. Thwaites (ed.), "Brackenridge's 'Journal,'" *Early Western Travels* (Cleveland, 1904), vol. VI, p. 86; and Patrick Gass, *Journal* . . . (Minneapolis, 1958), p. 126. Coyner mentions the need to dry these boats in Chapter 13.

unknown river, through an unknown country, here and there lashing his canoe to the willows and planting his traps in the little tributaries around. The upper part of the Arkansas (for this proved to be the river upon which he was trapping) is very destitute of timber, and the prairie frequently begins at the bank of the river and expands on either side as far as the eye can see. Captain Williams saw vast herds of buffalo, and as it was running season, the bulls were making a wonderful ado, making the plains roll with their low, deep grunting or bellowing, tearing up the earth with their feet and horns, whisking their tails, and defying their rivals to battle. Often they would come together in fierce battle, with a fury and force that reminded the spectator of the collision of two steamboats. Smaller game was also seen by Captain Williams in great abundance. Large gangs of wild horses could be frequently seen grazing on the plains and hill sides. As it was the spring of the year, the neighing and squealing of the stallions might be heard at all times of a still night. Captain Williams never used his rifle to procure meat, except when it was absolutely necessary, and when it could be done with perfect safety. On one occasion, when he had no beaver flesh, upon which he generally subsisted, he killed a deer, and after refreshing an empty stomach with a portion of it, he placed the carcass, which he had cut up, in one end of his canoe. As it was his invariable custom to sleep in his canoe, the night after he had laid in a supply of venison he was startled in his sleep by the trampling of something in the bushes on the bank. Tramp, tramp, tramp went the footstep, as it approached the canoe. Captain Williams first thought it might be an Indian that had found out his locality, but an Indian would not approach him in that careless manner. Although there was a beautiful star-light, yet the shade of the trees and a dense undergrowth, made it very dark on the bank of the river. Captain Williams always adopted the precaution of tieing his canoe to shore with a piece of raw hide about twenty feet long, which let it swing from the bank about that distance. This precaution he adopted at night, that in an emergency he might cut the cord that bound him to the shore, and glide off without any noise. During the day he hid his canoe in the willows. As the sound of the footsteps grew more and more distinct, the captain observed a huge grizzly bear approach the edge of the water and hold up its head as if scenting something. He then let his huge body into the water and made for the canoe. Captain Williams snatched up his axe as the most suitable means of defending himself in such a scrape, and stood with it uplifted and ready to drive it into the head of the huge aggressor. The bear reached the canoe, and immediately placed his fore paws upon the hind end of it, and nearly turned it over. Captain Williams struck one of his feet with the edge of his axe, which caused him to relax his hold with that foot. He, however, held on with the other foot, and Captain Williams inflicted another blow upon his head, which caused him to let the canoe go entirely. Captain Williams thought the bear sunk in the water, from the stunning effects of the blow, and was drowned. He saw nothing more of him, nor did he hear any thing. The presumption was, he went under the water. His aim was to get at the fresh meat in the captain's canoe. The next morning there were two of the bear's claws in the canoe, that had been severed from one of his feet by Captain Williams' axe. They were carefully preserved by the resolute captain for a number of years, as a trophy which he was fond of exhibiting, and the history of which he delighted to detail.

We have said that Captain Williams subsisted principally upon the flesh of the beaver, which he caught in his traps. This animal, when the hide is taken off and dressed, weighs about twelve pounds, and its flesh, although a little musky, is very fine. Its tail, which is eight or ten inches long, is flat and oval in its form, and is covered with scales about the size of those of a salmon fish. It is a great dainty in the estimation of the mountain trapper.[2] He separates it from the body of the beaver, thrusts a stick in one end of it, and places it before the fire with the scales on it. When the heat of the fire strikes through so as to roast it, large blisters rise on the surface, which are very easily removed. The tail is then perfectly white, and very delicious. Next to the tail is the liver. This is another favorite dainty with the trapper, and when prop-

---

[2] "A beaver of average size weighs between thirty and forty pounds, but fifty- or sixty-pound adults are not uncommon." Robert G. Cleland, *This Reckless Breed of Men: The Trappers and Fur Traders of the Southwest* (New York, 1950), p. 11. Coyner's description of trapping methods and of beaver is generally sound, perhaps because he obtained his information from former trappers. The beaver tail, all agreed, was a delicacy, and Lewis and Clark recorded that it was large enough "to afford a plentiful meal for two men."

erly cooked, constitutes a delightful repast in the eye of these mountain epicures. This animal is exceedingly wily, and is sometimes too
cunning for the most experienced trapper. If, by scent, or sound, or
sight, he has any intimation of the presence of a trapper, he puts at
defiance all his traps. The trapper, therefore, finds it necessary to practice great caution when in the neighborhood of a beaver lodge. He
avoids riding over the ground, lest the sound created by the feet of his
horse might strike dismay among the furry inhabitants beneath the
surface. Instead of walking on the ground, he wades in the water, lest
he might leave a scent behind by which he might be discovered. He
also plants his traps under the surface of the water, where they can be
neither seen nor smelt. But one kind of bait is used, because no other
kinds are needed, and this kind is the best. The beaver has two pair of
testicles, one containing the semen, by which he propagates his race,
and the other containing the matter that gives to his body the musky
smell that is peculiar to it. These testicles are opened, and their contents are put in separate horns, which the trapper carries by his side.[3]
When he uses it for bait, he thrusts a small stick in both of his horns,
about an inch deep in the matter, and then plants it upright in the
water, between the jaws of the trap, leaving the baited end of it several
inches above the surface of the water. A natural propensity prompts
the beaver to seek the place whence the scent issues, and he is taken.
In this respect the beaver resembles the dog, that always seeks to smell
the place where one of his kind may have spent his urine. It is worthy
of notice, that the beaver feeds exclusively on the bark of trees and
shrubs, whilst the otter lives on fish and reptiles; the consequence is,
the flesh of the former is very fine, whilst that of the latter is very offensive to the taste. An experienced trapper always aims so to set his
traps as to drown the beaver when they are taken. This is accomplished
by sinking the trap several inches under water, and driving a stake
through a ring on the end of the chain, into the bottom. When a beaver
finds himself fastened in a trap, he pitches and plunges about until his

---

[3] Castoreum, obtained from scent glands located beneath the skin in front of
the genital organs of both sexes, served as a common lure. It was often mixed
with nutmegs, cloves, or cinnamon to give it extra pungency. Semen, however,
was not used. Branches of green poplar or cottonwood also made effective bait.

strength is exhausted when he sinks down and is drowned. If a beaver succeeds in getting to shore, he always extricates himself by cutting off the leg that is in the trap.

This animal is furnished with several large front teeth that are curved, by which he is enabled to cut down trees that are from six to twelve inches in diameter. Armed with these formidable tusks, he will cut a dog that ventures upon him, immediately into pieces. They bestow a great deal of labor and pains, in the construction of their dams, and generally make them so firm that a man may pass over them on horseback with perfect safety. The last thing that I shall state, at present, by way of description of the beaver is, that his fur, which is of the finest quality and remarkably thick on the hide, very much resembles in color, the fur of our common wild rabbit.

But let us return to our solitary trapper, as we find him gliding about in his cotton-wood canoe on the bosom of an unknown river, upon the banks of which, no white man had ever been present, to leave his foot-prints behind him. We confess that we never contemplate this part of Captain Williams' history but with a feeling of astonishment, as well as unrestrained curiosity. What contempt of danger, or rather superiority to it! What zealous perseverance in the prosecution of his purposes; and at the same time, what caution and constant vigilance must he have practised, to avoid being discovered by the natives. For several months, he was certain, that no eye saw him, but that of his God, nor did he see the face of a fellow-being, civilized or savage. He communed with none but his own heart, nor did his eyes rest upon the face of any mortal, except that of himself, as it was reflected back from the surface of those wild waters. Day after day did he add to his stock of rich peltries; but day after day passed away without bringing any light as to the destiny before him. Week after week had he descended this river, and no frontier cabin greeted his return. Wildness and solitude still reigned every where. But Captain Williams was a man of as much patience as fortitude, and possessed a cheerful disposition, that made him look upon the "sunny side" of every thing, and "always hoped for the best." Solitary as he was, and exposed to danger all the time, he frequently spoke of this kind of life as having its peculiar attractions.

But it would have been a miracle if he had entirely escaped the observation of the savages. Circumstances occurred that led to his discovery, and threw him into their clutches. As he was descending the river, with his peltries, which consisted of one hundred and twenty-five beaver-skins, besides some skins of otter and other smaller animals of the fur-bearing race, all of which he had procured since he parted with Workman and Spencer, he overtook three Kansas Indians, who were also in a canoe descending the river as he learned from them to some post, to trade with the whites. They manifested a very friendly disposition toward Captain Williams, and expressed a wish to accompany him down the river. He learned from them, to his great gratification, that he was on the Big Arkansas, and not more than five hundred miles from the whites. By this time Captain Williams had learned how much confidence he could repose in Indians and their professions of friendship. He had learned enough to know that they would not let a solitary trapper pass through their country, with a valuable collection of furs, without, at least, making an effort to rob him. The plan of these Kansas would be to decoy him into a friendly intercourse with them, and then, the first suitable opportunity to strip him of every thing he had. He resolved, therefore, to get rid of them as soon as possible, and to effect this, he plied his oars with all diligence. The Indians, like the most of their lazy race, had no disposition to belabor themselves in this way: but took it more leisurely, being satisfied to be carried along by the current of the water. Captain Williams soon left them, as he supposed, far behind him, and when night came on, as he had labored hard all day, and slept none the night before, he resolved to turn aside into the willows to take a few hours of sleep. But he had stopped scarcely thirty minutes before he heard some Indians pull to shore just above on the same side of the river. He immediately renewed his fire, loosed his canoe from shore, and glided smoothly and silently off and away, and rowed hard and faithfully for two or three hours, when he again put to shore and tied up.

But again, a short time after he had landed, he heard some Indians going in to shore on the same side and just above him. A second time the vigilant captain slipt out from the willows, and glided stealthily away from that dangerous ground, and pulled ahead with great industry until some time after midnight, when he supposed he could with safety stop to snatch a morsel of repose. Captain Williams was apprehensive that he was in a dangerous region; the anxiety of his mind, therefore, kept him awake, and it was a lucky circumstance, for as he lay in his canoe, invoking sleep, he heard for the third time a canoe land, as before. He was now satisfied that he was dogged by the Kansas whom he had passed the day before. In no very good humor, therefore, Captain Williams snatched up his rifle and walked up the bank to the place where he had heard the canoe land. As he suspected, they were the three Kansas, and when they saw the captain they renewed their expressions of friendship, and wished him to partake of their hospitality. Captain Williams stood aloof from them, and shook his head in anger, and charged them with their villainous purposes. In the short, sententious manner of the Indians, he said to them "you now follow me three times; if you follow me again, I kill you," and wheeled about abruptly and returned to his canoe. A third time our solitary trapper pushed his little craft from land, and set off down stream, to get away from a region where to sleep would be extremely hazardous. Captain Williams faithfully plied his oars the balance of the night, and solaced himself with the thought that he was very lucky, when no evil had befallen him, except the loss of a few hours of sleep. But whilst he was escaping from the villainous pursuers behind him, he was running into new dangers and difficulties. The following day he overtook a large company of the same tribe (Kansas), headed by a chief, who was also descending the river. Into the hands of these Indians he fell a prisoner, and was conducted to one of their villages.[4] The principal chief took all of his furs and traps, and all his chattels. A very short time after this, the Kansas went to war with the Pawnees, and took Captain Williams with them. In a battle in which the Kansas gained a most decided victory, Captain Williams acted a distinguished part, killed a number of Pawnees, and, indeed, by his very efficient services, caused the affair to terminate in favor of the Kansas. When they returned to the Kansas village, the captain, who had always been treated with kindness, was now thought to be a great brave, and could have been advanced to all

[4] Kansas Indians captured Williams about 150 miles from the Verdigris on June 23, 1813, and held him until mid August. See Editor's Introduction.

79

their honors, and been made one of their principal chiefs. But, as the Kansas had set him at liberty for the services he had rendered them, in their late difficulty with a formidable and inveterate foe, he determined to return to the white settlement on the Missouri.

But they retained his furs, and indeed all his chattels except his rifle, with as many rounds of ammunition as would be necessary to secure him provisions along his route. Captain Williams was the more reconciled to the loss of his furs, as he believed the Indians would preserve them with a view of taking them to a trading post, where he formed the purpose of being present to secure them again. As to the furs that were *cached* before he parted with Workman and Spencer, he intended to return for them as soon as he could get a sufficient number of men to accompany him. As Captain Williams knew not where he was at the time he *cached* his furs, whilst he was with the Kansas he was able to procure some facts in relation to the country that were of value to him. When he left the Platte, which he supposed to be the Arkansas, he descended a stream that interlocked with the main branch of the Platte, and is an affluent to the Big Arkansas.[5] They *cached* their furs near the mouth of this stream. Here, and indeed for a long distance below, the Rocky mountains are to be distinctly seen, covered with perpetual snow. When he separated from Workman and Spencer, they set off up a stream emptying also into the Arkansas, (supposing it to be the main stream) and coming from the south. This proved to be what, in those days, was called the third fork of the Arkansas,[6] on the west side. The captain also learned, whilst with the Kansas, that they expected to repair, the following spring, to Fort Osage,[7] on the Missouri river, to receive some annuities due them from the United States, and he knew that his furs would be found there at that time. There was a fort of

[5] Perhaps Coyner had in mind Fountain Creek which flows into the Arkansas at present-day Pueblo.

[6] St. Charles River which empties into the Arkansas to the east of Pueblo. Zebulon Pike identified it as the "third fork" and thought it a good route to Santa Fe. Jackson (ed.), *Journals of Pike*, vol. I, p. 349.

[7] Fort Osage, built in 1808, was designed as a government-sponsored trading post or factory for the Kansas and Osage Indians. It was located about forty miles below the mouth of the Kansas River.

white men at that time, called Cooper's Fort,[8] somewhere on the side of the Missouri opposite the post of trade where the Kansas expected to assemble. He therefore set off for that point on the Missouri, to be ready, the following spring, to regain, if he could, his peltries that were in the hands of the Kansas.

[8] Cooper's Fort, a stockade surrounded by log houses, was built during the War of 1812 by Colonel Benjamin Cooper to protect a settlement near present-day Glasgow, on the Missouri, in the Boon's Lick country downriver from Fort Osage.

Chapter 12

Mixing and intermarrying between white and red men—A numerous hybrid race—The consequence, an improved race—Captain Williams in great perplexity and somewhat frightened—A mysterious affair—Reaches Fort Cooper—Cibley secures the lost furs to Captain Williams.

Oₙ ᴛʜᴇ ᴏᴜᴛꜱᴋɪʀᴛꜱ of civilized society then, as now on the frontier of the West, there has always been a certain motley class of men, trappers, traders, renegadoes, and refugees from justice, who seem to have become disgusted with the tameness and monotony of civilized life, and made exiles of themselves, by going where the restraints and the security of laws are not felt. For these men, who by the way are very numerous, savage life seems to have its peculiar charms. They take to themselves wives, and domesticate themselves among the different tribes in the west, and live and die among them. If one of these men should happen to return to the abodes of his white brethren, he feels like a fish out of water, and is impatient and restless, and seeks the earliest opportunity to get back to the country of his choice. The result of this intermixing and intermarrying, has been the springing up of a numerous hybrid race of beings, that constitute a medium, through which, it is hoped, at no distant day, the laws, arts, and habitudes of civilized life may be successfully introduced among the tribes of the west, and be the means of reclaiming them from the ignorance and barbarities in which they have been so long enthralled.

These half-breeds are already very numerous, and it is difficult to distinguish them from white men; for they seem just as intelligent, and just as decent as to their exterior; and speak our language just as fluently, as our own citizens, and really vary but little from them in the color of the skin. As Captain Williams was journeying from the Arkansas to the Missouri, he met with one of those white men, that had taken up his residence among the Osages, and was to some extent, engaged in an effort to teach that tribe how to cultivate the soil. He had married quite a good looking squaw, with whom he was living, and by whom he had several black-eyed little children. He had erected two or three comfortable cabins, around which he had several acres of ground under cultivation. Captain Williams came upon his residence late in the evening, and was received by him with a real backwoods hospitality. As he was much fatigued, he stayed with him that night. It was now late in the fall, and the cold winds had already began to sweep over those extensive prairies. He was not only fatigued, but hungry, and after enjoying a very abundant repast, he became very sleepy and stupid, and expressed a wish to lie down. The landlord accordingly conducted him to one of the cabins, in which there were two beds, standing in opposite corners of the room. Captain Williams threw himself upon one of the beds, and was soon in a very deep sleep. About midnight, his slumbers were disturbed by a singular and very frightful kind of noise, accompanied by struggling on the other bed, in the opposite corner of the room. What it was, the captain was entirely at a loss to understand. There were no windows in the cabin to furnish any light, the door was shut, and it was as dark as Egypt.[1] A fierce contest seemed to be going on. There were deep groans and hard breathings; the snapping and gritting of teeth was constantly going on. Occasional struggling took place, in which great muscular power seemed to be employed. For a moment the noise would subside, with drawing the breath, at long intervals, as if death was taking place. Then again the struggling and scuffling would be renewed, accompanied as before with groaning and deep sighing and grinding of the teeth, and the exercise, it would seem, of great physical power. The bed clothes, that

[1] Apparently a reference to the "ninth plague" in which the Lord had Moses darken Egypt to force Pharaoh to let the Israelites go. *Exodus* 10:21.

consisted of a blanket or two and a buffalo robe, were pulled about and very much torn. At last slam-bang the whole mysterious affair fell upon the floor, and carried on in the same frightful and unearthly way. Captain Williams stated that in all his difficulties with the savages, his fortitude had never been so fairly tested, as on this night. *"To be able to see danger,"* said he, "takes away at least one half of its terror." But here was a mysterious, formidable, invisible something, which he could not *see*. He did not know where to find the door, as he had forgotten where it was. As for his rifle, that had often saved his life, he now recollected, that he had left her in the cabin occupied by the family. He had a knife, but it was attached to his hunting coat, which he had hung on the corner of the other bedstead, but the danger was between him and his knife.

For a moment the sounds would subside as in death, and then again every power seemed to be wakened up, and the same unseen and mysterious and dreadful tragedy repeated. All over the floor it shifted about, until it got under the bed of Captain Williams. Here, as by convulsive efforts, it lifted the bed, with the perplexed captain on it, off the floor several times; and after belaboring itself dreadfully for several minutes, it moved rather to the side of the bed. Captain Williams then raised himself to a sitting position on the bed, and threw around him a buffalo skin, to protect himself, if an effort should be made to injure him; but in an instant the skin was snatched and pulled off, and the captain left uncovered and unprotected, at least so far as a buffalo robe might prove a shield. Another violent snatch took away a blanket upon which the captain was seated, and nearly took him with it. As the next thing might be a blow in the dark, he *felt*, as he jocularly remarked (if he could not *see*) that it was high time to shift his quarters. So he made a desperate leap from his bed, and alighted on the opposite side of the room, and called for the landlord, who came immediately to his relief by opening the door. The captain told him the devil, or something as bad, he believed, was in the room, and he wanted a light. The accommodating host hurried back, and in a moment returned with a light, that soon revealed the awful mystery. It was an Indian, who, at the time, was struggling in convulsions, which he, it appears, was in the habit of having. He was an old chief, who the captain ascertained to be a relative of the wife of the land-lord, and generally made his home there. Being absent when the captain arrived, he came in at a late hour, when all were asleep, and repaired to the bed he usually occupied. It was not known to any one that he was on the premises, until he was found in the above miserable condition. The poor fellow had dreadfully mangled himself by tearing his flesh, particularly his arms, with his teeth. His nose, which was uncommonly large, was much bruised and skinned. He was removed out of the cabin, and our guest, who was not to be frightened out of a night's rest, soon again sunk into a profound repose. Captain Williams reached Cooper's fort in the beginning of winter, which was at that time occupied by a few white men, having been absent one year and eight months.[2]

When Captain Williams reached Cooper's fort, he learned that a United States' factor, (trader) C. Cibley,[3] was expected from St. Louis that winter, to go up to fort Osage to meet the Osages and Kansas, and pay them their annuities. Mr. Cibley came up the Missouri as far as Cooper's fort, but was not able to get to fort Osage, on account of the ice and the severity of the winter. The Indians were therefore compelled to come down the river to a place now called Arrow Rock,[4] where they were met by Mr. Cibley. Captain Williams was present, and there met the very Indian chief that had robbed him of his furs on the Arkansas. The agent of the United States had already been apprised of the whole affair, and informed the Kansas chief that as Mr. Williams was a citizen of the government for which he was acting, he would not pay them their annuities, unless they returned the furs properly belonging to Mr. Williams. They at first were unwilling to admit their villainy, but Mr. Cibley was very positive and determined, and finally succeeded in bringing them to an acknowledgment of the deed. In compliance with the orders of the agent, the guilty-looking fellow sneaked off to their lodges to bring out the furs, and returned with four pack-

---

[2] By Coyner's reckoning, Williams would have returned around December 25, 1809. In fact, he reached the Missouri in the autumn of 1813 after an absence of over four years.

[3] George C. Sibley, then U.S. Factor at Fort Osage.

[4] Sibley's letter to Clark (Editor's Introduction) confirms that the meeting occurred at Arrow Rock. Coyner's account, which follows, seems somewhat overdone.

ages, which Captain Williams proved by the initials of his name, E. W., which were on them. The agent inquired if that was all. Captain Williams replied, there were eight more. The fraudulent chief said there were *no* more. Mr. Cibley peremptorily demanded the whole of the furs. Three more packages were then brought out, which the chief affirmed made up the number he had taken. Mr. Cibley gave them every assurance that he would not pay them their annuities, if they did not comply with his orders. One after another three of the bales of skins were reluctantly brought forward, until they numbered eleven. Mr. Cibley demanded the twelfth, but "it could not be found," said the Indian chief. "But it must be found," said Cibley. The old Kansas chief went away, and after an absence of an hour, during which time he was busy searching among the lodges for the lost pack, returned and told Mr. Cibley that "*he could not find it,* and he believed that *God Almighty could not find it,*" by which he meant to be understood, that such a bale of fur did not exist. Captain Williams, who was much amused with the answer of the chief, suggested to Mr. Cibley the great probability that one of the packages might have been lost, and stated, furthermore, that he would not insist upon their returning it. Here the matter ended, and in the end it resulted to the great advantage of Mr. Williams, as he got rid of the very difficult job of conveying his peltries to the Missouri river.

The following spring Captain Williams took his furs down the Missouri and sold them in St. Louis, and then returned to Cooper's fort, for the purpose of raising a body of men to go with him for the furs he had *cached* on an upper tributary of the Great Arkansas.

Chapter 13

Captain Williams met with difficulty in raising another party—
Camanches and their horsemanship, and way of fighting on horseback—On 25th of December Joseph and William Cooper set out
with Captain Williams—Fort Osage, Osage river—Neasho river—
Their sufferings—Want of food—Walnuts—They kill eight squirrels.
Indian camps and Osage Indians—An Indian squaw prepares a
repast for the men—One of the men faints—Kill two buffalo bulls—
Strong wind—Wild horses—Wolves, their nature—A poor little
wolf and a fat coon—An old wild stud killed—His meat rank—They
reach the *caches*—Kill their horses—Kill six buffalo—Make bull
boat—Suffering from cold—The Plum thicket—A band of wolves
after a bull—A prayer-book is burnt—Party discovered by Camanches—Move to another thicket—Set off down the river—Again
reach the Missouri.

THE GLOOMY and melancholy account that Captain Wil-
liams had to give of his expedition, and the horrible representations
that he was compelled to make of the great majority of the western
tribes, was by no means favorable to Captain Williams' purpose of
raising a body of men to accompany him back to the mountains, for
his furs were *cached* where the Great Arkansas issues from the Rocky
Mountains. Nor did his accounts as to the great abundance of valuable
furs in those regions seem to have much effect. The most dreadful
stories had been told about the savage cruelty of the piratical Sioux,

the ferocity of the ruthless Black-feet, and the treachery of the thieving
and dishonest Crows, and they were most abundantly confirmed by
the fate of Captain Williams' party. His furs, too, were in a country
infested by bands of marauding Camanches, a tribe that was not behind any other tribe in the far west in point of strength and ferocity.
They were represented as the best horsemen in the world, and as
having the fleetest horses. Their mode of fighting was always on
horseback, and they would hang by one leg on the withers of their
horses, throw themselves on one side, so as to make a breast-work of
their horses, and shoot their arrows from under their necks whilst their
horses were at full speed. And they could shoot an arrow completely
through a man, horse, or buffalo, with all ease. Again, a body of men
should be large to go through those regions of danger, and such a body
could not be raised any where above St. Louis, as there were very few
white people at that day above said town.

These were the difficulties which met Captain Williams, whenever he
made an effort to collect men to go with him. The summer passed away
and autumn came on, and not a single man as yet had agreed to go;
and it was not until the latter part of December that two young men
informed Captain Williams they would join him. They were very
young, and as there was a strong probability that their friends would
interfere, and persuade them to abandon a trip so very dangerous, the
captain found it to be good policy to start within two or three days
after they consented to go. On the 25th of December the old veteran
trapper, with his two youthful companions, Joseph and William
Cooper left Cooper's fort, again to brave the perils of the wilderness.[1]
They set out on horses, with ten day's provisions, and traveled up the
Missouri to fort Osage, where they left the river and went a southwest
course until they struck the Osage river. Here they found fine grass for
their horses. In the prairies there was a deep snow, and the wind blew
very cold. Leaving the Osage, they journeyed a west course until they
came to the Neasho [Neosho] river, which is an affluent to the Great

[1] Coyner neglects Williams' first attempt to retrieve his furs, when he left
Cooper's Fort for the Arkansas in May 1814 with B. Cooper, May, and Philibert's
party. The journey here described may be a rough approximation of Williams'
second journey to the Arkansas, which did occur in the winter of 1814-15.

Arkansas, and interlocks with the tributaries of the Kansas. Two days before they reached the above river, their provisions failed, and not a living thing was to be seen on the face of the earth; if there had been any game, they probably could not have secured it, as there was a thick, hard crust on a deep snow that covered the prairie, and when they walked on it, it created a cracking sound that could have been heard a great distance. They encamped before night in a walnut grove on the bottom of the river, wearied, cold, and weak from hunger. For two days, traveling over bleak prairies, pierced with merciless winds, they had nothing to eat.

The thought presented itself to their minds, that there might be walnuts under the trees composing the grove where they were encamped. They therefore immediately began to remove the crusted snow and found this fruit very abundant; and whilst they were busily cracking nuts, the sun came out from behind some dark winter clouds, and shone warm and beautiful, and the party were cheered with the sight of some squirrels that made their appearance. They succeeded in killing eight of them, and ate three of them that night. The next day they resumed their journey, and trudged along for three days, having nothing on which to subsist but five of the eight squirrels they had killed. On the fourth day they came to the Verdigris, another tributary of the Great Arkansas, and found two Indian camps. They were the Osages, who had been out on a buffalo hunt, but their supply of provisions was scanty. They, however, manifested a very friendly disposition, and very promptly furnished the men with something to eat. Men as hungry as they were, are not disposed to be very fastidious as to what they eat, or the manner in which it may be prepared and served up. A squaw, for the purpose of cleaning a wooden bowl, set it out of the lodge that the dogs might lick it, and when this was done by the canine part of the house-hold, it was filled with a kind of porridge, in which there was meat and Indian corn. To season this, an old snaggle-toothed squaw added some small pieces of buffalo tallow. As she labored under the disadvantage of not having a knife to cut it, she resorted to the expedient of *gnawing off* piece after piece and *spitting* it into the bowl.

On the next day Captain Williams and his two men left the lodges of the Osages, taking with them five quarts of corn, which they parched, to eat along the way. After traveling two or three days, William Cooper fainted on the prairie, from hunger and fatigue; but Captain Williams and Joseph Cooper carried him to a point of timber where they raised a fire. Here fresh buffalo signs were abundant, and Williams and J. Cooper went out and killed two bulls. They took as much meat as they could carry to camp, and when they had all eaten of it, their faces as well as their prospects seemed to brighten up, and they felt ready as well as renewed for the resumption of their journey. For seven or eight days they continued to go westward, being favored with good weather, except one day the wind blew so hard from the west that they were compelled to stop, as they could not get along against it. About the fifth of February another snow fell, and the weather turned intensely cold. The little party had been traveling on the north side of the Arkansas; they now crossed that river, to reach a warmer climate. They report the cold as being so great, that it was with difficulty that they saved their horses from being frozen to death. Continuing a south-west course, within a day or two they came to a region where there was no snow, and grass was very abundant. A great many wild horses were to be seen on the prairies, elevating their heads and tails when the men would approach them, and snorting, and wheeling, and curveting around. They were of all colors. Large gangs, also, of buffalo and elk were feeding about, and on the outskirts of the buffalo herds there were the usual appendages: that is, bands of hungry wolves sitting about, watching the buffalo. Encouraged by numbers, and mad from hunger they frequently make the most desperate assaults upon the buffalo, and even run down deer. Whilst in this region of good weather, grass and game, the party lived high and were in good cheer. When they wanted meat they would kill the buffalo cows, which were very fat and fine. But the weather turned cold; as they approached the mountains, the buffalo disappeared, and there was nothing to be seen but wild horses and restless packs of wolves gadding about, pinched with cold and hunger. It is an old saying, *"Canis non est canem,"* (dog does not eat dog).[2] The same may be said of wolves. *Lupus non est*

---

[2] Coyner's Latin seems to have become rusty. One of my colleagues, Professor Jon Sutherland, reports that Coyner should have said "canis non edit canem."

lupum, (wolf does not eat wolf). Yet their ravenous propensity is so great as to prompt them to attack every thing else but their own race.

Captain Williams and his men again found themselves destitute of provisions, in the midst of winter, and suffering from hunger. When they looked out upon an ocean of prairie, they could see nothing but a little half-starved wolf, that frequently came to gnaw some buffalo bones. Hunger constrained them to shoot it. "Within ten minutes," say the notes of their journal, "his hide was taken off and some of the meat was cooked and ready to be eaten." They speak of his flesh as having a good flavor, and being very refreshing to their hungry stomachs. They also cleaned his entrails, and carefully preserved them for future necessities. Such are the means to which the early adventurers in that country were compelled to resort to prevent starving to death.

The party also procured a racoon, which being fat, made a fine repast. One day an old wild stud was seen by the men, pawing the ice to get to water, at a considerable distance from the party, in the prairie. J. Cooper took the advantage of some sand hills, and got within one hundred and forty yards, (as he supposed) when the horse trotted up within eighty yards, and received a shot in the bulge of the ribs, which only caused him to snort and prance about for the moment. Cooper then shot him the second time, in the point of one of his shoulders, which made him run off a short distance, and lie down. Cooper was so weak from hunger that he was compelled to make a rest of his gun stick and wiping stick, before he could hold up his gun with sufficient firmness to shoot with any degree of accuracy. Captain Williams observing the inefficiency of Cooper's shots, came up and shot the horse in the head. They skinned him, and supped upon his flesh. His hide they preserved for tugs to bind up their furs, as they were now only a short distance from the *caches.* This flesh, to some extent satisfied the cravings of their hungry appetites, but it was very coarse and strong, and as they expressed themselves, "not fit for a white man to eat." It would remain in the stomach for a long time, in a state of indigestion, and for several days, (eight or ten they said), "they belched up the old stud as strong as ever."

They reached the *caches* about the 10th of March. They found them undiscovered by wolves or Indians, and of course undisturbed. Up to this time they had lost none of their horses, and now that they had reached the point, both of place and time, beyond which they would not have much need of their services, they were not much concerned about their preservation. Indeed, as they intended to take their furs down the river, and as their horses might betray them into the hands of Indians, the safety of the party required that they should get rid of them, some way. It would not be safe to turn them loose. They would wander about, be picked up by the Indians, and lead to their discovery. They, therefore, determined to shoot them, and preserve by drying some of their flesh, and throw them into the river.

Within a day or two, after they reached the *caches*, a herd of buffalo made their appearance, but on the opposite (north) side of the river. They were moving toward their camp. The men crossed the river, and met them about eight miles from camp, and killed six of them. They skinned three of them, and took as much meat as they could carry with the three hides back to their camp. By the time, however, they had finished the work of skinning and cutting night came on, and they were compelled to spend the night in the prairie without fire. They broke some of the bones of the buffalo and procured a supply of marrow, upon which they supped, in its raw state. They thought it a great luxury. But their bedding was at their camp, and they could get no wood to make a fire, as the timber on that side of the river seemed, at least, twenty miles off. In this emergency, they spread one of the raw hides on the ground, upon which they stretched themselves, whilst they used another of the hides for a covering. But as the weather was very cold, their covering froze very hard and would not fit down and around them. The consequence was, the cold wind blew under their covering, and they suffered greatly from cold during the night. The next morning very early they returned, crossing the river to the south side to their encampment. They now went to work to construct what are called bull-boats, to convey their fur down the river, when the spring rise should come down, caused by the melting of the snow in the Rocky Mountains. This kind of boat is made by stretching a green buffalo hide over a light frame of willows or some other wood. It is then turned up to the sun to dry before it is launched. It is a very convenient kind of water craft, and answers a good purpose, where timber cannot be had to make canoes. In crossing streams that cannot be forded, they are generally used, as they are very easily constructed, and made in a very short time. They, however, very soon begin to leak, and it is necessary to take them out of the water and dry them.[3] In a few days they begin to rot and are of no farther use. Williams and the two Coopers made three boats of this kind, and after drying them, concealed them so as to have them ready for the spring freshet.

As there was no rise in the Arkansas that spring, our little party for the sake of greater security, went down the river to a large plum thicket, into which they crept. In the centre of this fastness they cut away the brush so as to open a place spacious enough to allow them to lodge there at night. They also opened a narrow path from the centre to the outside to admit of their passing in and out. At the same time they cut a small hack-berry bush which they made to answer the purpose of a gate. At night it was placed in this narrow path, and made it perfectly impassable. In the morning it was rolled out of the path upon the thicket. Here they took up their residence, until the river should rise, or some marauding band of Indians should find them. Whilst here, and at a time when they were almost destitute of anything to eat, as they were lounging about the border of the plum thicket, peering over the prairies, they saw at a great distance a large bull attacked by two wolves; he was coming toward the thicket, and as he passed the men the number of the wolves had increased to about fifty. He betook himself to the river, which was but a few steps from the camp. The wolves dashed into the water after him. As the river was very low and the water shallow, no part of him was covered but his legs, sometimes he was covered with the wolves gnawing him in every part. At last they cut his ham-strings, which caused him to sink down. The men then shot the buffalo and drove away the wolves and took possession of his carcass.

During their imprisonment in this thicket one day seemed as long as four, as they had no way to amuse themselves, and were compelled to spend day after day, and night after night, in and about their sequestered lodge. They were in a region full of danger, as they fre-

[3] See p. 73

quently saw Indians on the prairie. Joseph Cooper had a small prayer-book, that he read every day to his two companions, and in the evening he was in the habit of sticking it up in the fork of a little hackberry tree. It would appear that the lessons read from the prayerbook were not very acceptable to the company, as one morning the book was found in the ashes and burnt. Joseph Cooper seemed not to miss his book, but occasionally recited from his memory an exercise equally as dry and tasteless as the book.

After being there about twenty long days, the monotony of the place was interrupted by three Camanches, who discovered the men, and shot several arrows at them before they got into their place of security. Two of the Indians remained to watch the men, whilst the other one put off to communicate the news to their party. During the absence of the one, Captain Williams spoke to the two that stood as guard about sixty yards from the thicket, and such were the answers he received, that he went to them and succeeded in getting them to the camp. The men gave them the best they had to eat, and got them in a very pleasant and talkative mood. About three hours after they saw a great fog or dust, and after a little time they discovered that it was made by many Indians on horse-back. They came ready for battle, naked, except a flap, and furnished with bows and arrows and arrow-fenders or shields. When they came within forty yards of the camp they were met by the two that had remained at the camp, and after a talk among them that lasted about five minutes, they dismounted and stripped their horses to remain there all night. Having regulated matters about their camp, they went to that of Captain Williams. They had a great curiosity to know something about the white man's gun, which they had never seen before.[4] They expressed a wish to see it used, and made a small circle, which they drew with a piece of charcoal on a piece of cottonwood, at which Captain Williams shot to show them the dexterity of the white man in the use of the rifle. The captain shot and nearly drove the centre of the circle. They were delighted with the performance, and expressed a wish to see the other men shoot. Captain Williams told

[4] It seems unlikely that after a century of exposure to Spaniards and French traders a group of Comanches could be found who had not seen "the white man's gun."

them that these two men would put their balls just *there,* pointing at the same time to the centre.

The party were certainly very fortunate in getting on the right side of these savages. The Camanches are one of the most ferocious and barbarous tribes in the far west, and notorious for their cruelty to those who fall into their hands, and for many years subsequent to that day for being the implacable foes of the white man. The Camanche Indians may be justly called "the terror of the Santa Fe trade." Captain Williams found it necessary, for their escape, to practice some deception upon them. The Camanches were very shortly going to war against the Pawnees, and were actively engaged in preparing for it. This fact the sagacious captain learned from the two that had remained to watch their lodge. He professed to have sustained injuries from that tribe, and to entertain designs of revenging them, and offered to join the Camanches against them. This plan acted like a charm. They treated the three men with much friendship, and informed our men that they were going to one of their villages, and that they would return in four days, and when they returned it was a mutual understanding that the three white men were to accompany them against the Pawnees. The Indians, after spending the night with them, left the next morning. Early the following night our little party hurried away from the place where they had made so narrow an escape. They took the trace made by the Indians down the river, and followed it for several miles. Their policy in doing this was to prevent their own trace from being perceived. They traveled hard that night, and waded the river three or four times, and about sun-rise they reached another large plum thicket on an island in the Arkansas, in the heart of which they opened room for another lodge. Here they laid themselves down to take that rest they so much needed, and a snow fell upon them about three inches deep. Although it was the latter part of April, the proximity of this region to the Rocky Mountains made the weather at that time of the year quite cold. They were afraid to move, as there was a snow on the ground, and therefore remained not only that day, but that night also, wrapped up in their buffalo robes under the snow, without fire or any thing to eat.

They remained on this island until the middle of June, during which they found a plenty of game on the island for their purposes. They then started back up the river, which was then rising, went to their *caches*, raised their fur, and set off with it with all haste down the river, in their bull-boats. They glided along smoothly and quietly for ten days, when they were compelled to stop and dry their boats. After starting for the second time, and traveling a few miles, they saw a large company of Indians, who had been encamped a short distance from the bank of the river, and were taking up their lodges to leave. The men glided along under a bluff bank which prevented them from being discovered. Their boats lasted only four days longer, when they began to leak, and the party were compelled to stop and kill buffalo, and make new boats of this kind, as they had not yet come to timber of which canoes could be made. These boats proved to have less durability, than the first they made, as they lasted but nine days, when they were abandoned as useless. By this time, however, they had come to timber, and they went to work with two axes and made two canoes, which they lashed together, and in which they put their furs. In these they resumed their journey, and floated down with the current, without any thing occurring to excite unusual apprehensions of danger, until the fourth day, when they, as they were descending the river, heard below them the report of guns, and the sound of that which seemed to be bells. They therefore pushed their canoes to shore and concealed them by hacking down bushes over them; and remained there until about ten o'clock in the night. They then very cautiously pushed their canoes into the current, and as the night was dark and rain was falling, they passed without being seen by the savages. As it frequently lightened, when they were passing the Indians, they unexpectedly found themselves passing down considerable falls in the Arkansas, of which they had no knowledge. They passed over without any unfavorable accident. Two days journey from these falls they overtook eight Cherokee Indians going down to one of their villages. At first they were very shy and alarmed, but the party laid down their guns and made signs of friendship and they then met Captain Williams and talked with him. He procured from them some salt and tobacco, luxuries by the way, which they had not tasted for the last six months. When the interview ended between the captain and the Indians, they both moved on in their canoes. The Indians showed a disposition to keep with the captain, and the captain knowing the treacherous character of the savages, was as anxious to get rid of them. For two or three days they hung about our little party in spite of all that they could do to prevent it, landing when they would land, and traveling when and only when they would travel.

When they drew near a Cherokee village, these fellows went ahead, as it afterwards appeared, to communicate to their people the fact of these men being on the river, and to prepare to rob them. For when they approached the village, the river was absolutely covered with canoes, playing about on the surface of the water, and a drum and fife were making music; and when Captain Williams' canoes came opposite to their village, the Indians rowed up by the side of them, sprung into them, seized the rifles, claimed the three men as prisoners, and tumbled all the furs out on shore and carried them off. In the meantime Williams and the two Coopers were ordered to follow a large Indian, whilst they were guarded by about fifty with guns. They were conducted about ten miles, to an agent for the United States, a Mr. Lovely,[5] for trial, as they were suspected for being three men who had robbed the Osages, and whom Lovely had authorized to be apprehended. They were detained about three days, when, having satisfied the agent that they were not the men they were supposed to be, they were discharged, and their furs were restored to them.

Down the river Arkansas our three adventurers continued to float in their cotton-wood craft, delighted with their success in escaping all the dangers behind them, and with the prospect of soon being within the limits of the country inhabited by the white man. They soon reached, after passing the Cherokee village, a trading post, not far above what is now the seat of government of Arkansas, where they disposed of their furs for the snug sum of about five thousand dollars,

[5] Cherokees, pushed out of their lands in Georgia and the Carolinas, had begun to move up the Arkansas after 1808. By 1813 they were so numerous that the United States government sent William L. Lovely as an agent to the Cherokees on the Arkansas. John Joseph Mathews, *The Osages: Children of the Middle Waters* (Norman, Okla., 1961), pp. 408-10.

to a white trader, whose name was M. Murry.[6] Those furs would now bring double that amount. From this point they crossed to St. Louis, and from thence up the Missouri back again to Cooper's fort, after an absence of about one year.

[6] Ezekiel Williams finally sold his furs at "Arkansas Post," located about 45 miles above the mouth of the Arkansas, in the late spring or early summer of 1815. Voelker, "Ezekiel Williams," p. 27. I have been unable to identify M. Murry.

Chapter 14

Before we return to the narrative of the events that attended the wanderings of Workman and Spencer, we will furnish a few facts in relation to the Arkansas river and the country through which it passes. This great affluent to the Mississippi, from its mouth to its source, is upwards of two thousand miles in length, and is navigable to the mountains during the spring freshet; at any other time of the year its navigation is extremely uncertain that high up. It has one peculiarity, noticed by all who have seen it, and that is, about two hundred miles from its source it has a deep, navigable stream any season of the year,[1] whilst for an extent of four or five hundred miles below the mountains the bed of the river is wide and a perfect sand-bar, which, in the summer season, is so near dry that the water does not run, but stands about in ponds. The water no doubt sinks. "The borders of the Arkansas river," says one who explored that country in 1807, "may be termed the terrestrial paradise of our territories for

---

[1] This description of the Arkansas and the quotation which follows are taken from *The Journals of Zebulon Montgomery Pike*, edited by Donald Jackson (Norman, Okla., 1966), vol. II, p. 25. Here, Coyner misread Pike who did not say that the upper Arkansas was navigable at any season.

the wandering savages. Of all countries visited by the footsteps of civilized man, there never was one, probably, that produced game in greater abundance, and we know that the manners and morals of those erratic nations are such as never to give them a numerous population; and I believe that there are buffalo, elk and deer sufficient on the banks of the Arkansas alone, if used without waste, to feed all the savages in the United States' territory one century." The above extract is from Pike's journal, and although it may seem extravagant, it is most abundantly confirmed by the observation of all men who traveled through those regions at that early day. A gentleman now living in Missouri, whose word is as good as that of any living man, and who was among the first traders to Santa Fe, informed me that his wagons were stopped for two hours by a frightened herd of buffalo, that threatened to overrun their caravan. They succeeded in dividing the multitude, by firing their guns and shouting at the top of their voices, and they passed on both sides. As far as they could see, in every direction from the point they occupied, the face of the country seemed to be densely covered with the moving mass of living animals. How immensely great must the herd have been, when their passing the caravan consumed about two hours. We could give many other similar statements, if it were necessary, made by a gentleman of veracity, going to prove the abundance of buffalo at that time, on all the western and south-western waters. The earliest adventurers were under the impression that game could not become scarce, and that there would be an abundance for the savages for many ages to come.

Let us compare these statements with those found in Captain Frémont's expedition in the years 1843-4. "A great portion of the region inhabited by this nation (the Shoshonees) formerly abounded in game, the buffalo ranging about in herds, as we found them on the eastern waters, and the plains dotted with scattering bands of antelope; but so rapidly have they disappeared within a few years, that now, as we journeyed along, an occasional buffalo and a few wild antelope were all that remained of the abundance which had covered the country with animal life. The extraordinary rapidity with which the buffalo is disappearing from our territory will not appear surprising, when we remember the great scale on which their destruction is yearly carried on. With inconsiderable exceptions, the business of the American trading posts is carried on in their skins; every year the Indian villages make new lodges, for which the skin of the buffalo furnishes the material; and in that portion of the country where they are still found, the Indians derive their entire support from them, and slaughter them with thoughtless and abominable extravagance. Like the Indians themselves, they have been a characteristic of the west, and like them they are visibly diminishing."[2]

About twenty-five years ago, near the sources of the Colorado and Bear river, buffalo existed in great abundance, and seemed to be an inexhaustible source of subsistence upon which the savages might safely depend for a century to come. But the buffalo are gone from that region, and the poor destitute natives are frequently exposed to starvation. There is reason to believe that buffalo were never so abundant in and west of the Rocky Mountains as they were on the eastern waters. Throughout all the country east of the mountains are found what are called buffalo paths or routes, that continue for hundreds of miles, from several inches to several feet in depth. These ancient vestiges are not met with west of the mountains.

The time was when expeditions crossing the plains from Missouri to Santa Fe, and from Missouri to the Rocky Mountains, could almost at any time see bands of buffalo ranging about, and could safely depend upon them for subsistence. Now an expedition does not think of depending upon the game of the country to sustain them on their journey, but are always supplied with provisions to take them through. A company going either to Oregon or Santa Fe would have to travel several hundred miles from Independence, a frontier town of Missouri, before they would see buffalo, and when they see them, they may look out for Indians as they now, like the wolves, follow the buffalo.

To give the reader some idea of the extent of the trade in buffalo skins, as carried on by the different companies, we would state that Captain Frémont gives a statement furnished him by a partner of the American Fur Company, which fixes the total amount of robes annual-

[2] John Charles Frémont, *Narratives of Exploration*, edited by Allan Nevins (New York, 1956), pp. 232-33. Most of the three paragraphs which follow also come from Frémont, pp. 187-89.

ly traded to the different companies at ninety thousand. But we are to remember that there are a number of tribes of Indians who depend upon the buffalo for subsistence, who furnish no skins for trade. The Indians, too, generally kill the greatest number of buffalo in the summer and fall seasons, to avail themselves of a hot sun to dry the meat for winter provisions, and yet at this time the skins are not fit for purposes of trade. The skins that are good for dressing are only those that are procured in the winter, when the wool and hair is long. To this is to be added the fact that the hides of bulls are not taken off and dressed at any season. And then again an immense number of calves are killed by the wolves.

Immense, therefore, as the herds of buffalo may have been, from the above statements, it will not be difficult to see that the day is not far distant when the race of that animal will be almost if not quite extinct on the plains and prairies of the far west. The question may be asked, what will be the means of subsistence left the different tribes when this takes place? We answer, those tribes are diminishing and disappearing as fast, if not faster, than their means of subsistence. Such are the dreadful conflicts that are constantly taking place between the different tribes, such the massacres and burning of each other's towns and villages besides acts of cruelty perpetrated by individuals, that scarcely the name remains of tribes that were once very numerous and formidable. And if these savage customs are kept up, as they in all probability will be, the race of the red man will diminish so fast that they will not furnish any obstruction to the expansion of our population and the occupation of their territory. When their country may be needed to receive the surplus of our rapidly increasing population, there will be no necessity to prompt us to get it by conquest or by purchase. The original proprietors will not be there to vindicate their claims to it, or to waylay the white man and take his scalp.[3]

Captain Williams speaks of the country near the Arkansas as generally beautiful and rich, as admirably adapted to the raising of stock

[3] Although he derives much of this chapter from Pike, Coyner was more optimistic about settlement of the West and did not believe, as Pike did, that Americans would "leave the prairies incapable of cultivation to the wandering and uncivilized aborigines." (*Pike*, vol. II, p. 28.)

of every kind.[4] Any number of horses, cattle and sheep could be kept there, as the earth, both winter and summer furnishes spontaneously an abundance of food. The difficulty in the way of that country being densely populated is the total want of timber in many parts. But it has been satisfactorily demonstrated that timber can be raised with success in the rich soil of the west. The discovery of coal, no doubt, will make the country habitable. In many places in the prairie states, coal has been found in abundance, supplying the absence of timber.

We have said that Williams, Workman and Spencer supposed they were on the Red river, and the little knowledge they had of the country led Workman and Spencer to think that, if they ascended this (Red) river to its source and crossed a mountain range of the Rocky Mountains, they would be in the Spanish country, and somewhere near Santa Fe, the seat of government. And they would have reached Santa Fe by this route, if they had really been on Red river, but they were on the great Arkansas. Laboring under this mistake, our two trappers set off up the river, resolved to follow the main branch to its source, from which they must have been at that time not less than three or four hundred miles.[5] Fortunately they were but a few days' travel from the Rocky Mountains, and passed over that part of their journey, by the exercise of a great deal of caution, without being detected by the savages. When they reached the mountains, they observed game was diminishing in quantity, which was a circumstance in their favor, as the country was not likely to be overrun with prowling bands of Indians.[6] Indeed they saw very few signs of Indians, and what they saw were very old. When they entered the mountains, they traveled on the south side of the river, for two or three days, and then crossed to the north side. They speak of a very high peak that was visible nearly all the time they were on that river. Its top was covered with snow and

[4] Coyner has taken the ideas in this paragraph from Pike, not Williams. Ibid., p. 26.
[5] Here is another example of Coyner's carelessness. In chapter XIV Coyner says that Workman and Spencer left the Arkansas and started up the "third fork," which would have taken them in a southwesterly direction. Now, we find them on the Arkansas again.
[6] Pike points out that game became scarce as he approached the mountains, "owing to the vicinity of the Spanish Indians and the Spaniards themselves." (*Pike*, vol. II, p. 26.)

103

glistened in the sun. It seemed so very high, to use their own words "that a cloud could not pass between its top and the sky." It was, most probably the peak, the altitude of which was taken by Lieutenant Pike, the year before, (1807), and found to be about eighteen or nineteen thousand feet above the level of the ocean. This peak is so very remarkable as to be known to all the savage nations for hundreds of miles around, and to be spoken of with admiration by the Spaniards of New Mexico, and was the bounds of their travels north-west.[7] Pike speaks of it, as not being out of sight, for twenty-five or thirty days. It is characteristic of the very high peaks, in the Rocky Mountains, that they can be seen a very great distance, although they may appear to be within a day's ride. The top of some of these peaks are inaccessible, from obstructions that are in the way, and from the fact, that they are covered with deep snows. Workman and Spencer whilst on the Arkansas observed the trace of a party ascending the river, which was old, and proved to be that of Pike's party in 1807, as they saw the names of the men occasionally engraved on rock and trees and the name Red river also, a circumstance that confirmed them in their notion, that they were on that river. This fact was calculated to encourage them, as they were not aware of the fact, that lieutenant Pike himself was laboring at the time that he was on the Arkansas, under the same mistake, and found himself on the Rio Del Norte,[8] in the Spanish country, to his great regret, and contrary to his intentions. They, therefore, aimed to follow the trail of Pike's company, as it would lead them to the source of Red river, whence they would cross into New Mexico. As it was summer season, Workman and Spencer fared much better than they would, if it had been winter. They traveled all day when they thought it safe to do so, and killed no more game than was necessary to supply them with provisions. As they approached the source of the Arkansas, the altitude of the country seemed to be very great, and there were a number of peaks of vast elevation, that were nearly all the time to be seen, distinctly covered with snow. The country was generally destitute of

[7] This, of course, is Pike's Peak, elevation 14,110 feet. Coyner has copied this sentence from Pike, including Pike's error that New Mexicans would travel northwest to reach the peak. (*Pike*, vol. I, pp. 353-54.)

[8] The Rio Grande. That Pike was mistaken is generally believed.

timber, except here and there clumps of trees, that were a variety of pines. Some cedar was also to be seen.

In giving an account of the ramblings of these two trappers in this terra incognita, it is proper to state that they ceased to make notes of the events of their travelings. They found it inconvenient, and it consumed time. Indeed they had not paper nor the disposition. As they were anxious to extricate themselves from those labyrinths in which they had been entangled so long, they thought but little about enlightening the minds of others, especially as they thought it very doubtful whether they would ever again reach the abodes of civilization. All the facts, therefore, which they were enabled to furnish, connected with this part of their expedition, were drawn from memory, and although interesting, they must constitute but a small amount of that kind of valuable information which a journal faithfully kept would have furnished about a region and its inhabitants, of which, even yet, but little is known.

They represent beaver, as they ascended this river, as very abundant, frequently furnishing their principal food. As they had no traps, they used their rifles to procure them. Another article of food was what is commonly called mountain mutton, which is very delicate and sweet. It is the flesh of the mountain sheep, which is variously called the bighorn by the trappers, the asahto by the Mandans, and the argali and ibex by others. They go in flocks, and generally frequent the cliffs of the mountains, and if they are alarmed in the valleys, into which they sometimes descend, they escape to the highest precipices, where they indulge their curiosity by gazing on all below them. They generally seek the places among the rocks that are the most inaccessible to man. They are said not to be very wild, and to fall far behind the antelope in the grace, and ease, and fleetness with which the latter animal moves over the ground. A little caution on the part of the hunter enables him to get within shot of it, when it is on ground on which he can approach it. It is called the bighorn from its horns, which are very large, and twisted like those of a ram. They are very long also, and a gentleman now living in Missouri informed me that he had seen them used by the Upper Nez Pierces for the purpose of blowing. The big-horn has short hair like a deer, and resembles it in shape, except as to its head and horns, which resemble those of a sheep. It abounds in the Rocky Mountains, from the sources of the Missouri and the Columbia to California. It is of the size of a large deer, and the horns of a full-grown, large male, are frequently three feet six inches long, and one foot and three inches at the base. North of the country ranged by the big-horn is found the woolly sheep, which is sometimes confounded with the big-horn. It is, however, a very different animal, and in its habits and appearance resembles the goat, and more properly belongs to that genus. Its covering is a growth of long white wool, interspersed with long hair. Like a goat, it has a beard, short legs, a deep belly, and is not very active. Its horns, which are from four to six inches long, have a polished surface, and are very black. They are by no means very abundant, and not much can be said in favor of their flesh as an article of diet. The trappers represent the fleece of this animal as exceedingly fine, and would be very valuable, if it could be procured in sufficient quantities.[9] The Flat-head Indians are said to use the skins of these animals for purposes of clothing. The flocks of the big-horn seen by Workman and Spencer increased as they approached the head of the Arkansas, and could be seen on the brow of mountains, and often standing on the edge of very high and shelving rocks. They seemed to enjoy a great deal of security when they had reached some extreme height, and added much to the wild and imposing character of mountain scenery. When they killed a young one, which was sometimes the case, they had a fine repast, as its flesh was very tender as well as fat.

It was when Spencer was making an effort to shoot a "mountain mutton" that he sustained an injury in one of his feet that caused them to suspend their wanderings for two weeks. It was in the neighborhood, as they believed, of the head springs of the river whose courses they had been following so long and so faithfully. This interruption caused them to select a clump of pines, in which they fixed up a lodge on such a plan as to defend themselves with more success, if they should be molested by savages. Here they whiled away the slow revolving hours of twelve or fifteen long summer days, devising every plan "to *kill* time" of which they could think, and which they could safely adopt.

[9] The foregoing description of bighorn sheep and "wooly sheep" was probably derived from Irving, *Astoria*, p. 234, or *Bonneville*, pp. 31-32.

Every circumstance seemed to combine to make time irksome and tedious. They were lost in their own minds as to their precise locality. They had abandoned all hope of seeing the country from which they had set out. They were seeking safety from the savages by betaking themselves to a country, the inhabitants of which could not boast of a very great degree of civilization, and were at that time not very favorably disposed towards our citizens. And then they had lost the trail of Pike's party, and might not be on the right route, or even any route, to the Spanish country.

The sacred Scriptures tell us that we shall have grace given us according to our day and trials. It would seem that there are *latent energies* in man, which are wakened up whenever, and only when their exercise is necessary, to raise us above our trials and hardships, or to enable us to combat our difficulties with success. These energies or capabilities of buffeting difficulties, in the case of some men, may never be developed, because they may never be surrounded by circumstances that make their exercise necessary. We are not, therefore, to suppose that they did not exist, and that such men, under certain circumstances, would not also be patient in enduring hardships and trials, and brave in the hour of danger.

In the midst of their perplexing difficulties these men avow they kept in good cheer. Now and then Workman killed some game, as they needed it, and it was his daily business to reconnoitre the country around, to ascertain whether there was any thing to be seen calculated to awaken apprehensions of danger. By means of nooses on the end of long, light poles, they caught several birds, (magpies) as they thought. These, after cropping one of their wings to prevent them from flying off, they would throw into the branches of the trees, and then they would practice with bows and arrows which they made, trying to bring them down in Indian style. Whilst Workman was beating about one day in the vicinity of their camp, he saw a huge grizzly bear, about the fourth of a mile off, jogging along down a small stream, and going (he was pleased to observe) directly from their camp. They had had no thoughts about such unwelcome visitors, as they had observed no signs of their presence in that neighborhood.

These men were now in a region, as they think, that gives rise to the

107

Platte, the Yellow Stone, the great south-western tributary of the Missouri, the Arkansas, the Rio del Norte, and the Rio Colorado of California. Speaking in reference to this particular region, Lieutenant Pike says: "I have no hesitation in saying that I can take a position in the mountains, from whence I can visit the source of any of these rivers in one day."[10] This assertion may be true, and we do not know that any discoveries that have been made prove it untrue. There is one thing, however, certainly true, and that is, that region to this day remains, to a great extent, unexplored; and the statements Pike received, and which he seemed to credit, about some of these rivers, were incorrect, as subsequent discoveries will show. "By the route of the Arkansas and the Rio Colorado of California, I am confident," says he, "in asserting, (if my information from Spanish gentlemen of intelligence is correct), there can be established the best communication on this side of the Isthmus of Darien, between the Atlantic and Pacific oceans; as, admitting the utmost, the land carriage would not be more than two hundred miles, and the route may be made quite as eligible as our public high-ways over the Alleghany Mountains. The Rio Colorado is to the Gulph of California what the Mississippi is to the Gulph of Mexico, and is navigable for ships of considerable burden opposite to the upper part of Sonora."[11] This information, furnished Lieutenant Pike about the Colorado, or Green river, as it is now sometimes called, has been proved, by subsequent discoveries, to be entirely incorrect. Its length is about twelve hundred miles, eight hundred of which are broken into falls and rapids, so numerous and dangerous as to defy navigation in any way whatever. From one to two hundred miles of its lower part is in all probability navigable for vessels of the larger class. But more about the Rio Colorado in another place.

We have said that Workman and Spencer gave it as their opinion, that there is a region, (in the opinion of Pike of no great extent) which constitutes the great fountain head of the great rivers we mentioned. This region is the most remarkable and highest of the Rocky Moun-

[10] Jackson (ed.), *Pike*, vol. II, pp. 26-27.
[11] Ibid., pp. 25-26. In correcting Pike, Coyner apparently used Lansford W. Hastings, *Emigrants' Guide to Oregon and California*, p. 73, first published in 1844.

tains, and is a bed of lofty mountains, covered with eternal snows. It is said to be about one hundred miles long, and about thirty in breadth, and is now called the Wind-river mountains. Although Workman and Spencer may have wandered about in the south extremity of what is now understod to be the Wind-river sierra, yet we think the Arkansas and the Rio Del Norte perhaps have their fountain-heads further south. It is now well known that the Columbia, Colorado, and the main affluents to the Missouri, can be traced to this grand treasury of waters.[12]

One of the highest peaks in the Rocky Mountains is in the Wind-river range, and is probably fifteen thousand feet above the level of the sea.[13] Various estimates have been made of the height of the Rocky Mountains, and it is believed that when justice is done to their real altitude, they will be only second to the highest mountains on the globe. Their height has been diminished to the eye by the great elevations from which they rise. They consist, according to Long, of ridges, knobs, and peaks, variously disposed. They were called by some of the first discoverers, the Shining Mountains, from the fact that the higher parts are covered with perpetual snows, which give them a luminous and brilliant appearance. By the joint means of the barometer and trigonometric measurement, one of the peaks has been ascertained to be twenty-five thousand feet, and there are others of nearly the same height in the vicinity.[14]

Workman and Spencer relate a phenomenon, that, at first gave them much anxiety of mind, and that was the reports or singular explosions among these mountains, resembling heavy distant thunder. They could be heard at all times of the day and night, and more particularly in clear, calm weather. At first they had various conjectures about the cause. They thought at one time it was distant thunder and again they supposed it to be the report of artillery. A third ex-

[12] Irving, *Bonneville*, p. 44, similarly describes the Wind River Mountains of western Wyoming.

[13] Gannet Peak, highest in the range, rises to 13,785 feet.

[14] Although Coyner mentions Stephen H. Long, he did not utilize the account of Long's explorations. Rather, Coyner took his description of the Rockies from a letter of Professor James Renwick, published in the Appendix to Irving's *Astoria*, p. 518, and Irving's comments on this letter. Renwick overestimated the height of the Rockies. Mt. McKinley, North America's highest, measures 20,321 feet, and the highest peaks in the West are in the 14,000-foot range.

109

planation was, that the mysterious sounds were produced by volcanic irruptions [eruptions]. The existence of this phenomenon in the Rocky Mountains, is mentioned by Lewis and Clarke, and others who have been in those regions. It is a mystery, which excites the admiration and awe of the various tribes, and some of them regard it as the voice of the great Wacondah, (Supreme Being) who holds his residence, as they believe, in those mountains.[15]

When Spencer was able to walk, the two solitary trappers, with their rifles in their hands, struck out for the sources of the Del Norte, traveling a west course. They state, that the country through which they passed was generally mountainous prairie, abounding in fountains and lakes and vast beds of snow, that are the sources of those mighty rivers, east and west of the Rocky Mountains. A few days' faithful journeying brought them to an elevation in the mountains, where there was a delightful spring of water, remarkably pure and cold. It ran a west course; and this, in their view, must be the source of the Del Norte. Now their hearts were glad, as they fancied they had struck a stream which would lead them out of the extensive wilderness in which they had been lost so long a time. Here I would remark, the subsequent history of these two wanderers will show, they were again mistaken. The bubbling fountain which they supposed to be the source of the Del Norte, was one of the many fountains of the Colorado.[16] They followed a small streamlet, until it swelled into a mighty river, that dashes its waters against rocks and precipices, and rolls on and widens and deepens, for more than a thousand miles. When the stream acquired a magnitude that, they thought, would justify it, they went to work with a light axe, which they had retained, and constructed a small canoe, which they hoped, would save them many a long and weary tramp, in those Alpine regions. Whilst Spencer was making this little craft, Workman consumed a day in examining the river, to ascertain if it was navigable. He reported that he had reached a very high point near the river, from which he had a most delightful view of

---

[15] Irving discusses these noises in similar terms in *Astoria*, p. 232.

[16] Here Coyner has his lost trappers cross from the drainage of the Arkansas, over the continental divide, to an affluent of the Colorado. Since this portion of the book is entirely fictional, I will not try to outline their "route."

its banks and course; and that its surface seemed to be remarkably placid and free from falls. Its banks were also very low and destitute of timber.

This discovery seemed almost, in their minds, to put an end to their difficulties. In a few days more they would glide on the beautiful surface of this peaceful river into some of the Spanish settlements, which would be a home to them when compared with their present forlorn situation. But they were doomed to more disappointments. New and fresh difficulties and mazes were before them. When they had procured a supply of meat that would last them several days, and had put it into their little boat, they committed themselves to the current. They glided along in fine style for the first fifty miles. Through this distance a beautiful undulating prairie, without a stick of timber for many miles, stretched out from the banks of the river in every direction. Towards sun-set, however, the aspect of the country before them began to assume a wild, romantic, and forbidding character. A frowning mountain enclosed their prospect, and seemed to hem in the river. As they approached this unexpected obstruction, the surface of the water began to be irregular and rough. They did not think it safe to travel after night-fall; they therefore pulled to shore to await the disclosures that might be furnished by the light of another day. The next morning very early, with rifles in hand, they left their canoe and walked ahead to gain some point from which they might be able to examine the country and the channel of the river, and learn something about both. After several hours of toil and ascent, they reached an elevation where they had a view of the scenery before them, that was wilder and more imposing than anything they had ever seen before. The bed of the river, which had generally been from three to four hundred yards in breadth, was now contracted to a passage not more than forty yards wide, and walled up several hundred feet high by tremendous battlements of basaltic rock. Through this narrow defile the river flowed almost with the velocity of an arrow. Beyond these rapids there were evidently falls, as their tumultuous roar could be distinctly heard, and clouds of spray could be seen suspended in the air. For an hour or two our trappers remained seated upon the ground, gazing with mingled feelings of disappointment and astonishment at this magnificent scene.

111

At one time the roaring of the distant cataract would rise and swell with the breeze that bore the lulling sound to their ears. Again, as the gentle gale would sink, the tumult of angry waters would for a while die away in the distance. The feeling of disappointment, for a time, was lost in those of wonder and awe, and the trappers seemed to forget their situation, as they mused upon the picturesqueness and romance of this exhibition of nature. Seeing satisfactorily that quick destruction awaited them if they should attempt to pass the narrow defile, they returned to their camp to get a few articles they had left in their canoe, as well as some provisions. But when they came in view of the place where they had left their canoe they saw three savages in it, and in the act of pushing it from shore. The trappers made signs to them, which seemed only to frighten them, and to cause them to make the greater effort to cross the river. Understanding how to manage such a water craft, they soon reached the opposite shore. As they now felt secure, they paused on the bank to gaze with curiosity and surprise at the two men, when Workman raised his rifle and fired it towards them. The report of his gun and the sight of the fire struck a panic among them, that caused them to break and run. The trappers were particularly concerned about their axe, which they supposed was in the canoe, and was of course taken away, but fortunately they had left it on the land, and it had not been seen by the savages. *Who* these savages were, and *how savage* they were, the trappers were entirely ignorant, as they could not be brought to a parley. Their bodies were nearly naked, and they presented a most degraded appearance. They belonged, perhaps, to a tribe of *"les dignes de pitie,"* (objects of pity), as such Indians are sometimes called, who constitute a mere link between human nature and the brute.

Workman and Spencer now resumed their journeyings over land, aiming to follow the river as near as they could. When they had passed the narrow passage, the Colorado expanded again to its usual breadth, and poured over falls about forty feet high. The river in the falls was full of large rock, many of which projected above the surface of the water. Against these the waters of this great river dashed, and rebounded, and boiled up, until the whole surface seemed to be in a perfect rage. After spending the day in clambering the sides of very rough mountains, and winding round and round to avoid obstructions and to find ground on which they could travel, they succeeded in getting below the falls, where the river again assumed a tranquil and placid surface, and a beautiful and delightful prairie country came to the very banks. These men would have made another canoe and tried it again, but there was no suitable timber, and they thought it the better policy to ascertain something more about the navigation, before they should again commit themselves to its uncertain current. They therefore followed it from day to day, as near as they could get to its banks, until they were satisfied that it was filled with rapids, and rocks, and other obstructions, that not only rendered the navigation unsafe, but utterly impossible. Necessity, therefore, reconciled them to the toil of traveling on foot. They kept near the river, resolved to follow it, let it take them where it might. The country was sometimes very broken and mountainous, and very often they would have to turn back and retrace their steps, and make a circuit of several miles to find a way through which they could pass. They frequently passed places where for several miles the banks rose up into precipices of an awful height, from the tops of which they sometimes took a view of the river below, as it whirled, and dashed about, and foamed, and struck the basaltic rock, impatient, furious and wild. These men give it as their opinion that the scenery of the Rio Colorado is equal, perhaps, to that of any other part of North America. Their statements are very applicable to the Snake river scenery, which is also represented as being wild and grand beyond description. Indeed it may be noticed as a characteristic of the rivers west of the Rocky Mountains, that they are marked by a wild majesty, produced by the frequent recurrence of rocks and rapids, that place them in striking contrast to the smoothness and placidity of the streams east of said mountains. This distinction in favor of the eastern rivers will operate against the navigation of the western waters, and, of course, against the interests of the country through which they pass, if those countries should ever be settled by a civilized people.

Having descended this river for several hundred miles, still believing it to be the Rio del Norte, and wondering why they had not reached

Santa Fe, they came to a place which seemed to have been much used as a crossing.[17] There were a great many signs of horses and mules, but they were old, and all pointing an east course. Indeed the signs were so numerous that Workman and Spencer conjectured there must have been several thousand. Without the least hesitation the trappers resolved to follow this great trail, and to take the way the signs indicated the last caravan had gone. They felt confident that this trail had been made by the Spaniards, and not by Indians. They traveled it two days, when they met a caravan of Spaniards (forty or fifty) on the trail, but going an opposite direction. They at first entertained fears they were Indians, but when they found out they were Spaniards, their joy was too great to be described. Neither of the trappers could speak the Spanish language, but there was an Englishman in the caravan, and one or two Spaniards who could speak the English language with some fluency. They therefore found no difficulty in communicating to the company what had been their history in the mountains, and the fact that they were now seeking security in their country.

The caravan then selected a suitable place for encampment, for the purpose of adopting some plan for the protection of the two men who had thrown themselves upon their mercy, for these Spaniards were, by no means, insensible as to their situation. Until midnight they listened with thrilling interest to the details, as the trappers gave them, of their trials and hardships since they had left the United States. They informed Workman and Spencer that the river which they had descended was the Rio Colorado, and that they were about five hundred miles from Santa Fe. In passing over that distance they had met with a good deal of trouble from the Indians, and they gave it as their opinion, that the two trappers could not pass through to Santa Fe without being cut off by the savages.

The caravan was going towards Puebla de los Angelos (*sic*), a town in Upper California, near the coast of the Pacific, in which region of country they expected to be engaged in trading until the following

[17] This, supposedly, was the Spanish Trail connecting Santa Fe with Los Angeles. Actually, the trail did not come into use until 1830-31. Had Workman and Spencer really made such a journey, they would have struck the Spanish Trail in eastern Utah near today's Moab.

spring, when they expected to return to Santa Fe with horses and mules. Part of the company were men who lived in Upper California, but they had accompanied a caravan the last spring to Santa Fe, and were now returning home. Workman and Spencer determined to join the company and go to California, where they would spend the approaching winter, and in the spring return with them to New Mexico, whence they hoped some opportunity would present itself of getting back to the United States. They were therefore regularly taken into the service of the company, which was under the direction of a captain, and furnished with mules and such articles as they needed.

The company next morning set out, and were about twenty days' travel from San Gabriel, on the Bay of San Pedro.[18] In passing over this distance a great deal of the road was very rocky and rough. The season was dry (a circumstance, by no means unusual in that country), and the company had often to perform long and toilsome journies before they could reach water. In one or two cases the distance from one watering place to another was not less than one hundred miles, and very often from thirty to fifty. The surface of the country was often, too, a bed of sand, which furnished nothing to sustain their mules. It will therefore be seen that there are through this country regular jornadas (as the Spaniards call them) and stages where grass and water can be had for caravans, whilst the country intervening is almost as desolate as the Sahara of Africa. By making these regular jornadas or day's journey and reaching those regular stages, caravans are able to make their way through from California to Santa Fe. If a caravan breaks this regular chain of stages, their toils and sufferings are often very severe. These caravans are often very great, numbering sometimes several thousand horses and mules, which sweep away all the grass near their route, and leave the earth very bare. As they journeyed along, Workman and Spencer observed the bones of animals scattered about in great profusion in some places, and upon asking for an explanation, they were informed that they were the bones of horses and mules, that were lost by caravans from a disease very common in that region called the "foot evil," which sometimes causes the loss of whole

---

[18] Mission San Gabriel Arcángel, near the Pueblo of Los Angeles.

bands of horses and mules. It seems to be aggravated, if not really created by traveling over hot-sandy plains and deserts, and suffering from want of water. After crossing the Colorado and traveling north-west several days, the company turned and traveled a south-west course until they reached the Spanish towns on the Pacific. On the right of their route, very high mountains were all the time visible, the peaks of which were white with snow. This range of mountains, (no doubt what is now called the Wahsatch Mountains)[19] seemed to be infested with predatory bands of Indians, whose regular business was to beset the route of these caravans for the purpose of plunder. As this company passed, they could be frequently seen on the tops of the mountains, peering over the plains, and reconnoitering their movements. We would briefly state, that our two trappers spent the winter of 1809 in Upper California, which time Workman spent in examining the country and traveling from place to place to gather all the information he could of a country, about which our citizens at that time knew but little or nothing. As it is our object in another part of this volume, to give a short, but we hope a faithful account of California, it is our intention to interweave all the statements of Workman in that account. We will, therefore, suspend for the present, his descriptions of California, that they may appear in a more proper place, and we will ask the reader to go with us to Santa Fe, where in the summer of 1810, we find our two mountaineers and trappers safely landed, with a large caravan of mules and horses, both in fine health and good cheer.

[19] Coyner seems to have been describing the Sierra Nevada on the "right." His description of the Spanish Trail is taken in part from Frémont's account of his return from California to the Wasatch Mountains in 1844. Frémont, *Narratives*, pp. 398-417.

Chapter 15

The two trappers try their luck in Santa Fe for several years—Santa Fe trade opens—An opportunity to return to the States—An escort sent by the Governor of Santa Fe—Captain Viscano's dreadful fight with the Camanches on the Semirone—Several killed on both sides—The nocturnal tramp express to Captain Riley on the Arkansas—Mysterious horse and thousands of mysteries—A bold attempt, result amusing.

W<small>ORKMAN AND</small> Spencer being men without families in the States, and being foiled thus far in their efforts to make fortunes, resolved to try their luck in Santa Fe, as gold and silver seemed to be very abundant. They, therefore, took up their abode at the seat of government (Santa Fe) with the purpose of remaining there for several years, if their success should justify it, and when they had amassed a sufficiency of the precious metals, they thought of returning to the United States, if a safe opportunity should present itself. This shows how men become weaned from the habitudes of civilized and cultivated society, and are so charmed with the wild adventure connected with savage life, that they are seldom satisfied, unless they are braving the toils and difficulties of the wilderness, and realising all the excitement belonging to such a life. Workman and Spencer remained in and about Santa Fe, for fifteen years, and had abandoned all thought of regaining the place of their nativity. But the Santa Fe trade was opened up, and large companies every spring crossed the plains from Missouri to

New Mexico, with goods which they exchanged at a great profit for gold and silver. One of the first of these large companies was under the direction of Captain Means,[1] who with part of his men were killed by the Camanches, whilst the others barely escaped with their lives, leaving everything they had, to be carried off by these ruthless savages. In consequence of this disaster, the General Government sent a company headed by Captain Riley,[2] to escort the next trading expedition, the following spring [of 1829] over all the dangerous ground to the Big Arkansas, where Captain Riley was ordered to remain until a specified time, awaiting the return of the trading company to conduct them back to the States. This company reached Santa Fe in safety, and after disposing of their goods in that mart, turned their faces towards the States. They were fortunate enough to meet with an opportunity to go under the protection of the Spanish government, a circumstance that was brought about in this way. Some half a dozen of wealthy Spaniards residing in Santa Fe had been found guilty of some treasonable designs against that government, and had the privilege of leaving the country in so many days, or being hung. They of course preferred the former kind of punishment and determined to go with their families and fortunes to the States.[3] The governor of Santa Fe, therefore ordered a Captain Viscarro with sixty men, ten of whom were brave Purbulo [Pueblo] Indians, living near Santa Fe, to conduct these exiles and the company until they should meet Captain Riley on the Big Arkansas, from which point he was to return to New Mexico.[4] Workman and Spencer, when they saw this very safe opportunity of getting back to

[1] The Santa Fe Trail opened to steady commerce in 1821. The *Missouri Intelligencer* reported the death of Captain John Means of Franklin on October 24, 1828. Means's death was one of a series of incidents that resulted in the government action described by Coyner.

[2] Major Bennett Riley. His experience on the Santa Fe Trail is told in Otis E. Young, *The First Military Escort on the Santa Fe Trail, 1829* (Glendale, Calif., 1952).

[3] A decree of March 20, 1829, from Mexico City, ordered the expulsion of Spaniards from all of Mexico. Ten Spanish men and six women left Santa Fe for Missouri, about September 1, with the 1829 caravan.

[4] Colonel José Antonio Vizcarra, former governor of New Mexico, 1822-23, had sixty regular soldiers under him as well as militia and camp keepers—about 220 men altogether. Pueblo Indians were among them. Young, *First Military Escort*, p. 142.

the States, felt the love of their native land, which had been almost extinct, revive in their hearts, and they determined to join the party on their homeward route.[5]

They had been quite successful whilst in New Mexico in advancing their fortunes, and now they would make an effort to return to renew their acquaintance with those whom they once knew, but from whose memory all recollection of them had now perhaps passed away, as of those long ago dead and gone. At that time, a trip from Santa Fe was very dangerous, and the savages had been very successful in frightening the mules of caravans, and causing them to break loose and run off. But the company got along very smoothly until they were within sixty miles of the Arkansas.

When near the Semirone river, and just when the company were driving up to a spring around which they intended to encamp that night, a large party of Indians on foot, perhaps one hundred and fifty, emerged from a covert, and arrayed themselves on open ground, in a right line facing the traders. "What tribe are they?" was a question that was quickly asked, and as quickly passed around the camp. "Camanche," was the answer from one who knew.[6] And that was enough, for the company knew what they were to expect. In the Camanche Indian is embodied every trait of a savage, whose hand is raised against every man, and who is even more blood-thirsty than the gangs of hungry wolves that roam over those extensive plains. They made known their hostile feelings, and challenged the traders by brandishing and flourishing their arms, and acting the mad buffalo, which consists in gathering the dust in one hand and then in the other, and throwing it into the air, after the manner of that animal when he is provoking one of his peers to combat. So menacing was their aspect, that the

[5] Workman and Spencer (had their story been true) would have had ample opportunity to return to Missouri from 1821 on. There was no need for them to wait until 1829.

[6] The remainder of this chapter describes the fight on the Cimarron and its aftermath. Josiah Gregg, whose *Commerce of the Prairies* (1844) was available to Coyner, says that 120 Gros Ventre attacked the party. Coyner clearly had not read Gregg, however, and must have heard the story from a contemporary. His account contains details which appear nowhere else, and much of it seems plausible. Other accounts agree with Coyner that some 150 Comanches attacked the caravan.

119

traders hesitated as to holding a parley with them, and indeed few, if any, were willing to undertake it.

Finally, one of the company went out, and was met half way by one of the Camanches, with arms in one hand and his cross in the other. But they had scarcely met before two other Camanches broke the line and dashed up to the party. This movement being not understood by the traders, two of them, Barnes and Wallace,[7] ran up to protect their man, if it should be necessary. A momentary and fearful pause ensued. The parties stood for the half of a minute in perfect silence, keenly eyeing each other, with their fingers upon the triggers of their guns. The savages seemed eager to begin the work, and but for one circumstance the combatants, the next moment, would have been thrown into dreadful conflict. That circumstance was this. The ten Purbuloes who, under the Spanish captain, Viscarro, were accompanying the traders to Big Arkansas river, and who had gone out on a hunt that afternoon, were at that time near at hand upon a ridge, skinning and cutting up a buffalo which they had killed. They had a full and fair view of all that was taking place below them, and abruptly leaving the carcass of the buffalo, they raised a dreadful war-shout, and came bounding down the hill, and charging and pitching like mad horses, and rushed up into the very faces of the Camanches.

The sudden and unexpected sight of these braves perfectly electrified the Camanches; not that they dreaded ten Purbuloes, but because they conjectured that a party (perhaps large) of that war-like tribe were concealed behind the adjacent ridge. One of the Purbuloes, a game youth about sixteen, observing a very gaudy pair of socks under the belt of a Camanche, laid violent hands upon them, and by way of pay gave the owner of them a tremendous kick in the posteriors, that nearly lifted him off the ground. The insult was received by the crestfallen Camanche without resistance.

Balked in their designs by the circumstance just mentioned, the

[7] Thomas Barnes and George "Wallis" were with the 1829 caravan, Young, *First Military Escort*, p. 184. Perhaps Coyner learned the details of the fight on the Cimarron from one of them. Thomas Barnes's brother Abraham married Grace Jones, a step-daughter of Ezekiel Williams, in 1823. William S. Bryan and Robert Rose, *A History of the Pioneer Families of Missouri* (St. Louis, 1876), pp. 313-14. Voelker, "Ezekiel Williams," p. 41.

Camanches began to make professions of friendship, in which some of the traders were foolish enough to confide. Indeed the whole company, with a few honorable exceptions, were overawed by the savage appearance and disposition of the Camanches. This the Purbuloes perceived with surprise and great indignation. They assured their party that the Camanches intended to attack them, and that their only alternative was to fight. The Spaniards under Captain Viscarro excused themselves by stating that they had recently entered into a treaty of peace with the Camanches, and did not wish to violate their faith. The Purbuloes knew this was only an excuse, and therefore charged them with cowardice. They told Captain Viscarro that they would no longer submit to him as an officer, for he had not the bravery of a squaw.[8] Becoming furious, they threw their shields upon the ground, by way of appeal to the courage of the company, and proclaimed themselves ready to fight without any thing to defend them against the darts of the enemy. All this, however, had no effect upon their quailing, faltering spirits. They did not intend to strike the first blow, let the provocation be any thing short of a real attack. This was discovered by the Camanches, and prompted them to come nearer the company, and to be more impudent. In fact, in their reprehensible timidity, the company had permitted the daring Camanches to mix among them to some extent. The Purbuloes kept their eyes constantly upon them, and only grew the more impatient, as they observed that the Camanches were waiting for a favorable opportunity to make an assault. One of them, a tall, stalwart and distinguished warrior, perceiving something among the enemy very suspicious, sprang to his feet and seemed to look wild. Seizing a moment when the eyes of the company were generally turned away from them, the Camanches fired, and in a kind of headlong hurry ran across a creek that was near the camp to reload. The worst predictions of the heroic Purbuloes were realized. Four of their greatest warriors fell dead, and a number of the tame and spiritless Spaniards. A great uproar now prevailed. Some flew to their frightened

[8] The behavior of Vizcarra and the Pueblos, as described by Coyner, seems out of character. Vizcarra was regarded as a courageous Indian fighter and an admirable horseman. The Pueblos apparently had some respect for him, for according to Josiah Gregg a Pueblo placed himself in front of a bullet aimed at Vizcarra.

mules, to prevent them from breaking loose, some flew to their arms, and some, there is reason to believe, flew to the wagons for safety. As the Camanches crossed the creek, one of their number received a ball from the rifle of Workman, who pulled the savage to the ground by his long hair and passed on. Although mortally wounded, and unable to get upon his feet, the indomitable Camanche, as he lay upon the ground, reloaded his gun, and as one of Captain Viscarro's sergeants rode up with a sword in hand to dispatch him, shot him between the eyes. The Spaniard instantly fell lifeless from his horse. The six surviving Purbuloes, deeply mortified at the miserable management of the company, would not join in the fight, but remained near their dead brothers, chagrined, disgusted, and filled with sullen rage. The Camanches had but two or three rounds of balls and powder, which they speedily used, and then betook themselves to flight. Sixteen of the traders followed them. But a few of them, however, had the presence of mind to get their horses, and they found that the Indians could out-leg them.

Away they went on foot, and on horseback, and shooting as they went. Among those in the chase was a Spaniard on horseback, but he had no arms and he did not appear to desire any; his aim and business being to rob the slain and to get the spoils. He had collected a sufficient number of bows, and arrows, and buffalo robes, and blankets, and trinkets and trumpery of all sorts, to completely cover and conceal the horse and his rider. Barnes and Wallace, (old Wallace as he was called) of whose bravery we have sufficient proofs, of course were in the number. The former was well mounted. Wallace was in his glory, but he was on foot, and an old man in the bargain. He applied to the Spaniard for the use of his steed: but the Spaniard thought too much of his plunder, to part with the means of conveying it to the camp. Barnes thought the emergency would justify Wallace in taking the horse, *vi et armis.*[9] The suggestion was scarcely made before it was carried into effect. In a moment the venal Spaniard came heels over head, upon the ground, with his bows and arrows, and dry buffalo skins, and trinkets and trumpery of all sorts rattling around his ears, and in a moment

[9] "By force and arms."

Wallace was on his horse and away. As the affair began between sunset and dark, nightfall soon came on, and all the pursuers turned back to the camp, but Wallace and Barnes. They held on until nine or ten o'clock, shooting and pursuing, and pursuing and shooting; until their guns became so hot by frequent firing, and so dirty, they were compelled to desist. The moon shone as bright as day, and an open and extensive plain spread around. Barnes and Wallace thought, they followed the Indians for seven or eight miles, and they stated that they retreated all that distance, in a right line, nor was there at any time any confusion, or breaking of ranks. They farther reported, that they saw at some distance off, what they believed to be another party of Indians, that seemed to be very large. On the part of the Camanches this was a very unsuccessful adventure, and dearly did they pay for their impudence. They were most sadly drubbed, and lost many of their greatest warriors, as was ascertained the following year.

The night passed, not, however, with its usual rest and repose. The company had a sample of Indian fighting, Indian treachery and Indian cruelty, which was by no means calculated to invite sleep. They were at that time in a country infested by hordes of savages of the most ferocious character; who would perhaps dog them for hundreds of miles. They had just had a fight with a party of them, and other parties, perhaps very large, were in the neighborhood. The company of men, sent by the governor of Santa Fe under Capt. Viscarro, to protect them to the Big Arkansas, had proved timid and cowardly in the affray, that had taken place. They therefore could not safely depend upon them for aid in a difficulty.[10] Captain Riley by this time had in all probability left Big Arkansas and turned his forces towards the United States. They had many and strong reasons to fear, that they would be unprotected throughout the whole of the dangerous route, that lay before them. The next day they expected the Camanches to return with renewed and multiplied forces, to slay and rob. Under these circumstances, and with these gloomy prospects and feelings, the light

---

[10] Although Coyner charges the Mexicans with cowardice, the Mexicans were themselves revolted by the barbarity of the Americans who pursued the Comanches, scalping them whether dead or alive and even skinning one of them. Young, *First Military Escort*, pp. 143-44.

of the next day dawned upon them. After the fight on the previous evening, two of the Camanches that were badly wounded, were seen scrambling along on the ground to a ledge of rocks, in which they hid themselves during the night. The Purbuloes being apprised of the fact, hurried to the spot and found them. One of them was dead. The other was living, and the partial opportunity to sate their thirst for blood was embraced with savage greediness. He was dragged out by the infuriated Purbuloes, and cut to pieces. Their scalps of course were taken. As these crown their original owners, they crown and complete the victories of those who take them. But the dead were to be buried, this morning, and the company had to prepare for the anticipated difficulties of the day; and these they were afraid would be many and trying.

Every arrangement would be made to meet them. Accordingly, after an early, and we may conjecture a hurried breakfast, graves were dug, and the slain were put in the ground as decently as circumstances would admit. In the meanwhile the mules and horses were permitted to fill themselves with grass, and then brought within a circular fortification made of the waggons and baggage. Their arms were put in a state of readiness, and sentinels were placed out on elevated points, to reconnoitre the surrounding country, and to report every thing that appeared above the verge of the horizon. The day passed, however, and, contrary to their calculations, they saw no Indians, but the slain that lay here and there, who, as they were now objects of no great terror, were still less, in the estimation of the company, entitled to the rite of sepulture, but were doomed to lie on their native plains, to feed the hungry wolf attracted that way by the scent of their putrescent bodies. Although they had not been molested that day, still the company knew that they were on very dangerous ground as large bands of hostile Indians were believed to be hovering about their route, seeking a suitable opportunity to make an attack. It was about sixty miles from Big Arkansas, where it was hoped Captain Riley might still be, awaiting their return, although it was a week past the time to which he was limited, and when he had expected to set out on his return to the United States.

As the distance could be rode on good horses in a night, it was proposed to send an express to Captain Riley, (if he should still be there), to apprise him of their exposed situation, and to request him to wait until they should come up.[11] But who would undertake it? If the company were in danger, the express would certainly be much more so.

The route lay through the most dangerous part of the country, between Santa Fe and Independence. The moon was full and shone very bright, but if this circumstance would facilitate the undertaking, it would at the same time expose the party to the danger of being more easily discovered by Indians. The wealthy Spanish exiles, who seemed to be very much alarmed, offered large rewards in gold and silver to any party that would undertake to carry an express to the Arkansas that night. The danger was great, it was true, but the reward was too tempting to be withstood. Remember, reader, it was *gold* and *silver*, and every one knows what gold and silver has done and can do. A small party agreed to go, and, mounting their horses, set out.

But in less than an hour they came back at the top of their speed, dreadfully frightened, and stating that they had seen a great many Indians. "Where did you see them? what number did you see? what were they doing? were they encamped or moving?" These questions and many others were put to them, first by one and then by another. But as the answers returned were not very satisfactory, and the statements of the party somewhat conflicting, the company doubted whether they had seen any Indians at all. They finally said they *thought* they had seen Indians. The wealthy Spaniards increased the reward, and another party set out. But they returned also in a short time, frightened half to death and telling the same story. They, too, gave the company reason to believe that the Indians seen were only imaginary.

This second failure aroused the game spirits of Wallace and Barnes, and as they had no time to lose, they told the company that if they were furnished with the best men and best horses belonging to the expedition, they would undertake it. The proposition was immediately

[11] Riley had left the Arkansas on October 11 after the caravan was one day overdue. Later that morning messengers from the caravan who had been riding all night caught up with Riley and he halted his march. The caravan, which had been twenty-four miles from the Arkansas, joined Riley on October 12. Hence, Coyner's account which follows has some basis in fact.

accepted. The selection of men was easily and soon made. The rich exiles furnished the horses, as their animals were very superior. Wallace, Workman, Barnes, the six Purbuloes, and seven others, constituted the band that were not to be so easily deterred. They took a full supply of arms, leaped into their saddles, which they had girted very tight upon their horses, and put off. Away they went, silently and swiftly careering over the plains, and keeping a most vigilant look-out in every direction. The moon shone with a brightness inferior only to the light of a vertical sun. The deep and sepulchral silence that prevailed was sometimes broken by the shrill neighing of the elk, and by the howling of hungry, saucy gangs of wolves, that sometimes whipped across their route. They had traveled more than half the distance before they saw any thing that was calculated to excite apprehensions of danger, or to interrupt their nocturnal tramp. As they were approaching the edge of a bluff that overlooked an extensive plain, a horse came up the bluff towards them, and when he noticed the party neighed, and seemed to be perfectly tame. Here was a mysterious circumstance, a mysterious horse, to be understood before they could venture any further in safety. "How came he there?" As he was tame, he must belong to some Indian encampment, that might be very near. After holding a consultation and interchanging opinions for a few minutes, it was determined to secretly reconnoitre the plain that lay beneath the bluff, particularly as the mysterious horse came from that direction. Wallace, (Colonel Wallace I will call him, for he ought to have been a colonel), who was always the first to dash into danger, and upon dangerous ground, gave the reins of his horse to Barnes, and crept along to the edge of the bluff.

After making a thorough examination, he returned cautiously to his party, reporting that the plain that lay beneath the bluff was covered with thousands and thousands of animals, that might be Indians and Indian horses, but he saw no fires; a circumstance, however, that he said did not signify any thing, as Indians always put out their fires after eating, or leave them and go somewhere else to encamp. Barnes, who was always the right hand man of Colonel Wallace, next crept up to the edge of the bluff, and after making a careful examination returned, stating the same thing, that the plain below was covered with thousands and thousands of something, but he could not say what it meant. Workman then went, and after an absence of a few minutes returned, reporting the same thing, to wit, that thousands and thousands of animals covered the plain, which he took to be Indians and Indian horses. The six Purbulo braves must next go and see for themselves, and satisfy their curiosity. After prying and peeping most cautiously for some time, over the bluff, they brought back the same account, that animals lay by thousands and thousands over the plain, which they conjectured were Indians.

"Well, under the circumstances, what are we to do?" was the problem, the solution of which was not very easy. The present party were prompted not so much by the prospect of a great reward in gold and silver, as by a nobler impulse, that made them insensible to danger, and raised them superior to it. They determined to dash through any and all obstructions that might be in their route, or sacrifice their lives in the attempt. To turn back, therefore, was not to be recognized by them at any time, as a way of avoiding or getting rid of a difficulty. A free interchange of views and notions resulted in that of adopting the following purpose and plan. They resolved to surprise and route the mysterious things, though they might prove to be thousands and thousands of Indians and Indian horses. To effect this they were to go down to the plain and approach the encampment, or whatever it might be, as secretly and as silently as possible, the six Purbuloes going before. Their aim would be to strike a panic among the horses of the Indians by a general yell, and frighten them off. "And what can an Indian do on foot," said they, with feelings of anticipated triumph. Accordingly, every one adjusted his saddle and arms, and down they went, creeping along in breathless silence, the Purbuloes leading the way. When they were sufficiently near, they raised a tremendous shout, and dashed ahead. In a moment the whole plain was alive and moving. The mystery was solved. Thousands and thousands of wild buffalo and wild horses darkened the plain, and fled in headlong confusion. This vast assemblage of wild animals was easily explained. The season was very dry, and they had come and congregated there for water. The mysterious horse had saddle marks on him, and was really tame. He was most probably a stray from some Indian encampment, perhaps not far off.

The headlong and continued running of the buffalo and horses created a rumbling sound that was heard for more than an hour, and resembled distant and prolonged thunder. The party then, in fine cheer, pushed on, and without any thing to interrupt their course, arrived at the Big Arkansas the next day some time in the afternoon, at the place where Captain Riley had encamped. But he was not there.

They knew, however, from fresh signs, particularly the remains of buffalo killed but a few hours, that he had been there the previous night, and following on, they overtook him the same day. Captain Riley, after hearing of the exposed condition of the expedition, resolved to await their arrival.

The company followed the express the next day, and traveled very hard, to get away from a country so full of danger. For two days the Purbuloes kept up a constant howling and lamenting, that was very annoying to the company. On the third day they ceased their wailings, wiped away their tears, and were in fine cheer. Two days' travel brought the company up to Captain Riley. Captain Viscarro here turned his face back to New Mexico, whilst the company going to the States continued their journey under the protection of Captain Riley's forces, and safely reached Independence.[12]

[12] Independence, five miles east of today's Kansas City, was founded in 1827. When Franklin was washed away in a flood in 1828, Independence became the most important outfitting point for Santa Fe caravans.

Chapter 16

People of California—Priests—Missionary establishments—Amusements—Bull and bear fights—Immense number of horses and cattle.

W<small>E HAVE ALREADY</small> said that Workman and Spencer remained about six months in Upper California, during which time Workman was generally engaged in traveling about, collecting information by personal observation, concerning the climate, face of the country, and its productions, and the customs of the people who inhabit that country. We also promised the reader, that we would give him a short account of that country, as furnished by Workman, which we believe to be strictly true, because it harmonizes exactly with the accounts of several other gentlemen who have been there, and who are regarded as incapable of *intentionally* misrepresenting anything.[1]

That country is divided into Upper and Lower California. Lower California is a peninsula about seven hundred miles in length and about sixty wide, with the Pacific on one side, and the Vermillion sea, (or as now called, the Gulph of California) on the other. A part of Lower California is in the torrid zone, and the climate must therefore be very hot. A great deal of this peninsula consists of sandy sterile plains and mountains, that give to it an aspect, that is rather stern than inviting. Frequently for many miles deserts of hot sand spread in

[1] The account of Baja California which follows is taken entirely from Irving, *Bonneville*, pp. 287-88 although Coyner has at times oversimplified Irving's description.

every direction, on the face of which not a single sign of vegetable life can be seen. And then again the face of the country swells into barren mountains, that are equally as destitute of any kind of vegetation. In some parts of Lower California, however, there are valleys of great fertility, in which are to be found all the productions of the tropics, such as olives, oranges, dates, figs, citrons, pomegranates, sugar cane and indigo.

This part of California was settled in 1678 by the Jesuits, an order of the Romish church, who, it seems, were successful in gaining the affections of the natives, and acquired a powerful and extensive influence over their minds. A number of missionary establishments were built in different parts of Lower California, to which the natives gathered from different portions of the country to be initiated in the principles of the Catholic faith. It cannot be denied, that the efforts of these Jesuit fathers effected a complete change in the habitudes and customs of these savages, and they succeeded in persuading them to abandon their barbarous practices, and to adopt, to some extent, the arts and habits of civilized life. But the Spanish government, fearing the growth of the power and influence of the Jesuits, caused them to be banished from the country. The Jesuits were succeeded by the Franciscans, and the Franciscans by the Dominicans.[2] After the expulsion of the Jesuits, to whom the natives were affectionately devoted, the aspect of the various missions became worse and worse, and *now* all of the missionary establishments are in ruins, except one that continues a monument of the former power and prosperity of the order. This establishment is situated in a beautiful valley, and was once the residence of the principal of the Jesuits in that country. Although a monument of the strength of a very powerful order, it is now as silent as the grave, nor is there a human being living at this time within thirty miles of the place. The edifice is of hewn stone, one story high, two hundred and ten feet in front and about fifty-five feet deep. The walls are six feet thick and sixteen feet high, with a vaulted roof of stone, about

[2] Jesuit Juan María Salvatierra founded the first permanent settlement in Baja California in 1697 at Loreto. Jesuits founded twenty missions before being expelled in 1768. Franciscans founded one mission before turning their attention to Alta California. Baja became a Dominican province in 1773, but the Indian population continued to decline and the area languished.

two feet and a half in thickness. There is but little in Lower California to invite immigration. The greater part of it is traversed by barren mountains and sandy plains, that make a very unfavorable impression upon the minds of those who visit that region. A few settlements of *whites* have been attempted, but they have nearly all failed. The population of the peninsula is supposed to be about 12,000. This includes savages, converted Indians and whites. So much for Lower California.

We come now to Upper California, the hunter's Elysium, the tramontane paradise, and land of milk and honey, to which so many thousands and thousands are now turning their eyes, as their future home, and which, by the way, constitutes a *ne plus ultra*,[3] beyond which the restless, roving emigrant can not go.

Workman represents the Spaniards as a people who devote the greater portion of their time to sporting, and various kinds of amusements.[4] This is owing to the fact that very little exertion is necessary to secure a competency of food and raiment. The peculiarity with which he was very much struck was their superior horsemanship, and their equestrian exercises, in which they are constantly engaged. The vast number of horses, both wild and tame, in California, makes every one a cavalier, who is, nearly always, in the saddle, and there is no country, perhaps, in the world, where there are better riders. They commence this kind of exercise when they are very small, and many of their children are killed; and when they have strength to manage a horse, it is no uncommon thing for them to noose a horse perfectly wild, and then mount him in the open prairie and let him go. The frightened animal darts off with great and desperate speed, rearing and plunging to rid himself of his terror, until he worries himself down by his violent exertions, and submits to the government of his rider. It is remarkable that the wildest horse, sometimes in two hours, will become perfectly passive and tractable. A boy ten or twelve years old is generally a good horseman, and it is difficult to get him to do any thing on foot, and any Californian would think less hard of riding

---

[3] "Limit."

[4] This paragraph and the five that follow are taken (sometimes verbatim) from Walter Colton, alcalde at Monterey in 1846, some of whose letters Coyner must have read in an Eastern newspaper. See Walter Colton, *Three Years in California* (New York, 1850), especially pp. 102, 111-13, 116-17.

one hundred miles than he would of walking four hours on foot. They do the most of their labor on horse-back, such as taking care of cattle and horses, and catching wild cattle and horses with the lasso. On horseback, with the lasso, they noose bear, and it is very common to draw their wood to their houses by means of this cord, which they, without dismounting, will throw around the end of a log. The California horses are of a hardy nature, as may be seen by the inhuman manner in which they are generally treated by the natives. If a man has to travel from thirty to forty miles from his residence, he saddles his horse and mounts him; on his arrival at his place of destination, he ties him to a post. He may, in some cases, give him a drink of water, and should he remain away from home four or five days, his horse gets nothing but water, without food all that time; and if he is a horse of the middling class of California horses, he will travel those thirty or forty miles back again, with the same free gait at which he started on a full belly and in good condition. Of course this is only in summer season, when the grass has substance and the horse is in good order. It is customary with the Indians, as well as the Californians, when they wish to perform a long, hard, and perhaps a dangerous ride, to tie up their horses for several days, and give them nothing to eat. When a horse is equipped for a journey in that country, he generally carries, besides his rider, a weight of from fifty to sixty pounds of saddle-gear, and should the weather be rainy, and the saddle get wet, the weight is doubled. It requires two large tanned ox hides to fit out a California saddle; add to this a pair of wooden stirrups three inches thick, the saddle-tree, heavy iron rings and buckles, with a pair of spurs weighing from four to six pounds, a pair of goat skins laid across the pommel of the saddle, with large pockets in them which reach below the stirrups, and a pair of heavy holsters, with the largest kind of horse pistols. Notwithstanding this burden, their horses are active, and travel very freely.

In California the inhabitants are not only said to be almost born on horse-back, but to be almost married in the saddle. Workman's statements correspond with those furnished by one now living in that country about the marriage ceremonies. When the marriage contract is agreed on by the parties, the first business and care of the bride-groom is to get, by buying, begging, or even stealing, (if necessary), the best horse that can be found in his district; and at the same time, by some of the above means, he must get a saddle, with silver mountings about the bridle; and the over leathers of the saddle must be embroidered. It matters not how poor the parties may be, the articles above mentioned are indispensable to the wedding.

The saddle the woman rides has a kind of leathern apron, which hangs over the horse's rump, and completely covers his hinder parts as far as half way down the legs; this, likewise, to be complete, must be embroidered with silks of different colors, and gold and silver thread. From the lower part upwards it opens in six or eight places, each of which is furnished with a number of small pieces of copper or iron, so as to make a noise like so many cracked bells. One of these leathern coverings will sometimes have not less than three hundred of these small jingles hanging to it.

The bridegroom must also furnish the bride with not less than six articles of each kind of women's clothing, and buy up every thing necessary to feast his friends for one, two, or three days, as the inclination of the attendants may dictate. The day for the celebration of the wedding being come, the two fine horses are saddled, and the bridegroom takes up before him, on the horse he rides, his future god-mother, and the future god-father takes before him on his horse the bride, and away they gallop to church. I say *gallop*, for you will never see a Californian going at any other gait than a brisk hand-gallop.

As soon as the ceremony is over, the new married couple mount one horse, and the god-father and god-mother mount the other, and in a hand-gallop gait they return to the house of the parents of the bride, where they are received with squibs and the firing of muskets, and before the bridegroom has time to dismount, two persons, who are stationed at some convenient place near the house, seize him and take off his spurs, which they retain until the owner redeems them with a bottle of brandy or the money to buy it. The married couple then enter the house, where the near relations are all waiting in tears to receive them. They kneel down before the parents and ask a blessing, which is by the parents immediately bestowed. All persons, at this moment, are ex-

133

cluded from the presence of the parties, and the moment the blessing is bestowed, the bridegroom makes a sign or speaks to some person near him, and the guitar and violins are struck up, and dancing and drinking is the order of the day.

The moment a child is born on a farm in California, and the mid-wife has had time to clothe it, it is given to a man on horse-back, who rides post-haste to some Mission with the new born infant in his arms, and presents it to a priest for baptism. This sacrament having been administered, the party return, and the child may rest sometimes for a whole month, without taking an excursion on horseback; but after the lapse of that time, (one month), it hardly escapes one day without being on horseback, until the day of sickness or death. The above statements will show how much *truth* there is in the assertion that the Californians are almost born and almost married in their saddles.

Workman represents the whole of California as given up to pleasurable amusements,[5] some of which are very cruel, but suited to the minds of a priest-ridden, degraded, ignorant, and semi-barbarian people. These are bear and bull fighting, and cock fighting, and fandangoes; amusements in which they generally indulge on the Sabbath, and to which they generally repair after divine service, led on by a priest-hood who are more frequently to be seen in cock-pits and amphitheatres, or at card tables, than in the sanctuary of the Most High. These amphitheatres vary as to their area, according to the size of the towns, in the vicinity of which they are always made.

Mr. Workman was frequently present at their exhibitions, and witnessed their performances in an amphitheatre of very great size. He states the assemblage was always immense, and the excitement and noise very great. A bull-fight always draws forth the greatest concourse;—a real, old-fashioned—old Spain bull-fight. Thousands and thousands come and cram the seats, that are fixed up, one rising above the other, around the amphitheatre, and make a multitude, at last, that would seem to be the whole population of California. A wild bull of the fiercest kind, which has been taken with their lassos, and exasperated until he is in a tremendous rage, is turned loose upon the arena, and is

[5] The discussion which follows is derived from Hastings, *Emigrants' Guide*, pp. 128-31.

134

followed by the bull-fighters, some of whom are on foot and some on horses armed with spears and swords. And now the contest begins, for the moment the bull sees his adversaries, he makes a desperate spring at them, and all the equestrian skill and tact of these distinguished horsemen are put into practical exercise to keep beyond the reach of his horns, and, at the same time to dispatch him. No horse is taken into an amphitheatre, that is not well trained to bull-baiting, and it is therefore generally the case, that the horses which are used on these occasions show as much tact as their riders. Yet it *sometimes* happens that horse and rider are killed in the contest, and it *often* happens that men and horses are badly gored. During the contest, as the enraged animal variously attacks the foot-men and horses, he is pierced and goaded with spears and lances, which make him the more furious. Finally exhausted from rage, violent exertions, and the wounds he has received, he lolls out his tongue and bellows, which being an omen of victory on the part of his assailants, elicits one tremendous burst of applause after another, from the excited multitude. In the meantime the goading and piercing is kept up, until the bull is dispatched amid the shouts of thousands and thousands. The dead bull is then removed from the amphitheatre, and another bull is then brought in, and the same scene is acted over again. Sometimes a bear is turned in with the bull, and then the amphitheatre is smaller, so as to bring the combatants more immediately together. A contest between a bear and a bull is generally soon terminated, as one of the combatants or the other, by acquiring some advantage at the outset, very soon dispatches his adversary.

The constant indulgence in such cruel and inhuman amusements and exhibitions as the above, will lead the reader to see that the inhabitants of California are not a very refined and enlightened people. It is true, there are a number of missions, that are occupied by Catholic priests, whose *ostensible* object is to propagate the principles of the Christian religion: but what can a set of men do in an undertaking of this kind, when in their own mode of living, they daily violate and trample under their feet, every principle of that faith, in the spread of which they profess to be engaged! What importance can the savages of that country attach to the Christian religion, when they are told that such priests are its divinely authorized representatives? If the one half be true that is told of the abominations of the priesthood in that garden spot of the globe, that order *there* must be a perfect embodiment of every wicked attribute that darkens the character of corrupt human nature. Mr. Hastings, who was in that country in 1843, and who is now residing there, gives a very well delineated account of the religious condition of California;[6] and when I read his statements about the missions, and those who occupy them, I confess, that I viewed them as the exaggerated and distorted representations of a mind laboring under some strong prejudice. But when these statements were fully supported by the testimony of Workman, and several other citizens of this country, who have visited California, I am constrained to believe them to be entirely correct.

These missionary establishments are the residences of the priests, to each of which are attached fifteen square miles of land, which is divided into lots to suit the native converts belonging to the establishment.[7] On these lots the converts, (or I should rather call them, poor humbugged vassals and dupes) dwell in their miserable huts, in the most degrading submission to a sacerdotal domination.

As the produce of the lands and all the stock about these establishments, as well as the proceeds resulting from sales, are entirely at the disposal of the priests, the wealth of these religious dignitaries is sometimes very great. Over these fifteen square miles, allotted to each mission by the government, vast droves of horses, numbering several thousands, and herds of cattle even more numerous and sheep, and hogs, may be seen, watched by servile Indians, who, like the stock, are the property of the priests. Appertaining to these establishments are also extensive vineyards, that yield an abundance of wine for the use of the priesthood. In the midst of this domain sits enthroned a fat, pursy, pompous, wine-drinking, debauched priest, who is lord of all the country and consciences, within the above named limits (fifteen miles square).

We have said that the Californians are a very ignorant and degraded people. Indeed they are but little above the Indians, with whom

[6] Ibid., pp. 105-08, 113-14.
[7] Coyner has again used Irving, *Bonneville*, p. 289.

they have intermarried, and to whom they are in all respects assimilated. It is the policy of their religious rulers to keep them in this condition, to perpetuate their wealth, power, and influence. But it is gratifying to be able to say that this deplorable state of things seems to be destined very shortly to mutation. The great fertility of the soil, the remarkable salubrity of the climate, its various valuable productions, and its vast resources of every other kind, are now acting as a charm, and inducing many of our intelligent citizens, and the citizens of other countries, to seek their fortunes in that land of great promise. They are hailed as benefactors by the people, although they may be viewed with suspicion by the priests and those in authority. The principles of civil and religious liberty are being introduced [there and] a strong partiality is expressed by the people to our forms of government and religion; and unless measures are adopted by that government to prevent our people from immigrating into that country, a revolution in favor of our institutions must take place, and who would not be delighted to see such a happy change? Who does not desire to see the twenty thousand semi-barbarians[8] of Upper California, now in a state of wretched vassalage, elevated to the condition of a people enjoying the blessings of education, and the liberty of a free and enlightened conscience? Will the government of Mexico venture to say that our citizens, and those of any other civilized and christian country, shall not take up their residence in California, because, perchance, her duped, downtrodden, priest-ridden people may get a little too much light, and see and feel their own situation, and the tyranny by which they are now oppressed? The juxtaposition of the two governments, (ours and that of Mexico), the constant intermingling of their citizens, the opportunity which the natives of New Mexico and California have of becoming acquainted with our citizens, and trading with them, and of learning something of the excellency of our various institutions, all have the effect of prepossessing them in favor of our principles, and have already caused thousands of anxious eyes to be turned to the United States as their friends and future benefactors.

In writing on this subject, I derive my information from gentlemen

[8] Coyner seems to have meant California Indians, whom Hastings estimated as numbering 20,000 in 1845. Hastings, *Emigrants' Guide*, p. 112.

who have been engaged for a number of years in the Santa Fe trade, and those who have traveled through all of California. I have heard these gentlemen frequently assert, that when our forces in the present war with Mexico shall march into Santa Fe and Monterey, the capital of Upper California, instead of meeting with resistance, they would be hailed as their deliverers. In fulfilment of these prophecies, look at Colonel Kearney, as he enters Santa Fe and lifts and unfurls the flag of our country, greeted by the united voices of a people who feel that deliverance has at last come.[9] Look also at our flag at Monterey, the capital of Upper California, as it waves in the breezes of the Pacific, and infuses joy into thousands of hearts. And look at our little exploring party of sixty men only, led on by Captain Frémont, as they put to flight and pursue, without the loss of a single man, Castro, the Mexican governor of California, with all his forces,[10] and tell me what these things mean, if they do not clearly show that the majority of the people are with us.

In support of what has been stated above, we will give an extract from a letter written by a gentleman, one of our own citizens, who is, at this time, chief magistrate of Monterey, in Upper California.[11] "I was elected," says he, "by the suffrages of the people. The vote polled was a very large one, though no officer or seaman connected with our squadron went to the polls. I mention these facts as an evidence of the good feeling that prevails here toward our flag. Any hostility must have defeated my election. The office is one which I do not covet; it is full of labor and responsibility. It covers every question of civil policy in Monterey and reaches to the lives and fortunes of the inhabitants through an immense jurisdiction. General Castro's officers and men have returned to their homes, and signed a parole not to take up arms

[9] Col. Stephen Watts Kearny entered Santa Fe on August 18, 1846. Although his welcome was not enthusiastic, New Mexicans offered no open resistance.

[10] A reference to Frémont's "Bear Flag" rebellion, in which the ill-equipped governor of northern California, José Castro, fled to the south to avoid certain defeat.

[11] The letter which follows was written by Walter Colton and apparently published in an eastern newspaper where Coyner saw it. Colton wrote a similar account in his *Three Years in California*, which appeared in 1850. Colton was appointed alcalde of Monterey on July 28, 1846, by Commodore Robert Stockton, then was elected to that office on September 15.

against the authority of the United States, or say or do any thing to disturb the tranquillity of the present government. This puts an end to all further war in California; indeed there is no disposition here among the people to offer resistance. The masses are thoroughly with us, and right glad to get rid of Mexican rule. Had it been otherwise, they would never have elected me to the chief magistracy of Monterey. We are all regarded more in the light of benefactors than victors. Their friendship and confidence must never be betrayed. California must never be surrendered to Mexico. If that country has still good claims to her, let those claims be liquidated by an equivalent in money. But it would be treason to the lives and fortunes of the best inhabitants to surrender the province itself. Let Congress at once annex her to the Union as a territory, and establish a civil government. We require a new judicial system; the present one throws all the responsibility on the alcades (justices of the peace). I broke through the trammels of usage a few days since, and empannelled the first jury that ever sat in California. The first men in Monterey were on it; the case involved a large amount of property, and the allegation of a high crime. No one man should decide such a case. The verdict of the jury was submitted to without a murmur from either of the parties. The community seemed much gratified with this new form of trial; they think, and very rightly too, that twelve men are less liable to partiality, prejudice and corruption, than one.[12]

"It was the establishment of trials by jury here that probably led to my election as magistrate. Mr. [Robert] Semple, an emigrant printer, and myself, have established a small paper here, the first ever published in California. It is issued every Saturday; its appearance made not a little sensation. We found the type in the forsaken cell of a monk, and the paper is such as is used here for segar wrappers, and was imported for that purpose. It is printed in English and Spanish. We are going to send, at once, to the United States for larger paper and a fresh font of type. With this new engine of power we are going to sustain the genius of American institutions here. Three thousand emigrants from the United States, it is understood, have just arrived at San Francisco,

[12] This trial occurred on September 4, according to Colton. The newspaper, which he describes next, first appeared on August 15, 1846.

in two companies, one commanded by Captain Hastings, and the other by Captain Russel, and ten thousand more on the way."[13]

So much for the people of California, and their present condition and future prospects. In our next chapter we will give the reader a description of the country, as to climate, health, productions, soil, and local advantages.

[13] Parties led by William H. (Owl) Russell and Lansford W. Hastings reached California in late summer of 1846. Colton exaggerated the number of emigrants they brought, however, for the total that year was only 1,500. Dale L. Morgan, *Overland in 1846: Diaries and Letters of the California-Oregon Trail* (2 vols., Georgetown, Calif., 1963), vol. I, p. 116.

Chapter 17

Description of the soil, climate, health, and productions of Upper California.[1]

As there are many in the United States who are now thinking of going to California, and no doubt many more will remove there if that country should be attached to our territory, I would state that Upper California is west of the Rocky Mountains, and between latitude 31° and 42° on the Pacific,[2] and about two thousand miles from the frontier of the state of Missouri, and the route, the greater part of the way, is the way to Oregon. Emigrants going to the two countries travel together to Fort Hall, at which place they are about twenty days' journey from their destination. The climate of California is a point upon which every man who thinks of going there will aim at obtaining all the correct information that can be had. The journey is very long and tedious, and the advantages gained ought to be many and valuable.

When an emigrant goes to the western frontier of our states, and finds a climate that is destructive to his health, it is very easy for him to find a very healthy region to which he may repair and rebuild a broken down constitution. Persons, however, who go to Oregon, or California, will, in all probability, bury their bones there, whatever

---

[1] Coyner has derived much of this chapter from Hastings, *Emigrants' Guide*.
[2] Irving, *Bonneville*, p. 289, said that upper California began at 31° 10′. Coyner rounded this off to 31°. Today, 32° would be more accurate.

the country may prove to be. For but few families would have perseverance enough to retrace their steps for two thousand miles, through a country not inhabited, except by savages. Although I met with persons, during my residence in the State of Missouri, who had moved with their families to Oregon, and staying there for a time, returned to the States, much dissatisfied, and of course, disposed to give the country a very bad name.

That California is healthy, must be evident from the fact, that it is a country of vallies and mountains. For it is generally the case, that the face of a country determines its character, as it regards health. A country of vallies and very high mountains is always blessed with a pure elastic atmosphere, and an abundance of fine water, which every one knows, are essential to good health. The mountains of California are much higher than the Rocky Mountains themselves. The remarkable phenomenon has been made known, that near the coast of the Pacific, and at the extremity of the continent, there is a range of mountains, (the Sierra Nevada) that is one of the highest on the face of the globe. Its lofty peaks, in all parts of California, and along the shores and far on the waters of the Pacific, may be seen covered with perpetual snow, and glistening in the sun. My authority for these statements, is Captain Fremont, who recently traveled through Oregon and Upper California, exploring the country and taking the altitude of the highest peaks and ranges of mountains. He represents a pass in the Sierra Nevada or Snowy mountains as 2,000 feet higher than the South Pass in the Rocky mountains,[3] and several peaks in view, that rose several thousand feet still higher. Those who have read Mr. Hastings' account of the Sierra Nevada, or as he calls them, the California mountains, will remember that he speaks of this range as "much less elevated than the Rocky mountains." We consider Captain Fremont as the best authority, as he did what Mr. Hastings did not, that is, he ascertained the altitude of those mountains by the use of proper instruments, whilst

[3] Frémont, *Narratives*, p. 367, measured Carson Pass at 9,333 feet. Actually, the summit of the pass is at 8,635 feet, making it over 1,000 feet higher than South Pass (7,550 feet). Although the Sierra Nevadas contain the highest peak (Mt. Whitney, 14,495 feet) in the continental United States (excluding Alaska), the Rockies are generally higher than the California mountains.

Mr. Hastings most probably was guided in his calculation by the unassisted eye, and information derived from others. It is easy, however, to conceive how two men, both of whom may be aiming to state nothing but that which is correct, may differ in opinions about a country, of which so much yet remains to be known. Trappers, who have been in the Rocky Mountains from six to ten years, have informed me that they have frequently come upon large rivers in those mountains, of the name and even the existence of which, they had no knowledge whatever and the course of which are not to be found laid down in any map of that country. Such is the great extent of that country, lying between the States and the Pacific, a great deal of which is now, and is likely to continue to be, unexplored regions.

But let us return to the climate of California, as this is a matter in which every emigrant to that country takes a deep interest, and about which he wants nothing but facts. The united testimony of all men, who have been in California, make it not only healthy, but equal, in this advantage, to any part of the world. It is not subject to the extremes of heat and cold, that are peculiar to the climate of all the States. In any part of Upper California snow seldom falls, and it soon and always disappears at the rising of the sun. This applies to the low lands, or the vallies and table lands, which are the parts of the country that are destined to be settled and improved.

The remarkable uniformity of temperature peculiar to California, and the mildness of its climate is owing to the fact that during the summer winds almost constantly prevail from the north and northwest, and, sweeping over vast bodies of perpetual snow, they are very cool and refreshing.[4] And during the winter there are regular warm sea breezes, which tend to diminish the cold. The heated and rarified air of the valleys and low lands ascends and gives place to the exhilarating and refreshing streams of pure air that come from the adjacent snow capped mountains. As there is very little cold weather during the winter, and no snow or frost to do any harm, there is perpetual life in the vegetable kingdom. This must be the case, otherwise there would

[4] This paragraph and that which follows are drawn from Hastings, *Emigrants' Guide*, pp. 83-84.

be no adequate means of subsistence for the thousands, and ten, and twenty, and fifty thousands of wild horses and cattle that are in California.

In the winter, (if they can be said to have a winter season), that is, during the months of *our* winter, all the productions of the earth are growing, some of them rapidly, refreshed as they are by frequent warm rains; and in the spring, at any rate in the beginning of summer, crops of all kinds are fully matured. This seems to be a wise provision of Providence, for in the latter part of summer there is generally not only a want of rain, but frequently severe droughts, which has made water and food to be so scarce as to cause the loss of thousands of stock. This is the only objection that I have ever heard urged against that country; and it must be acknowledged that it is, to some extent, an unfavorable trait in its character. It seems that the success of the crops depends upon the quantity of rain that falls in the rainy season, which is in the winter months. If a great abundance of rain falls during the winter, the crops the ensuing summer are said to be very abundant; and, on the contrary, if there be a lack of rain during the rainy season, the crops are not so abundant. But even in a dry season, such is the great fertility of the soil, the crops, compared with those in the states, are immense. The uniformity then of temperature, the dry summer and autumn seasons, the pure streams of water, an atmosphere remarkable for its elasticity and purity, the presence of very high mountains, whose peaks are always white with snow, must convince any man that Upper California cannot be any thing but a very healthy part of the world. All descriptions of this country, as it regards the climate, whether written or oral, with which we have met, speak of California in the same unmeasured terms of praise. And should it be attached to our domain, thousands of our enterprising citizens will be seen, every spring, taking up their line of march from the frontier of Missouri for that country. And then, again, the fact that at all seasons of the year the population are in possession of the most perfect health, and none of those diseases are to be seen prevailing that are so common in our new and western states, and make the happiness and the lives of the people so precarious.

We will state another fact (lest we may forget to do so elsewhere)

144

connected with emigrating to California or Oregon. It is the great improvement a trip to either of those countries, or to Santa Fe, is sure to make on the health of invalids who may undertake the journey. I have known many who were completely broken down by the diseases of Missouri, that took trips of this kind in search of health, and have always returned not only completely restored, but even more fleshy than they had been at any period of their lives. If there be a certain cure for diseased lungs in the world, I believe it to be a trip to one of those countries. Let no invalid be afraid to try it. If he thinks the trip too long to California or Oregon, let him go to Santa Fe, which is but about nine hundred miles from Missouri, and is *now* only a trip of pleasure. It matters not how reduced he may be, if he has strength to ride, his health will improve from the start. I have met with many gentlemen in the state of Missouri who were of the opinion that from ten to twenty years had been added to their lives by a trip to Santa Fe.[5]

An impression exists that California is not well supplied with timber; which is certainly very erroneous. It is true, timber is not as abundant in some parts of that country, as it is in the old states, and it is one of the advantages that it is not so abundant. There seems to be a great mistake in the minds of the majority of people, as to the *quantity* of timber necessary for the various purposes to which it is usually applied. When there is more than a sufficiency for said purposes, the surplus must be an expensive obstruction in farming operations.[6] For it must be cut down and removed off the ground, and this often costs more than the land is worth. And if the whole face of the country in California were covered with timber, so exuberant is the growth, it would be next to a physical impossibility to settle the country. One of the greatest facilities experienced by emigrants in settling the prairie states, is the absence to a great extent of timber. When they have made the rails and inclosed their land, their farms are made, and these farms are rich and beautiful in the bargain, and made in a few weeks. By the time they may want a new supply of rails to inclose their

[5] Coyner here reflects the best thinking of his day. He elaborates on his view of healthy climatic conditions in his letter "To A Friend In Virginia" in the Appendix.

[6] Hastings, *Emigrants' Guide*, pp. 85-86, describes California as having "ample timber," but less than in the States. Coyner carries this idea further.

145

farms a second time, timber will have grown up to sufficient size to make them. How different is the case with regard to the lands in some of the old states, that are covered with a dense and heavy growth of timber. It is the lot of many a "young beginner in the world" to have to go into the forest, alone and without any assistance, to open a farm. By the time the trees and stumps are removed off his tract of land, and he has things fixed to his notion and taste, he is an old, worn-out man, if not in years, at least in feeling. And what is worse, he has nothing to show for his time, and labor, and expended energies, but a farm that will not bring as much per acre, as it would have cost to remove the timber. I have known farmers, in Illinois and Missouri, to make their rails ten miles from their prairie lands, and haul them that distance, and make a prairie farm infinitely easier than they could have opened a farm in the woods. The timber in California is in abundance in the mountains, along the rivers, and coast, and grows to an extraordinary size and height. Workman affirms that he saw trees on the coast, that were not less than two hundred feet high, and without a limb, the first hundred feet, and about thirty feet in circumference. The principal varieties are oak, ash, fir, pine, spruce, cedar of great size, called red wood, cherry, willow. The prickly pear and wormwood are to be found, constituting the only vegetation in some parts of California, as well as Oregon and the Rocky Mountains. The forests abound in wild grapes, which fact, connected with the circumstance that there are extensive vineyards belonging to the missions shows, that California is admirably adapted to the cultivation of the grape. The fact, that there are orchards attached to those missions, that furnish every variety of fruit, northern and southern, settles another important question in regard to the fruits of the country.

Vegetables of all kinds are produced in the greatest abundance, and wheat, corn, rye, oats, hemp, tobacco, are cultivated with as much success as in any part of the world. In the southern part of Upper California, and Lower California, cotton, rice, coffee, cane, and the tropical fruits, such as oranges, pomegranates, citrons, lemons, et cetera, are cultivated and come to perfect maturity. Clover, flax, and oats, are in many parts, spontaneous productions of the earth, and may be seen in vast fields. The wild flax in California is the same as our variety, and is to be seen in Oregon and the Rocky Mountains. The wild oats and clover, almost in every respect, resemble those of the states.

Wheat may be sown, any time between fall and spring, and the time of cutting depends on the time it is sown. If it is sown in the fall, it will mature in the spring. The quality and quantity of tobacco cultivated is said to be equal to that of any portion of the world. Indeed all the experiments that have been made in cultivating the different kinds of grains and fruits, have resulted in the most satisfactory, and flattering developments. And every variety of spontaneous fruits found in the States are found there luxuriant and abundant.[7]

One of the most interesting characteristics of this country is the immense herds of cattle and gangs of horses, partially wild, that may be seen grazing on the prairies and plains. The almost endless number of cattle and horses, and their rapid increase, and the ease with which they are raised in California, makes it perhaps the greatest stock country in the world. Indeed, for many years, cattle were raised (if they can be said to be raised) for their hides, and were slaughtered by thousands for this object, whilst their flesh was left on the ground as food for wild beasts. Recently there has been an increasing demand for their tallow and beef, and indeed a great many cattle are driven to Oregon to supply the emigrants.

It would appear that the cattle of California are of an inferior quality, as the people of Oregon greatly prefer the cattle taken from the state of Missouri. Hence several droves of cattle (cows principally) have been taken to Oregon by speculators from Missouri, and sold at a very high price, four times as much, perhaps, as the price of a cow from California. The preference for our cattle may arise from the fact that they are more tame and easily managed. The California cattle are said to be very wild and ferocious, and from the fact that no pains are taken to cross and improve the race, they are, in all probability, very rough. They are certainly very large, and generally weigh more than our domesticated race, which excels them in neatness and gentleness of disposition.

[7] Hastings, *Emigrants' Guide*, pp. 86-89, provides a much more detailed discussion of field crops, from which Coyner has drawn.

The country is also very favorable to the raising of hogs and sheep, of which any number may be raised with little or no trouble. Horses are the favorite stock with the Californians. A Californian well mounted is in his glory. His equipments, in our idea, are awkward and clumsy. His saddle, which is after the Moorish mode, is high behind and before. The front part, called the pommel, is made very strong, as the Californians are in the habit of fastening their lasso to it when they have noosed a wild horse, cow, or bear. Indeed the lasso is always hanging coiled up on the pommel of the saddle, and it is astonishing to what a variety of uses they apply it, and with what dexterity they throw it. The tree of a California saddle is covered with two or three covers of raw hide, which is sometimes carved and embroidered. The stirrups, which are of wood, and very clumsy, are also sometimes carved. A tremendous pair of spurs, as large as pitch-forks, fastened by chains, jingle at the heels of the equestrian. As to the bridle, it often has such mechanical force that it is perfectly easy for the rider to break the jaws of his horse. The seat of the saddle is so deep that when the rider occupies it, it is almost impossible for the most vicious horse to dismount him.

In no part of the world are horses so numerous as they are in California. One man will frequently own from ten to twenty thousand, some of which are distinguished from those belonging to other men by being branded. These horses are slightly smaller than our horses, but they are very clean-limbed, active, and capable of enduring great fatigue. It is said to be very common for a Californian to ride one hundred miles in a day, or one hundred miles in ten hours, on the same horse. It is to be remembered, however, that the face of the country is very level and the roads very fine, circumstances that very much determine the distance a horse will travel in a day. Their horses, no doubt, are of the pony kind, and from the fact that no pains are taken to improve the race, they must be very degenerate. As numerous as horses are in California and Oregon, and as cheap as they are, there is a demand for our horses there, and one good horse from the states is worth twenty of those trifling little ponies.[8]

[8] Coyner has read too much into Hastings (ibid., pp. 92-93), who merely says California horses "are but slightly smaller than ours."

Chapter 18

Santa Fe Trade.

WE HAVE STATED, that our two lost trappers, Workman and Spencer, returned to the States with a company of Santa Fe traders. We have also alluded to the beneficial effect, which a trip to Santa Fe always has on the health of invalids, and we have recommended persons laboring under pulmonary diseases to take a trip of this kind as an almost certain cure.

It may not be improper to give the reader a short account of the Santa Fe trade, which is now a regular business, in which a number of our citizens are regularly engaged, and in which an immense amount of capital is invested. I am not able to state the year, when this trade assumed its present weight and importance: not long before 1824 or 5.[1] Although now and then a few adventurous individuals would venture through the immense wilds of Louisiana with a few light articles, before that time.

This trade differs in one respect, from the fur trade, and that is this. The latter is carried on by companies of very heavy capital. The Santa Fe trade is carried on by individuals. A man engaged in this trade buys his goods in the eastern market, and has them taken to the frontier of Missouri. There he hires a sufficient number of hands to drive his

[1] The Santa Fe Trade got under way in 1821, following Mexican independence from Spain. This chapter, apparently not drawn from published sources, is basically sound and seems to have been based on information that Coyner gathered from conversations with traders in Missouri.

teams across the plains to Santa Fe, and as many more, as may be needed for other purposes. His goods are conveyed in wagons, that were usually drawn by mules. Oxen are now substituted. A Santa Fe company generally numbers about one hundred men, and it was customary to depend upon game for provisions, but now every company takes a supply to carry them through. The buffalo have become wild, and it takes too much time to hunt and kill them. Moreover, serious disasters have befallen several companies, by permitting the men to leave their wagon teams to engage in buffalo hunts, as Indians have sometimes seized such times as a suitable opportunity to rush in upon a company and run off their mules, and perhaps cut off the party.[2] The Indians along that route, have learned that it is very easy to frighten a caravan of mules, and their policy is always to strike a panic among them, and a mule *frightened* is a mule frantic. They cannot be restrained, but break loose and dash off, pursued by the savages, who keep up the panic by a constant yell. Formerly the traders were in the habit of buying mules in Santa Fe, and bringing them to the States; but the Spanish mules are very small, and since our own citizens have engaged in the raising of mules, that kind of stock is not, at this time, ever brought to the States, from New Spain. Whilst mules were an object of trade, the traders met with many mishaps. Whole droves of mules, numbering from three to five hundred, were sometimes lost. Cattle are preferred to mules for another reason. They are stronger than mules, and can stand the heat as well. A duty of one hundred dollars is to be paid in Santa Fe, on every wagon, without any reference to the size and the amount of goods.[3] To take the advantage of this regulation, the traders have wagons made that will contain seventy or eighty hundred weight, with very wide tire. Oxen are better adapted, by their superior strength, to draw such heavy wagons, than mules. When the expedition approaches Santa Fe, the freight of three wagons is put into one, and the empty wagons are destroyed by fire, to prevent their falling into the hands of Indians. In this way, the traders manage

[2] Although experienced traders may have forsaken buffalo hunting when Coyner wrote, it was still widely engaged in on the Trail.

[3] This was the case, only the amount was $500 a wagonload. Max L. Moorhead, *New Mexico's Royal Road* (Norman, Okla., 1958), p. 127.

to avoid paying a great deal of duty. When they have sold their goods, they also sell their teams at a very fair price. One of these Santa Fe traders will buy up from eighty to one hundred pair of oxen every spring for his trip. From this it will be very readily inferred that there is quite a demand for oxen in Missouri, at least once a year. Gold and silver being the articles for which the traders exchange their goods, our citizens are required by the authorities of Santa Fe to pay a heavy duty on the precious metals they take out of that country. To avoid paying this tax, they have large false axle-trees to the wagons, in which they convey their money back to the States, which are excavated, and in which the precious metals are concealed. When the proper officer examines the contents of the wagons, he is perfectly unconscious of the artifice. A great deal of capital is invested in this trade. Some expeditions return to the State with fifty and as much sometimes as one hundred thousand dollars. By this means a great deal of Mexican coin is brought to this country.

During the first few years of this trade, indeed until very recently, the Indians between Missouri and Santa Fe were very troublesome, particularly the Camanches. The companies generally keep some cannon buried on the Big Arkansas, where the danger begins, and when they reach there they take them up and convey them through the dangerous country, and then bury again until they return. The caravans leave Independence in the spring, and, if they go no farther than Santa Fe, they return the following autumn, but, if they go on to Chihuahua, which is five hundred miles beyond Santa Fe, they are absent a year. Heavy capitalists now generally go on to Chihuahua.

As there is nothing else to induce our citizens to go to that country, but its precious metals, very few of them take up their residence there for life. The regular traders who have families leave them in Missouri, and it is a rare thing to see one of our female citizens in a company going to Santa Fe. A German who was going to Santa Fe to become a resident in that country, is said to have had a great deal of trouble in consequence of his having a wife with him. She was perhaps the first white woman that ever passed through that country (and for any thing that I know, she was the last), and when she was seen by the savages, their curiosity could scarcely be repressed. They gazed upon her beautiful white face with astonishment. They wanted the privilege (that is, some of the principal chiefs) of riding with her in the conveyance in which she was seated, and some even followed the train of wagons for two or three days, simply to enjoy the pleasure of gazing upon her. One of the Indians, a Camanche chief, expressed a wish to buy her, and offered her husband two *buffalo skins*, which the savage thought a very fair price for a wife. It is hardly necessary to state that the German had a very different notion about the value of a wife, and declined the offer of the Camanche chief. It is said that his mind experienced many anxious fears, lest he might lose his "better half," and he declared that if he succeeded in getting to Santa Fe with his wife, he never would again run the like risk of losing her, or put himself in a situation where he would again be taunted with two buffalo skins.

The Santa Fe trade is not now as sure a road to wealth as it was some years ago. There are too many engaged in it. Competition has reduced the price of goods, and the Spaniards themselves have recently engaged in it, and it is now somewhat overdone. Such is a brief account of a trade that has made many of our enterprising citizens very wealthy, and caused the precious metals to circulate in great abundance in this country.

Chapter 19

Fur trade—The fate of the Tonquin.[1]

As the traffic in furs is a pursuit which has taken many of our citizens beyond the boundaries of the states, and prompted them to penetrate the vast wilderness between the states and the Pacific, and to explore regions that, but for the efforts of these early adventurers, must have remained perhaps until this day a *terra incognita*, whose beauty, grandeur, and fertility there was no one to admire but the uncultivated savage; and as these adventurers acted the part of precursors as well as trappers, and went in advance of civilization, and discovered countries now occupied by the agriculturalists and mechanics, we propose giving the reader a succinct account of the fur trade, and some interesting facts connected with it.

The French, who settled on the banks of the St. Lawrence, were among the first who engaged in this trade on a plan somewhat extensive, and they seem to have been the first to discover the vast sources of wealth that were to be found in the rich peltries of the western wilderness. They procured large quantities of the most valuable furs from the natives, by giving them in exchange little trinkets that were of very little value, and in this way realized vast profits. When the French lost possession of Canada, the trade fell into the hands of British subjects, when it contracted to very narrow limits and seemed to labor with

---

[1] The first portion of this chapter, through the description of the "fate of the Tonquin," is a synthesis of Irving's *Astoria*.

difficulties. About four years afterwards it seemed to expand again, and was pushed on by an additional number of enterprising merchants, who enlarged the field of their operations, and penetrated deeper into the wilderness.

The field of adventure in this trade continued to enlarge in the course of time, until it covered the great chain of Lakes, the sources of the Mississippi and the Missouri, the sources of the Columbia and Colorado, and even reached within the arctic circle. A field of enterprise so wide, and abounding in such vast treasures of hidden wealth, would naturally call into existence a great many companies. The first company that was formed was the Hudson Bay company, which was chartered in 1669 or 1670,[2] by Charles the second, who granted to said company the exclusive privilege of establishing trading posts on the shores and the tributary waters of that bay.

After enjoying almost uninterrupted control of the trade for several years, this company found a rival in an association of several wealthy Scottish gentlemen, (merchants), who had established a trading post at Michilimackinac, which became the centre of the trade extending from lake Superior to the upper Mississippi, and to lake Winnepeg. The evils arising from the competition of trade, brought the two companies together under the name of the North-west company. After this, as the trade increased, one company after another sprang up, until at different times there have been eight or ten different companies, the names of which we will give. We have mentioned the Hudson Bay Company, afterwards called the North-west Company; the Mackinaw Company; the American Fur Company; the Pacific Fur Company; Missouri Fur Company; the Rocky Mountain Fur Company, and several others. It is not our purpose to furnish a history of each one of those companies, the name of which we have given, but simply to state some facts in relation to that trade, which we think will be interesting. The Rocky Mountains embrace the region in which this trade at this time is more particularly going on. It is about the streams and lakes in that vast wilderness, more than any where else, that the ad-

[2] Irving says 1670, which is correct. Why Coyner chose to be less precise is curious.

venturous trapper is to be seen passing away his solitary days, and intensely engaged in his efforts to take the beaver.

The first company that attempted to establish a trading post on the waters of the Columbia was the Missouri Fur Company, formed at St. Louis in 1808, at the head of which was Manuel Lisa, a Spaniard. He established posts on the Upper Missouri, and one on Lewis river, the south branch of the Columbia. This appears to have been the first post established by white men in the country drained by the Columbia; but the enmity of the Indians and scarcity of food caused it to be abandoned by Mr. Henry in 1810.

In this same year 1810, Mr. Astor of New York engaged in the bold scheme of establishing a number of trading posts on the Columbia and its tributaries, and along the shores of the Pacific, and the headwaters of the Missouri, with a factory at the mouth of the Columbia. His plan was to send goods from New York by sea to this factory to be exchanged for furs, which he intended to have conveyed to China, and bring back the silks and teas of that country to New York. In this magnificent scheme, Mr. Astor had associated with him, four gentlemen, under the firm of the Pacific Fur Company. Another part of his plan was, to send an expedition overland up the Missouri, destined also for the mouth of the Columbia. The object of the land expedition was to open a communication through the Rocky Mountains, to gather all necessary information about the country, and to plant trading posts along the route.

We have said that Mr. Astor's plan was to forward all necessary supplies by sea to the mouth of the Columbia. In the execution of this plan, he fitted out a large vessel called the Tonquin, with men, guns, and every thing that might be needed at his posts on the Pacific and the Columbia. This vessel was committed to the hands of a Captain Thorn, a man who may have known how to manage a ship, but he certainly did not know how to manage savages, to the best advantage, or at least for his own good. It has always been found to be good policy to treat them kindly, and not to regard them as civilized beings, who may be expected in all instances to do that which is right. The observance of this kind of policy has often prevented difficulties, that

155

would, in all probability, have resulted in very serious consequences. It seems to have been the misfortune of the captain of the Tonquin, that he was of a petulant disposition, and rough and stern in his manners. He was very impatient under any provocation, and it would seem conceived not only an unfavorable opinion, but a sovereign contempt for his crew, which were not of the kind of materials that he admired, or would himself have selected for the voyage. Entertaining this opinion, his suspicious disposition made every thing foster it. The relations between the splenetic captain and his men being of a very unpleasant character, their trip was by no means a pleasant one. After a voyage of five months, Mr. Astor's ship reached the mouth of the Columbia. And if the captain had his trials before he reached that point, his little stock of patience was now doomed to be exhausted. The mouth of the Columbia, according to all accounts, must bear a very frightful aspect, and as it is said to have extensive sand-bars, its entrance must ever be very difficult and dangerous; a fact that will always diminish the value of that river in a commercial point of view. There seems to be vast bodies of sand about the mouth of the Columbia, that are brought down by its current, and accumulate at its communication with the ocean. The constant swelling of the sea, tends to throw it back, and thus it becomes an obstruction that must ever be in the way of vessels that would enter that river. The Tonquin met with delay, difficulties, and disasters, when she reached the mouth of the Columbia. From shore to shore there was a wild confusion of angry waves, lashed by their collision into tumultuous uproar, that spread fear through the hearts of all the crew. The Tonquin stood out, aloof from the danger that was before her, for several nights and days.

In the meantime, the authoritative captain sent out a boat, under circumstances that seemed almost to insure its loss. His conduct seems to have been not only very reprehensible, but even cruel. Four of his men were ordered out in a whale boat, to ascertain the channel, and to examine the bar. The poor fellows submissively entered the boat, but they cast a look upon the Tonquin, accompanied with tears in their eyes, as they left her, that showed that they felt they were going to a watery grave. The mouth of this river is upwards of four miles wide, and at that time, an angry sea lashed into rage by a strong north-west wind, was throwing its white foam and surges against the shore, and across the mouth of the river. It was not long before the Tonquin lost sight of the doomed boat in the tumult of angry waters. A dark, tempestuous night ensued, and this authorised the men in the Tonquin to indulge in the most painful anxiety and fears about the fate of the whale boat. The next day another small boat was sent to hunt the channel, as well as to look for the missing boat. The fate of this boat was nearly as sad as that of the first, as it was capsized near the shore, and but two of the crew made their escape. The whale boat was no doubt lost, as no account could be had of it; thus, eight or ten of the crew of the Tonquin were lost before she found shelter from the storm. It is due to Captain Thorn, to say, that when he landed, he caused a diligent search to be made along the shore for the men that were absent, but they could not be found.

As this account of Mr. Astor's enterprise in the fur trade is only intended to be a hasty sketch, we would state that the crew selected a site for a trading post, and that all hands went to work to erect the necessary buildings; when these were put up, the Tonquin was relieved of her cargo, and Captain Thorn, in compliance with his orders, put out into the Pacific, to coast to the north. By the way, an Indian interpreter was picked up by the Tonquin, to aid them in their intercourse with the savages along the coast. This interpreter was well acquainted with the various tribes with whom the ship was likely to meet, and when she reached Vancouver's Island, he informed Captain Thorn, that that part of the coast was infested with a very treacherous and uncertain tribe, in whose professions of friendship no confidence could be reposed with safety. But the captain was a man of his own head, and did things in his own way. He landed at said island, where he was received with great apparent friendship, by the savages, who manifested a readiness to trade by bringing their peltries. Captain Thorn, expecting a prompt and ready sale, soon made quite a display of that variety of notions and trinkets that is sure to take the eye of the savage. He seems to have calculated, too, upon getting their peltries at a very reduced price; but the natives had dealt with other vessels trading along the coast, and had gained some tolerably correct idea of the value of their furs. When Captain Thorn learned their prices, he

157

treated them and their skins with contempt, and withdrew from them, much fretted and vexed. But he could not escape the importunities of the savages, who, perhaps had not as yet, conceived any bad designs against the crew and the ship. It is said, that among the savages there was an old chief who followed the captain to and fro, taunting him with his mean offers; holding out at the same time a sample of his skins, to tempt him to buy. This was more than the patience of the vexed captain could stand. He snatched the skin from the hands of the chief, rubbed it in his face, and then kicked him overboard. He then in a very rash manner, cleared the deck of skins and savages. The badly treated old chief, who, by his fall in the water, had been completely submerged, came again to the surface, and paddled his way in a dreadful rage to the shore, from which, as he cast his eyes upon the Tonquin, he seemed to mean to say, "I'll have revenge." And revenge he secured, as the sequel will show.

Some of the crew, who were better acquainted with Indian character than the captain, assured him, the natives would resent the indignity offered their chief, and that it would be very unsafe to remain there. The Indian interpreter also, added his testimony to confirm the above opinion. But a parcel of naked savages were no terror to his mind, nor was he a man to confess that any difficulty could be brought about, by indiscretion on his part, for he was not willing to acknowledge any indiscretion. On the next day, some of the savages, very early in the morning made their appearance, and came along side of the Tonquin, in a canoe, making signs of friendship, and manifesting a desire to trade.

As punctilious to a fault as the captain was in strictly observing the instructions of Mr. Astor, in other things, he here failed to do as his employer had advised him, and that was, to treat the natives kindly, and not to suffer too many, at a time, to go aboard of his ship. This precaution seems to have escaped the mind of the very scrupulous captain, as these Indians, notwithstanding the occurrence, were permitted to mount the deck. Indeed there seems to have been no restraint of this kind practised, as one company after another, as they came in their canoes, enjoyed the same unsafe privilege, and in the space of an hour, the Tonquin was completely surrounded with canoes full of Indians, and the deck was crowded. The interpreter, who, being an Indian himself, and knowing the perfidy of this tribe manifested great anxiety for the welfare of the ship and informed the captain that the greater part of the savages wore short mantles of skins, under which it was customary to conceal their arms. This suggestion met with no better reception from the captain, than the advice that was given at other times. But the crowd of canoes and Indians became so dense that he, at last, but when it was too late, became alarmed, and gave orders to push out from shore. The Indians, as the ship was about to depart, now intimated, that they would let the captain have their furs at his own price, and a brisk trade commenced. But they all wanted knives for their skins, and as fast as one party was supplied, another came forward. Every thing that occurred on this occasion, in the view of men at all acquainted with Indian character, was calculated to prove that these savages had some hostile scheme on foot.

And yet, *mirabile dictu*,[3] it seems, nothing of this kind entered the mind of the captain, until he was completely in their clutches. In the space of an hour's trading, almost every Indian had supplied himself with a knife. The number of the crew did not exceed twenty-five or thirty; whilst the Indians numbered several hundred on the ship and on the shore. Having thus successfully armed themselves, the Indians had, in this, accomplished one important part of their plan, and were ready for the work of vengeance. In a moment a yell was raised in one part of the deck, and was in an instant responded to in every other part. Knives and war clubs were now seen in the hands of the Indians, who rushed upon the crew. This melancholy affair is graphically described in Irving's Astoria, in the following language.[4] "The first that fell, was Mr. Lewis, the ship's clerk. He was leaning, with folded arms, over a bale of blankets, engaged in bargaining, when he received a deadly stab in the back, and fell down the companion way. Mr. McKay, who was seated on the taffrail, sprang on his feet, but was instantly knocked down with a war club, and fell backwards into the sea, where he was dispatched by the women in the canoes. In the meantime, Captain

---

[3] Meaning "wonder of wonders."
[4] The lengthy quotation which follows is taken, with a few minor changes, from *Astoria*, pp. 111-14.

Thorn made desperate fight against fearful odds. He was a powerful as well as resolute man, but he had come upon deck without weapons. Shewish, a young chief, singled him out as his peculiar prey, and rushed upon him at the first outbreak. The captain had barely time to draw a clasp-knife, with one blow of which he laid the young savage dead at his feet. Several of the stoutest followers of Shewish now set upon him. He defended himself vigorously, dealing crippling blows to the right and left, and strewing the quarter deck with the slain and wounded. His object was, to fight his way to the cabin, where there were fire-arms; but he was hemmed in with foes, covered with wounds, and faint with loss of blood. For an instant he leaned on the tiller wheel, when a blow from behind with a war club, felled him to the deck, where he was dispatched with knives, and thrown overboard.

While this was transacting upon the quarter deck, a chance-medley fight was going on throughout the ship. The crew fought desperately, with knives, hand-spikes, and whatever weapon they could seize upon in the moment of surprise. They were soon, however, overpowered by numbers, and mercilessly butchered. As to the seven who had been sent aloft to make sail, they contemplated with horror the carnage that was going on below. Being destitute of weapons, they let themselves down by the running rigging, in hopes of getting between decks. One fell in the attempt, and was instantly dispatched; another, received a death blow, in his back, as he was descending; a third, Stephen Weekes, the armorer, was mortally wounded, as he was getting down the hatchway. The remaining four made good their retreat into the cabin, where they found Mr. Lewis, still alive, though mortally wounded. Barricading the cabin door, they broke holes through the companion-way, and with the muskets and ammunition which were at hand, they opened a brisk fire, that soon cleared the deck. Thus far the Indian interpreter, from whom these particulars are derived, had been an eye witness of the deadly conflict. He had taken no part in it, and had been spared by the natives, as being of their race. In the confusion of the moment, he took refuge with the rest, in the canoes. The survivors of the crew now sallied forth, and discharged some of the deck-guns, which did great execution among the canoes, and drove all the savages to shore.

For the remainder of the day no one ventured to put off to the ship, deterred by the effects of the fire arms. The night passed away without any further attempt on the part of the natives. When the day dawned, the Tonquin still lay at anchor in the bay, her sails all loose and flapping in the wind, and no one apparently on board of her. After a time, some of the canoes ventured forth to reconnoitre, taking with them the interpreter. They paddled about, keeping cautiously at a distance, but growing more and more emboldened at seeing her quiet and lifeless. One man, at length, made his appearance on deck, and was recognised by the interpreter, as Lewis. He made friendly signs and invited them on board. It was long before they ventured to comply. Those who mounted the deck met with no opposition; no one was to be seen aboard; for Mr. Lewis, after inviting them, had disappeared. Other canoes now pressed forward to board the prize; the deck was soon crowded, and the sides covered with clambering savages, all intent on plunder. In the midst of their eagerness and exultation, the ship blew up with a tremendous explosion. Arms, legs and mutilated bodies were blown into the air and dreadful havoc was made in the surrounding canoes. The interpreter was in the main chain at the time of the explosion, and was thrown unhurt into the water, where he succeeded in getting into one of the canoes. According to his statement, the bay presented an awful spectacle after the catastrophe. The ship had disappeared, but the bay was covered with the fragments of the wreck, with shattered canoes, and Indians swimming for their lives, or struggling in the agonies of death; while those who had escaped the danger, remained aghast and stupified, or made with frantic panic for the shore. Upwards of a hundred savages were destroyed by the explosion, many more were shockingly mutilated, and for days afterwards the limbs and bodies of the slain were thrown upon the beach.

The inhabitants [of Neweetee] were overwhelmed with consternation at the astounding calamity which had burst upon them in the very moment of triumph. The warriors sat mute and mournful, while the women filled the air with loud lamentations. Their weeping and wailing, however, was suddenly turned into yells of fury at the sight of four unfortunate white men, brought captive into their village. They had been driven on shore, in one of the ship's boats, and taken at some distance, along the coast.

The interpreter was permitted to converse with them. They proved to be the four brave fellows who had made such defense from the cabin. The interpreter gathered from them some of the particulars already related. They told him further, that, after they had beaten off the enemy and cleared the ship, Lewis advised that they should slip the cable and endeavor to get to sea. They declined to take his advice, alledging [sic] that the wind set too strongly in the bay and would drive them on shore. They resolved as soon as it was dark, to put off quietly in the ship's boat, which they would be able to do unperceived, and to coast along back to Astoria. They put their resolution into effect; but Lewis refused to accompany them, being disabled by his wound, hopeless of escape, and determined on a terrible revenge. On the voyage out, he had repeatedly expressed a presentiment, that he should die by his own hands; thinking it highly probable that he should be engaged in some contest with the natives, and being resolved, in case of extremity, to commit suicide, rather than be made a prisoner. He now declared his intention to remain on board of the ship until daylight, to decoy as many of the savages on board as possible, then to set fire to the powder magazine, and terminate his life by a signal act of vengeance. How well he succeeded has been shown. His companions bade him a melancholy adieu, and set off on their precarious expedition. They strove with might and main to get out of the bay, but found it impossible to weather a point of land, and were at length compelled to take shelter in a small cove, where they hoped to remain concealed, until the wind should be more favorable. Exhausted by fatigue and watching, they fell into a sound sleep, and in that state were surprised by the natives. Better had it been for those unfortunate men had they remained with Lewis, and shared his heroic death: as it was, they perished in a more painful and protracted manner, being sacrificed by the natives to the manes of their friends, with all the lingering tortures of savage cruelty. Sometime after their death, the interpreter, who had remained a kind of prisoner at large, effected his escape, and brought the tragical tidings to Astoria." Such was the fate, and such is the melancholy story of the Tonquin. We have been somewhat minute in our details as regards this part of Mr. Astor's enterprise, because we regard the fate of his ship as the most tragical event belonging to the Rocky Mountain fur-trade. For a fuller and more accurate account of Mr. Astor's herculean enterprise, which failed, by his trading post or factory falling into the hands of the English, during the late war, we refer the reader to Irving's Astoria, a book, which is certainly one of the best of the many valuable productions of the popular author, Washington Irving.

After the return of peace, and when the trading post at the mouth of the Columbia was surrendered, Mr. Astor sought to renew his enterprise, and to start it afresh; but he was not successful in securing the fostering aid of the general government, and the factory at Astoria was transferred to Vancouver. The Hudson Bay Company[5] enjoyed a perfect monopoly and had the uninterrupted sway over all the country west of the Rocky Mountains, until 1823, when Mr. Ashley made a successful expedition beyond the mountains; and in 1826 the Rocky Mountain Fur Company of St. Louis commenced regular expeditions to the borders of the Columbia and Colorado.[6] The American Fur Company then extended their operations. Through all the intermediate country, also, that is, on the waters of the Mississippi, Missouri, Yellow Stone, Platte, Arkansas, &c. the various fur companies are carrying on their operations. Each company has a number of men (trappers,) in their employment, whose services are engaged at a fixed price, by the year. There is also another class of men, who are called free trappers, from the fact, that they are not hired by the year, but whilst they enjoy the protection of the company, they sell the peltries they obtain to said company.

In the mountains, these companies have their fixed places for their yearly rendezvous, where the scattered trappers come in from every quarter, bringing their furs, which they may have procured the past trapping season. At these places they are met by their employers, or their agents, who come from the states, generally from St. Louis, with

[5] In October 1813, Astor's partners in Oregon sold Astoria to the British North West Company which merged in 1821 with the Hudson's Bay Company, the name of the latter remaining.

[6] Coyner has the general idea of the sequence of events here. Ashley did first enter the Rockies in 1823, but the Rocky Mountain Fur Company was not established until 1830. Coyner seems to have shifted from *Astoria* to *Bonneville*, pp. 4-8, for his source of information.

their loads of merchandise. It is an annual meeting, when the hired trappers receive their pay, and the free trappers bring their beavers to trade. The Indians also, come in from the country around, and are present to trade. Some two months are generally spent by all parties at one of those grand stampadoes, as the skin of the beaver, at that time (July and August) is of no value, and the trappers have nothing to do. The scene that one of these yearly rendezvous presents is truly one that is *sui generis* [unique], and to a person that has witnessed nothing beyond the dull monotony of civilized life, very exciting and strange.[7]

After the brisk trade, that is usually kept up for several days, the men are seen resorting to every expedient to pass away their time; such as shooting, playing cards, horse racing, wrestling, foot racing, passing from camp to camp, cracking their jokes, and telling anecdotes, and hair-breadth escapes, dancing and courting; courting whom? the reader may ask. Why, courting the young squaws, who assemble there, to accomplish *their ends*, to wit: by their smiles, charms, and graces, to win the hearts of the trappers, who, in their view, are a superior order of beings. To be a trapper's wife, in the eye of a mountain belle, is the perfection of good luck, the heighth of her coquettish ambition. The reader must not be surprised, when we use the term *coquettish*. These dames of nature, like their sex in civilized life, are fond of conquests of this kind, and to obtain them, they paint and bedeck their persons, and flirt about, smile and look pretty, and cast their shy-loving glances on those upon whose hearts they may desire to make their impressions. And by the way, let me tell you, they often succeed in their love adventures, and can apply the language of another, as to their undertaking, and say, *veni, vidi, vici*. Many of those men engaged in the fur business, indeed a majority of them, have their Indian wives, and show to the world, that, if not in other things, at least, in this particular, they are disposed to revere the authority of that Book, which tells us "to marry, multiply and replenish the earth;" and that they are firm believers at least, in one doctrine of that Book, which teaches that "it is not good that man should be alone."

[7] Coyner describes the rendezvous as if it still existed in 1847. The last rendezvous was held on Green River in 1840.

Among the articles of trade, at these rendezvous, is a due supply of the "O ! be joyful," as the New Englanders call it, *alias*, alcohol, which is said to be retailed at four dollars a pint. It is diluted with water, so as to bring it to the strength of whiskey. It is taken into the Rocky mountains in the form of alcohol, because it is more portable. It is hardly necessary to say, that the excitement at these rendezvous is greatly increased by the use of this artificial stimulant.

The principal points of these yearly meetings of our trappers, are the Green (Colorado) river valley, and Pierre's Hole. Here hundreds and hundreds, of hunters, trappers, traders, and Indians are assembled from two to three months. Before this season of festivity and idleness comes to a close, the men become impatient, and desire again to dash into the wilderness and engage in their exciting employment. Two trappers generally go together. The outfit of a trapper is seven traps, a rifle of course, an axe, a hatchet, four pounds of lead and one of powder, several blankets, a knife, an awl, and a camp-kettle. He is furnished with two or three horses for his trip. Each trapping party takes some particular stream and region, as the field of their operations, to which they repair, and where they make the necessary preparations for their stay there.

In the trapping season, these adventurous men are scattered all over the Rocky Mountains, along every stream, and about every lake or pool of water, setting their traps for their favorite game, and in the midst of danger, eagerly pursuing their favorite avocation. Men who have spent several years in this kind of life, seldom relish a civilized life. When they come to the states, they soon become restless and impatient, and again seek the haunts of the wilderness.

The state of things on the waters east of the Rocky Mountains is somewhat different from that in the mountains. On those waters our citizens have their forts regularly and safely constructed, and some of them mounted with guns. These forts are constructed in reference to the trade that the company expects to carry on with the different tribes; for example, a fort that is intended to reap the profits of a trade with the Crow Indians, is situated in some place in their country most likely to enjoy that advantage. Again, as the various western tribes generally occupy a hostile attitude toward each other, a company trading with a particular tribe, must, apparently at least, go with that tribe in their hostile feelings toward a neighboring tribe. The Crows and Black-feet are deadly foes. A company trading with the Crows must unite with them against the Black-feet; and the Black-feet will regard said company as hostile to them, because they trade with their enemies, and will treat them as such. This attitude, which the companies are compelled to assume, or which, are rather assigned them, frequently involves them in difficulties that result in the loss of life. I remember a fact communicated to me by a free trapper, who was with a company forted on the Maria river, in the Crow country.[8] The captain of the fort had, as a wife, a Crow Indian squaw, who was so remarkably vigilant, that nothing could occur without her knowing it. Indeed she was said to have saved the lives of the men in the fort on various occasions, by giving them timely notice of their danger, and by her constant watchfulness.

On one occasion, she reported a band of Indians in the neighborhood of the fort, whose movements indicated hostile intentions. By the aid of a glass it was ascertained that they were Black-feet, who were disposed to hover around the fort. As it was in the latter part of the day, an eye was kept upon them until dark, when the men of the fort turned out to hunt for them, and found them within an old breastwork of logs, where they had intended to camp for the night. There were nineteen of them, and, as it was supposed, they were Black-feet. They were easily taken and conveyed to the fort, to be disposed of as the company might think proper. When they were taken into the fort, they asked some of the Crows, that were in the fort, to give them some water. Their request was granted, and when they received it, they asked the Crows to drink with them; this the Crows declined, by shaking their heads. At their request, something to eat was next furnished them; they desired the Crows to eat with them, which was also declined by a shake of the head. They then asked for a pipe, in the smoking of which they asked the Crows to join them. This was also declined in

---

[8] Coyner seems to have confused the facts concerning this story, for the Marias River was not in Crow country. Fort Piegan, built at the mouth of the Marias in the winter of 1831-32, was established for trade with Blackfeet. The story which Coyner heard could have occurred there.

the same manner. The object of these requests was to ascertain something about their fate, and when they perceived that the Crows were not disposed to do any thing that indicated an amicable spirit, the poor fellows seemed to know the doom that awaited them. The Crows joined with them in a conversation that lasted all night. The next morning one after another was shot, and thrown into the river. The company were not at liberty to pursue any other course, as they were in the country of the Crows, and trading with them, and enjoying their protection.

Such is the character of many transactions that make a part of the history of the fur trade; facts that cannot tend to conciliate the natives generally, and prompt them to regard the white man as their friend and benefactor. Notwithstanding occurrences of this kind, which are greatly to be deplored, the inducements held out to great gain, by this trade, have been the means of thoroughly exploring that vast wilderness between the states and the Pacific. Indeed it has opened the way to Oregon and California, and laid open those vast and fertile countries to invite the thousands that are now emigrating there, and to encourage thousands more to go. Such, however, has been the vigor with which this business has been prosecuted, that it seems destined to be soon extinguished, with the race of fur-bearing animals, that are fast vanishing from both sides of the Rocky Mountains.

Appendix

An Oregon Emigrant furnishes the following way bill to Oregon:

	miles
From Independence, Missouri, to Blue, at Burnett's trace	520
From Blue to Big Platte	25
Up Platte	25
Up the same	117
Across the North Fork of the same	31
Up North Fork to Cedar Grove	18
Up the same to Chimney Rock	18
To Scott's Bluffs	20
To Fort Laramie	38
From Fort Laramie to the Big Springs at the Foot of the Black Hills	8
To Keryene North Fork	30
To the crossing of the same	34
To Sweet water	55
Up Sweet water to the snow on the Rocky Mountains	60
To the main divide of the Rocky Mountains	40
To the waters running to the Pacific Ocean	2
To Little Sandy	14

[1] Professor Thomas Andrews of Pasadena College, a specialist in overland immigration of this period, suggests that this is a simplified version of Peter H. Burnett's waybill of 1843, perhaps once removed.

APPENDIX

	miles
To Big Sandy	14
To Green River	25
Down the same	12
To Black Fork of Green river	22
To Fort Bridger	35
To Koax river	35
Down the same to the hills that run through the same	57
Down the same to the great Sandustry	38
To Partinith, first waters of the Columbia	25
To Fort Hall, on Snake river	58
To Partinith again	11
To Rock Creek	87
To Salmon Falls	42
To the crossing of Snake River	27
To the Boiling Springs	19
Down the same to Fort Boise	40
To Burnt river	41
Up the same	26
Across to Powder, to the Lamepens	18
To Grand Round	15
To Utilla river, Blue mount	43
To Dr. Whiteman's	29
To Walla-walla	25
From Walla-walla to Dalles	20
From Dalles to Vancouver	100
Whole distance from Independence, Missouri, to Vancouver in	
Oregon is 2,021 Miles	2021

170

APPENDIX

EXTENT OF THE OREGON TERRITORY

On the east, it skirts eight hundred miles along the Rocky Mountains; on the south, three hundred miles along the Snowy Mountains, on the west, seven hundred miles along the Pacific ocean; on the north, two hundred and forty miles along the North American possessions of Russia and England. The area of this immense valley contains 360,000 square miles, capable undoubtedly, of forming seven states as large as New York, or forty states of the dimensions of Massachusetts. Some of the islands on the coast are very large —sufficient to form a state by themselves. These are situated north of the parallel of forty-eight. Vancouver's Island, two hundred and sixty miles in length and fifty in breadth, contains 12,000 square miles—an area larger than Massachusetts and Connecticut. Queen Charlotte's, or rather Washington Island, one hundred and fifty miles in length and thirty in breadth, contains 4000 square miles. On both of these immense islands, though they lie between the high parallels of forty-eight and fifty-five degrees, the soil is said to be well adapted to agriculture.

The straits and circumjacent waters abound in fish of the finest quality. Coal of good quality, and other mines of minerals, have been found.

THE SOUTH PASS

Captain Fremont describes this avenue to the Oregon territory as one of easy access and gradual elevation. It is situated not far north of the forty-second parallel, which is the boundary between our territory and that of Mexico.[2]

"The ascent had been so gradual, that with all the intimate knowledge possessed by Carson, who had made this country his home for seventeen years, we were obliged to watch very closely to find the place at which we had reached the culminating point. This was between two low hills, rising on either hand fifty or sixty feet. When I looked back at them, from the foot of the intermediate slope on the western plain, their summits appeared to be about one hundred and twenty feet above.

"From the impression on my mind at the time and subsequently on my return, I should compare the elevation which we surmounted immediately at the Pass, to the ascent of the Capitol hill from the avenue at Washington.

"The width of the Pass is estimated at about nineteen miles. It has nothing of the gorge-like character and winding ascents of the Allegany passes—nothing resembling the St. Bernard of Simplon passes of the Alps. For one hundred miles the elevation is regular and gradual. It presents the aspect of a sandy

---

[2] This quotation is from Frémont, *Narratives*, pp. 161-62.

plain; and the traveler, without being reminded of any change by toilsome ascent, suddenly finds himself on the waters that flow to the Pacific Ocean. The importance of this Pass is immense. It opens the way into the valley of Oregon, and is the only avenue to that country from the interior, for a long distance. By observing the map, it will be seen that three great rivers take their rise in the neighborhood of the Pass: the Platte, the Columbia, and Colorado. The first is a tributary of the Missouri; the second, draining all Oregon, discharges all its accumulated waters into the Pacific; the third flows southwardly, and empties into the bay of California. From the South Pass, then, as a central point, three great valleys are commanded. It is the key to California; it opens the whole Oregon country from the Rocky Mountains to the Western ocean; and it subjects both these great regions to the control of the Mississippi valley."

As the South Pass is in our undisputed territory, its importance will doubtless attract the attention of the government. Fort Laramie, on the Pratte, [Platte] about three hundred miles from the Pass, is mentioned by Capt. Fremont as a suitable point for a national post; it is now merely a station for traders. If the President's recommendation is carried out to construct forts and block houses on the route to Oregon, these important points will doubtless be regarded.

A LETTER FROM THE AUTHOR TO A FRIEND IN VIRGINIA

Boonville, Cooper County, Missouri, May 20th, 1846

My Dear Sir:
    In your last communication, which I had the pleasure of receiving, you state that you are thinking about emigrating from Virginia to Missouri, and perhaps to Oregon; if the inducements to engage in such an undertaking were sufficiently great, and if you can be satisfied that the descriptions you have had of this country and Oregon were true; and you ask of me, an honest and candid answer to a number of important questions, which you very correctly say, interest every one, who thinks of going to the west.
    In answer, then, to your letter, allow me to say, that I know not what you may have read, and what you may have heard about this country and that farther west; but I would state, there are two classes of witnesses, who bear a testimony pro and con, in relation to this country, to which I do not attach much truth. The first embraces those who indulge in the most extravagant language, as to the advantages of this country, and describe on paper a country that is not to be found on the face of the earth. Where such persons are believed, they of course mislead. Many persons, receiving their statements as true, emigrate to the west, and are disappointed, and of course dissatisfied. The second

172

class embraces those, who are so dissatisfied with the country, that they cannot say a word in its favor. They forward to their friends in the old states, very doleful and disheartening accounts of the country; and indeed many such persons return back to the place from which they emigrated. I have known some who incurred all the expense and trouble of coming here, and instead of examining the country, they became dissatisfied, and went immediately back to the old states, giving a miserable account of a country they had never seen. The information, which such persons give of the west, cannot therefore be relied on as correct.

You ask me to account for the mania for Oregon that prevails in Missouri, and you seem to think that it does not say much in favor of our State, that so many of our citizens are leaving it, to cross the Rocky Mountains; you also inquire, what is the general character of the people who are emigrating from this country to Oregon. You will remember that the distance from Independence to the white settlement on the Columbia and its affluents, is about two thousand miles, and that it takes the greater part of a summer season to make the trip; and you must know that no very small amount of means is essential to procure the necessary outfit. It may, therefore, be taken for granted, that the emigrants from our state who are seeking a home beyond the Rocky Mountains, belong to the most enterprising and patient and resolute portion of our population, and are very far from being the poorest people in the country. They are a class of people that are not easily intimidated by difficulties which they may meet in life, and who are in possession of the secret, that the way to be able to accomplish an object, is to *"believe you can do it, and you can do it."* They are rather different from those who have acted the part of pioneers in the western states, and whose object, in part at least, seems to have been to avoid the restriction of salutary law and order, and "to follow the game," which recedes before more well organized society. Among the hundreds and hundreds, that leave us, there are many, who are actuated by the very laudable purpose of carrying the principles of our religion and government to that part of the world, and laying the foundation of institutions, of a civil and religious character, that will prove great blessings to all who may settle there, as well as to the ignorant and degraded natives. It is true, many are going there without any other specific object, than simply to be *moving*, or to find a country where "they will be satisfied;" an object, by the way, which they in all probability, will never attain. They seem, too, to explain your question, why so many are leaving this state. When men have once dissolved the relations that bind them to the country of their nativity and education, to seek a location in the west, it may be said, with too much truth, of the majority of them, that they are unsettled for the remainder of their days. "Having moved once, they are ever ready to move again;" and then the finest country is always ahead. In this city (Boonville), now numbering between three and four thousand inhabitants, I have been told, the population has undergone an almost entire change within the last five years. That is, very few of the citizens who were living here five years ago, are here *now*. In the old states, you know, it is very difficult to buy a valuable farm almost at any price, from the fact that the proportion of good land is very small, and men do not like to dispossess themselves of comfortable homes. All over the western states, it may be said to be different. Beautiful and very fertile land abounds, in every direction, and a pretty, splendid farm seems to be no great *desideratum*, because every one may have it. In this country, too, the majority are disposed to sell, for no reason, that we can assign, except to be going ahead, and reaching that elysium, that fills the eye of the unsettled emigrant, and enchants him along, from country to country, until he finds himself on the waters of the Columbia, or Colorado of the west. These statements may serve to furnish one reason, why so many are leaving this country for Oregon. But many are emigrating from Oregon to California, for the same reason, that they move from this State to Oregon. As to going to Oregon, my opinion is, that if a man cannot do well in this State, where he can get as good land, as he can get in Oregon or California, and at government price in the bargain ($1.25 per acre), he cannot do better by crossing the Rocky Mountains.

I have read every thing that has been written, professing to give us a description of Oregon, and I have yet to learn in what respect that country has one advantage which this country does not possess. And I have frequently conversed with men, who have crossed to the mouth of the Columbia, and not only carefully examined all the intervening country, but have remained for several years in Oregon, and I have never been able to learn why that country is to be preferred to this. Yet I believe we should do nothing to discourage emigration to Oregon or California. Great good will result from it to the world. It will put that vast territory in the possession of a civilized and christian people, who will apply it to the purpose for which it was intended by the great Creator of the universe. It is certainly a thing to be desired, that all parts of the face of our earth should be reclaimed from savage life, and be occupied by an enlightened people. The good of the human family requires this, and the christian religion sanctions it.

The more territory there is in the far west to be occupied, the more reduced will be the price of land. This is another good resulting from the great emigration to Oregon. It tends to keep down the price of land in the western states, a circumstance that greatly favors emigrants to the frontier states, whose means are generally limited, if they have any means at all. The price of land in this State is said to have been higher twenty years ago, than it is now, and it is likely to continue low. For if our government should acquire the Californias, or Upper California only, I do not hesitate to predict, although I am not a prophet nor the son of a prophet, that the *emigration* from the frontier states, westward, will greatly exceed the *emigration* into those states. This must, of course, keep down the price of land in said states and territories. I am inclined, therefore, to think, that land in this State in your and my life-time, will not reach a very high price.

I have said that I did not *know*, for I never have been able to learn, what advantage Oregon has over this part of the world. Now it is generally conceded that Oregon is not a *corn country*, and this in my opinion is a very great objection to it. As long as I can find a corn country, I do not expect to live in any other. The great variety of useful purposes which this kind of grain answers (and answers better), than any thing else, must make the country that grows it more valuable than those countries that do not grow it. How would we, Virginians and Kentuckians, do without it. "We *must* have our "*hog* and *hommony*," and we never would be willing to live in a country, where we could not raise it. Such a country, I understand Oregon to be.

If any one does not know the advantages of a corn growing country, let him compare the many uses to which this grain is applied, with the very few purposes to which wheat is applied, and he will at once see that it is much easier to get along without wheat, than corn. Oregon is said to be a fine wheat country, and I have no doubt that the climate is better adapted to the growing of that kind of grain than any other; but then you may depend upon it, it is no better, for example, than north Illinois, Iowa, Wisconsin or Missouri. I hope you will not misunderstand me. I am only comparing Oregon with this country, with the view of answering your question. It is a fine country, but in my opinion not superior to this. Nor am I to be understood as aiming to discourage emigration to that country. I would rather encourage it, and say nothing that would cast a damper over the feelings of the emigrant, and cause him to abandon his purpose.

In answer to your question about the soil of Missouri, I reply, that it is as fertile as that of any country. I mean the river bottom land. The prairie (table) land is not so rich, and on that account the first settlements were made in the timber, which is pretty much confined to the water courses. For the last few years, the river lands have not been valued so high, from the fact that they are liable to be overflown once a year. The larger class of rivers in this State rise in the Rocky Mountains, and every spring they are swelled to an enormous size from the melting of the snow in those mountains. This is called the June rise, and at that season of the year can do a great deal of injury. On this account, the earlier settlers of this State, who located themselves on the bottom lands, have generally moved up on the high lands; that is, upon the prairies, where their crops are not exposed to the danger of being swept away every spring. You have read the various accounts in the newspapers, of the great flood of 1844 in our rivers, which go to strengthen what I have said.

Another advantage which the prairies have, is, they are healthier than the bottom, timbered lands. They are higher, and being destitute of timber to interrupt the currents of air, a gentle breeze sweeps constantly over their beautiful surface, that tends to keep the atmosphere pure.

If you will select a situation on some elevation in these prairies, on the west side of any pond of water, or stream that may be in your vicinity, you may have as good health here as you may enjoy any where else. I say the *west side*, for through the entire summer, there generally prevails a south-west wind, that will blow away the noxious miasma that arises from the surface of standing stagnant water. No opinion as to a healthy location, is more generally entertained in the west, than the one just advanced.[3]

You wish to know what kind of crops are the most profitable. That will depend, in part, upon the men who undertake to raise a crop of any kind, and convert it into money. Corn, wheat, hemp, and tobacco, are the staples of this State, and every man should engage in that kind of farming which he understands. I make this statement, because I observe a great many *here* engage in the raising of tobacco, who, from want of experience, do not know how to handle such a crop, and generally lose their labor. Many, too, raise large crops of hemp, but as they have no way or means of breaking it, these crops are frequently lost. To raise tobacco, and make it a profitable crop, I am certain, from what I have seen, that a man must "serve his trade at the business;" and to raise hemp with profit, a farmer needs several strong hands.

Stock of every kind, such as horses, cattle, mules, hogs, etc., are more numerous here than in Virginia, and of the very best blood. Our beautiful prairies, in the grass season, are dotted, everywhere, with bands of the different kinds of stock, in grass up to their bellies. And, it is worthy of notice, that the prairie-grass has the property of fattening stock much quicker than any of the varieties of tame grass. However poor an ox may be, if he has strength enough to get out upon the prairie, when the tender grass begins to shoot up, he seems immediately to spring up with new life; and, in a few weeks, his naked bones are clothed with flesh.

I observe that many persons, coming even a thousand miles to this State, encumber their trip with stock, furniture, etc., believing that these things cannot be readily (if at all) procured in this country. This is a mistake which creates much trouble and expense. A horse that you can sell in Virginia for sixty dollars, you may get here for thirty. A yoke of cattle, that will bring thirty dollars here, will bring from fifty to sixty dollars in Virginia. It is only recently that a yoke of oxen, in this country, would bring even thirty dollars. The Santa Fe traders, however, now use them instead of mules, and they buy a great many every spring, and this has brought them into demand.

Whilst you ask of me "nothing but truth," you say you "want *all* of the truth,"

[3] Coyner is correct. See Billy M. Jones, *Health-Seekers in the Southwest, 1817-1900* (Norman, Okla., 1967), pp. 6-10.

as to the health of this State. It cannot be denied, that this country has been very sickly for the last three or four years; but I am constrained to believe that Missouri will become one of the healthiest of the western states. The face of the country is very undulating, and I have yet to see one of those sloughs, so common in Ohio, Indiana, and Illinois. Indeed, if there be any objection to the face of the country, it is too dry. Springs of water are scarce, and many are compelled to use cistern-water; that is, rain-water conveyed from the roofs of houses to wells dug to receive it. In a very few hours, this water, which is very free from mineral, and noxious properties, and of course very pure, becomes very cool. You may think this a poor substitute for the fine springs in the hills and mountains of Virginia; but, believe me, my dear sir, when I tell you that the majority of persons, after using it awhile, become very fond of it.

Like all persons, who may be thinking and talking about moving to the west, you ask a question about the game in this State.

There are no buffalo within the limits of Missouri State, nor any within five hundred miles from the boundary line. There are some elk, in the unsettled parts of the State, and deer are also plenty in some places. But game of every kind, in a prairie country like this, will vanish much faster and sooner, than in timbered countries. I have no doubt as to the fact, that there will be deer in the old States, when there will not be one in the limits of our State. Game is scarcer about the boundary line, and for some distance into the Indian country, than it is in the interior. In consequence of this fact, the tribes, about the line, often ask permission to come within the limits of our State to hunt. This privilege is granted by the Governor, if there is no objection raised by the whites living where the Indians wish to hunt.

It is yearly becoming a question of increasing interest, "what is to be the fate of the tribes on our frontier?" That which constitutes their main dependence for a living, (the game), is fast disappearing, and the poor wretches must beg, steal, or starve. The day is not very distant, when our government will be compelled to do something to prevent the difficulties and annoyances to which our citizens will be exposed, from their juxtaposition to these frontier tribes.

Documents

EZEKIEL WILLIAMS TO JOSEPH CHARLESS, August 7, 1816

St. Louis *Missouri Gazette*, September 14, 1816

The circumstances under which Ezekiel Williams wrote this important and revealing letter are explained in the Editor's Introduction. The Williams' letter was republished in 1913 in the *Missouri Historical Society Collections* by Walter B. Douglas, who suggested that Williams' dates are off by one year. Thus, the correct dates have been supplied in square brackets in this reprinting of the letter. The letter also differs from Douglas' printing in that it is completely faithful to the original as it appeared in the *Gazette*. I have not attempted to correct errors of punctuation or spelling as did Douglas. Braxton Cooper's statement, which follows Williams' letter, is reprinted here for the first time.—D.J.W.

COMMUNICATION.

Mr. Charless,

I beg leave through the medium of your Gazette, to answer the enormous charges alleged against me by some unknown calumniator published in the '*Western Intelligencer.*' I am positively charged with the murder of Champlain, of which together with every other fact alleged relative to the affair, I trust I shall be able to disprove to the satisfaction of a just people.

In 1810 [1809], I went with the Fur Company up the Missouri, near the head of the river, where I hunted two years; there I first became acquainted with Champlain. In August 1812 [1811], a party started to go towards the south to hunt: there were in all near twenty men, each man on his own footing except two who were in Champlains employ; myself and Champlain were of the company. Manuel Lisa who was an agent of the Fur Company, commanded a fort on the Missouri, from whence we started, promised to keep up the fort, and a good understanding with the indians, so that our return should not be cut off. We journeyed south forty or fifty days, struck a river I since found to be the Arkansas, where we hunted the first fall unmolested. The next spring the indians commenced robbing and harrassing our company in every quarter. Some time in June [1812], we all assembled on the head of a river, since known to be the Platte, where we held a council and agreed to part. Eight or ten crossed the Rocky mountains about as many started southward along the mountain, Champlain and myself were with the latter party, we proceeded until we crossed the Arkansas, where we were informed by indians that the fort on the Missouri was broke up, that Manuel Lisa had fell out with the tribes near there, and that they were killing each other as they could find them. We now thought it impossible to return to the Missouri, we concluded to part again. Four of our company determined to find the Spanish settlement, six remained; Champlain, his two hired men, two other Frenchmen and myself. We then set out to hunt in October [1812], in a cove in the mountain, taking care not to go more than a few miles apart. About the first day of November, we found three of our men killed; there now remained Champlain, one Porteau and myself. We then took protection amongst the Arapahow nation of indians; there we found the horses and equipment of our three men just killed. The head chief advised us as the only means to save our lives was to stay with him, which we did, and passed a wretched winter, filled with despair of ever being able to return home. The indians told us that said Manuel's fort was broke up, and that if we attempted to go back that way we would certainly be killed. Champlain, and Porteau insisted that we should stay with the indians until some white person came there who would be able to give the necessary information respecting the Fur company, or the place where we were, and of the means of escaping from thence. I decided to find white people or some place of safety, or lose my life in the attempt. From the best information the Arrapahows could give me, the river that we were on lead into the country of a nation, which from their description, I thought to be the Osage, and therefore determined to descend that river; my comrades assisted me to make a canoe, and on the first day of March [1813], according to our reckoning, I was accompanied by my two companions and a numerous band of indians to the water side, where I took a final farewell of them. Champlain shook my hand and said farewell, the other turned his back & wept.—A few minutes before we parted, they told me

179

they would start about three days afterwards. I have never seen them since. I promised them to inform the people at St. Louis of their situation, if I should reach there before them. They made me a similar promise. I traveled down the Arkansas about four hundred miles, trapping for beaver the most of the way. I could proceed no further because of low water. About the first of June the water raised and I started down until the last (nearly) of said month, I was taken by the Kansas; they soon distributed my little property among themselves and bound me fast. Luckily I had but little except the skins I had caught descending the Arkansas; I had hid all my furs before that I left the Arrapahows, and never expected to see it again—The Kansas kept me with them. A party of the Osages were in that country, and heard the Kansas had a white man prisoner, and sent Messrs. Daniel Larisson & Joseph Larivee with ten Osages to demand me from the Kansas, they would not give me up to the Osages, but would keep me until they returned to their town and send me home: after forty days we set off. I gave my gun &c. to a mulatto man to be my friend and speak for me, the indians returned me part of my furs, the balance was since demanded by the Governor and surrendered. Four Indians and the mulattoe brought me in, on the first day of September [1813] I arrived at Boons Lick. I was shortly afterwards in St. Louis, where I seen Manuel Lisa, who told me all the above difficulties they had with the indians at the post where he was, that my comrades had not got in, but were certainly killed if they went that road, of which they talked when we parted. In the month of May [1814] following, I started from Boons-lick, to go and bring in my fur from the Arrapahows, in company with Morris May, Braxton Cooper, and 18 Frenchmen called Phillebers Company. When we arrived at the Arrapahows, I called a council of the chiefs in the presence of all the aforesaid men, two of whom Durocher and La France served as interpreters, and asked *"what has become of Champlain and Porteau, whom I left in this village last year*[?]*"* The chief said they had staid with them three days after my departure, then went up the river hunting, saying they intended to wait to see if some white men would come there, that they came back again to the village after being gone some time, and determined to wait no longer but try to get back to the fort on the Missouri. That they bought two other horses, loaded all their furs, &c. having then eleven horses and started towards the Missouri. That they were seen on the road by two parties of their nation, and that the Crow Indians told them they seen two whitemen dead in their camp, which they believed were my companions. The Arapahows in the same council confessed that it was their nation that killed our three men in the cove before we took protection among them. They also told us, "that three white men had come from the south,["] wintered with them and went back the same way with furs loaded on three mules and a jack, that they had left their traps. I insisted these were my companions; they produced the traps but they were not the traps of our company—I despaired now of ever finding them, hired Michael La Clair, one of Philleberts company, and with my two companions, Cooper and May, collected part of my fur and started down the Arkansas. We travelled down it about five hundred miles and could proceed no farther on account of low water. There we hid the fur and came on home foot, intending to return in the spring following and get it.

Sometime in the winter, I had information that my man La Clair had told of my fur, and that a company were about to start to steal it, to be piloted by said La Clair. In consequence of that information, I got two men to go with me, they were Joseph and William Cooper. When I arrived at the little Osage village, I was told that La Clair and the aforesaid company were then at the Cheniers, on their way. I pushed with all force and got there first, and waited the coming of the plunderers, but they did not appear. When the water raised in the spring [1815], we set off with my fur down the Arkansas, and when I arrived at the settlement I met Messrs John and James Lemon's [sic], who told me they were at the Cheniers village, when the party returned, which went to steal the fur, and were told by said party that they (said party) were employed by *certain men* in St. Louis, and that their orders were to kill us if we had got there first, and take the fur and bring it in. That they were to have as many indians to assist them as necessary, that they had hired a large party, but had not told them the particulars of their business until they had got within a few miles of the fur. When the indians were informed of it, they abruptly left them and went back home. Messrs Lemon's asked the party the reasons why they were directed to kill us, they told them that the fur belonged to a company in St. Louis, that I had stole it, and if they killed us they would not be *hurt for it*—! The above is a true and succinct statement of facts, the most important and material parts of which I am still able to prove by good men as any in our country. I refer my fellow citizens to all men of my acquaintance in Kentucky, where I was raised, for my character and conduct from my cradle until I came to this country. I beg leave to refer them to Mr. Reuben Lewis, brother of the late Governor Lewis, and to Andrew Henry of the Mines, and to all others who recollect the facts relative to the circumstances of the company that went with me towards the south from the fort on the Missouri. I refer them to the depositions of Braxton Cooper, and to Morris May and Phillebert's company relative to the facts stated in council by the Arrapahow chief, respecting Champlain and Porteau, and the other three men which were killed. I refer them to Messrs John and James Lemon's, respecting the facts stated, in which their names are mentioned, and finally *I* refer it to the impartial unbiassed opinion of all good men, if *I* was the murderer of my bosom friend Champlain? *I* profess myself an honest man and good citizen, and *I* believe have been so reputed and taken, until the aforesaid libellous and malicious charges have been propogated against me. *I* demand justice of my countrymen. *I* call upon the base *liar* who published the aforesaid slander, to put his name out publickly. Let him no longer stab me from behind the scene.

Ezekiel Williams

Boons-lick, 7th Aug. 1816.

181

DOCUMENTS

STATEMENT OF BRAXTON COOPER

Missouri Gazette, September 14, 1816

I do hereby certify on oath, that on the 16th of May, 1814. I started and went with Ezekiel Williams from this place to go to the Arapahows on the head of the Arkansas, to assist said Williams to bring in some furs he had in that country. There were in company with us, Morris May and seventeen or eighteen Frenchmen, called Phillebert's company, when we arrived at the Arrapahow town. Williams called a council of the indians to know what had become of his comrades, Mr. Champlain and others, whom he had left there there [*sic*] the year before. Two Frenchmen called Durocher and le France interpreted. The indians informed us that after Williams had left his comrades (Champlain and Portau) in their village, that they made a hunt up the river, returned bought two horses, and started towards the Missouri with these furs, &c. on eleven horses. That they were seen on road by two parties of their own nation, and that they had never seen them since, they believed that they were killed from the best information they had of them. They also stated, that their nation had killed William's other three companions before that he had left their nation: also, that three white men had come to their nation after that Williams left it, and wintered there and had gone off towards the south with furs loaded on 3 mules and one jack. William[s] insist[ed] that they were his companions, but the indians said they were not. They produced the traps of the three men, which Williams examined and found not to be the traps of his companions. Sometime in July, we left that town and headed down the Arkansas four or five hundred miles where we were compelled to leave the canoes and loading, the water being too shallow to descend further; from which place we returned home by land. Sometime in the winter afterward, said Williams received information that a party was forming at St. Louis to go and steal his fur, to be piloted by Le Clair, a frenchman in Williams employ, who was present when the fur was hid: in consequence of which Williams set out with William Cooper and Joseph Cooper to get it. They returned the summer following, and informed me that they had got off the fur before said party got there.

Braxton Cooper

Howard County, sct.

Braxton Cooper came personally before me a justice of the peace in said county, and made oath in due form, that the above statement contained the truth in every particular. Given under my hand this 8th day of August, one thousand eight hundred and sixteen.

John Munro, J. P.

Afterword

I̶T WAS JACK RITTENHOUSE, that perambulating card catalogue of Western Americana, who came up with the idea of publishing a critical edition of David Coyner's classic account of the fur trade, *The Lost Trappers*. Jack had enjoyed many careers—several concurrently—including printer, book dealer, editor, and writer. In 1968, when the idea struck, Jack had just gone to work for the University of New Mexico Press and closed down his own Stagecoach Press. He had printed exquisite small books on a hand-operated press; at the University of New Mexico he would have the opportunity to publish larger works. So he launched a series aimed at bringing important works of Western Americana back into print.

David Coyner's *Lost Trappers* stood high on Jack's list. Although the book represented a curious blend of fact and fiction and its author had become obscure, Jack knew that *The Lost Trappers* had historical value. "The original [1847] edition," Jack argued in a proposal to the press,

> undoubtedly influenced many of the men who went West . . . and it gave to the world a picture of Western life at that time. It still reads well enough to provide an evening's pleasure to the layman and will continue to be used by any student of the fur trade in the West.

Jack's judgment reflected the views of two specialists in Western history whom he had queried about the book: Ira G. Clark and William

183

H. Goetzmann. Each had affirmed the book's importance, with Goetzmann placing it on a par with the works of George Frederick Ruxton and William Drummond Stewart. Both specialists cautioned, however, that Coyner's work could not be reprinted without a scholarly introduction. As Clark put it, "More harm than good could come from a new edition unless the reader is placed on guard that it is not to be accepted as reputable history, but rather is illustrative of a type of literature which played a significant role in popularizing the Far West."

Despite the warnings that he needed a skillful introduction, Jack chose an inexperienced historian to write it. Jack and I were not strangers. Through his Stagecoach Press he already had published a little book of mine in 1967, *The Extranjeros*. He also knew that I had written my doctoral dissertation on an aspect of the fur trade and that the revised version then awaited publication at the University of Oklahoma Press (it eventually appeared in 1971 as *The Taos Trappers: The Fur Trade in the Far Southwest*). Nonetheless, as a newly minted Ph.D. with only one year of college teaching behind me, I was astonished to receive a letter from Jack in the autumn of 1968 telling me of the project, reporting that his Publications Committee had just approved it, and asking if I would be interested in editing a new edition of Coyner's work. We could talk, he said, at the annual meeting of the Western History Association in Tucson in mid-October. I agreed, and a contract followed with a characteristic note from Jack. He would have preferred "a deal made over a cup of coffee and sealed with a handshake. Alas, protocol requires something for the archives."

I finished the work the next summer. That fall *The Lost Trappers* went into production, and I received unpaged galleys to proofread for Christmas. Two months later we piled our two small children into the car and drove from San Diego through Central America, where I taught for the remainder of 1970 as a Fulbright Lecturer at the Universidad de Costa Rica. Newly arrived page proofs traveled with us. Even as I prepared lectures in Spanish for a course I never had taught before, my wife, Carol, and I indexed *The Lost Trappers* on 3 × 5 cards on our dining room table in San José. There we had Jack's instructions before us. Rio Grande Press, in Glorieta, New Mexico, had surprised both Jack and me by reprinting *The Lost Trappers* in facsimile the previous autumn, with a modest introduction and an index. Jack, ever attentive to detail, pointed out the weakness of our competitor's index and explained how we could do a better one.

Published in the early summer of 1970, our edition of *The Lost Trappers* received generous reviews. Of the reviewers, only Dale Morgan offered new information. He explained that a "Way Bill to Oregon," which Coyner had reproduced in an appendix, derived from a Missouri newspaper, the *Jefferson Inquirer* (April 15, 1846), and represented a shortened version of a waybill printed in the Fayette *Missouri Democrat* (December 17, 1845).

A few years before his death in 1991, Jack Rittenhouse sent me an unexpected package. It contained a worn copy of the 1850 printing of *The Lost Trappers*. One of its yellowing pages bore the signature of its most recent owner, A. B. Guthrie, Jr., who won the Pulitzer Prize for his highly believable historical fiction about the American West. Could one find a more appropriate owner for David Coyner's work? Jack was a bookseller then, but he had not sold me the book. He had simply given it to me because he wanted me to have it.

A sentimental man, Jack would have taken delight in the knowledge that this critical edition of *The Lost Trappers* remains in print — now in this affordable paperback edition from the University of Oklahoma Press.

David J. Weber
Dedman Professor of History
Southern Methodist University, Dallas
May 1994

Index